THE VISION OF HISTORY IN EARLY BRITAIN

The Vision of History
in Early Britain

FROM GILDAS TO GEOFFREY OF MONMOUTH

ROBERT W. HANNING

COLUMBIA UNIVERSITY PRESS

NEW YORK AND LONDON, 1966

Robert W. Hanning is Assistant Professor of English at Columbia University

This study, prepared under the Graduate Faculties of Columbia University, was selected by a committee of those Faculties to receive one of the Clarke F. Ansley awards given annually by Columbia University Press.

The drawing opposite the title page represents the liberation of Britain, 296 A.D. The Roman conqueror, Emperor Constantius Chlorus, is welcomed at the gates of London by a kneeling woman symbolizing the grateful Britons. (Adapted from *Arethuse*, Paris, Jan. 1924, Plate vii; Roman medallion at the Trésor d'Arras, France.)

To Barbara

Preface

History has been called a seamless garment; it can as aptly be considered a coat of many colors. The varying tinctures applied by men to the past reflect to a variable but definite extent the chief concerns or dominant ideas of the age in which they write. This is not to say that historical writing is merely or inevitably propaganda, or that the environmental spectacles through which the historian regards history render him unfit to speak responsibly or usefully of the past. Spectacles, after all, are not blinders; they serve to focus our vision, not to limit it.

Philosophical "focusing" and its effects on historiography have been the objects of considerable scholarly interest in this century, as is fitting for an age which also possesses a heightened sensibility of the factors controlling personal and social formation. The present study seeks a place among the many others in which twentieth-century scholars have recorded and explored the history of history. Some chapters of that fascinating story have indeed been written and rewritten, especially those dealing with the historiography of the Greeks and the Romans. Despite the masterly surveys of Collingwood, Thompson, and others, however, the art and imagination of the historians of medieval Europe have yet to receive their share of sympathetic attention. Accordingly, I have attempted in this study to redress the balance a bit in favor of medieval historiography.

This is not to say that the medieval explicators of the past have been entirely without astute analysts and even defenders in this century. It is now thirty-five years and more since Edmond

Faral, in *La légende arthurienne,* studied exhaustively the learned materials and traditions which shaped the Arthurian legend and other visions of the past in the early medieval centuries. More recently Charles W. Jones and Nora K. Chadwick have put a generation of medievalists deeply in their debt by illuminating the doctrinal and political contexts of medieval thought and writing on the subject of history. These are considerable achievements; there remains, however, a dearth of critical analysis at once wider in the scope of material covered and more narrowly concerned with the historian, his world view, and his artistic presentation of the past.

It is with this last phenomenon—with what may be called the creative imagination of the historian—that the following pages are primarily concerned. Insofar as the imaginative process ultimately defies rational analysis and categorization, my attempt so to analyze and categorize will inevitably fall short of complete success. In examining and discussing the fall of Britain texts, I have tried to keep before me the following questions, hoping thereby to render my quest as systematic and objective as possible: (1) What precommitments to the past led the historian to the subject of his history and guided him in writing it? (2) What traditions of expression and analysis did he find in his cultural environment and utilize in his historiography? (3) What historical, ideological, or ethical themes dominate and organize the complete work? It is my hope that the answers to these questions, as set forth individually with regard to each fall of Britain text, will provide a tentative guide to the characteristic modes of early medieval historical expression, and, more importantly, will be available as a foundation for further, more detailed, investigations.

There are, of course, many other and perhaps more profitable ways in which I could have approached the problem of characterizing early medieval historiography on the basis of a group of texts sharing a related subject matter and common provenance (if, indeed, the island of Britain, with all its political and social changes over a period of six centuries, can be called a "common provenance"). Specifically, it can cogently be argued that I have spent too much time on explication and too little on the study of sources. My reply to such an objection must be that the methods of this study reflect the primarily literary interests of its author. I have found the histories of Bede and Geoffrey of Monmouth, however different they may be in all other respects, to be alike in the excitement which they generate, in reading after reading, and I respectfully submit that if the craftsmanship underlying this excitement yields its secrets at all, it does so as effectively under predominantly literary scrutiny as it does through the more respectable study of origins and sources. In addition (and perhaps more to the point), the basic research on the fall of Britain texts has been completed to the point where some attempt at synthesis seems both possible and appropriate. Whether or not my contribution to the work of critical consolidation proves valid, I am not sorry to have labored at it, and will count myself amply rewarded if my conclusions prompt others to revise or refine them.

The debts I have incurred in completing this study are as difficult to discharge as they are pleasant to acknowledge. As the work progressed from visionary gleam to Columbia University doctoral dissertation, and finally to publishable manuscript, I profited by turns from the knowledge, patience, encouragement, and (of special value) the skepticism of many of my colleagues on the faculty of Columbia University, notably Professors Howard Schless, W. T. H. Jackson, Norman Cantor, and Joseph A. Mazzeo. Discussions with and suggestions from Professor A. Kent Hieatt, Professor Andrew Chiappe, Monsignor James E. Rea, and Dr. Leo Walsh defined and lightened my task on many occasions. Mrs. Marian Maury proved a most helpful and knowledgeable editor; Miss Barbara Henry prepared the manuscript efficiently and intelligently. My parents have been as enthusiastic and encouraging through this as they have been through every stage of my academic career. As to my wife, to whom this book is gratefully dedicated, suffice it to say that without the constant exercise of her editorial talents this study would neither have been legible to the typist, acceptable to the publisher, nor understandable to its readers.

Acknowledgment is gratefully made to The Catholic University of America Press for permission to quote from the translation by R. J. Deferrari of Eusebius' *Ecclesiastical History;* and to Columbia University Press for permission to quote from the translation by I. W. Raymond of Orosius' *History Against the Pagans.*

ROBERT W. HANNING

New York, N. Y.
February, 1966

Contents

THE VISION OF HISTORY IN EARLY BRITAIN

CHAPTER I

The Formation of the Early Medieval Historical Imagination

The period of Western history which we characterize inadequately as the Middle Ages was abundantly varied in its recording, understanding, and uses of the past. To medieval man "history" could mean the history of salvation, the history of Rome, the history of the Christian church, or the preconversion and postconversion history of a barbarian nation. The movements of history could be and were perceived separately and individually; often, however—and especially during the early medieval centuries—they fell into place as semi-autonomous parts of a larger design, usually the design of God in history.

It has often been claimed that medieval thought about history and its significance partakes more of theology, or possibly of philosophy, than of disciplines we recognize today as appropriate to the social sciences, and such claims are, for much medieval historiography, well founded. But whatever its speculative roots, medieval historical writing also reveals characteristic, though diverse, modes of expression—narrative conventions and techniques, themselves the products of interacting cultures and cultural traditions. In seeking to analyze the medieval view (or, more accurately, medieval views) of history, therefore, we must distinguish these component parts: the creed or system of the historian, and the methods he uses to embody it in history. A Christian historian of the early Middle Ages can express himself quite differently in works written for different purposes, while a single set of narrative and rhetorical conventions can be used to illustrate several different and not necessarily compatible systems.

The present study aims generally to distinguish varieties of medieval historical thought, and particularly to explore varieties of medieval historiographical expression. Limiting itself to the earlier medieval centuries (sixth to twelfth), it offers tentative analyses of the historical vision during those centuries as revealed in four works: *De excidio et conquestu Britanniae* by Gildas, a sixth-century monk; Bede's *Historia ecclesiastica gentis Anglorum*; the highly composite ninth-century *Historia Brittonum*; and Geoffrey of Monmouth's *Historia regum Britanniae*. Uniting these texts is an historical event which all record: the mass settlement of Germanic tribes in Britain during the fifth and sixth centuries. They share in addition an interest in the effects of the migration on the civilization of the native, Celtic Britons whom the Angles and Saxons displaced, and, in varying degrees, in British history before the *adventus Saxonum*, as well as in British and English history after the achievement of Saxon hegemony over the island.

In discussing the fall of Britain texts, as I shall hereafter call them, I seek neither to defend nor condemn the accuracy, fairness, or ability with which the authors presented their nation's past to their contemporaries. Rather, my aim is to explore and to distinguish ways in which the past seemed meaningful, in terms of the present and the future, to those writers, and to discuss the methods by which early medieval convictions about the worth and meaning of history became embodied in finished historical works, or in less unified compilations of sources. This goal can best be met, I am convinced, by first comprehending the medieval historical imagination.

By the historical imagination I mean the faculty which perceives the reality of the past; the response, evoked by the record (accurate or inaccurate) of history, which identifies that record with the human condition, seen as a timeless and continuing phenomenon. The historical imagination minimizes the temporal distance between past and present, and emphasizes instead their proximity and continuity. This it does by creating a vision of reality (be it sensual, intellectual, or spiritual reality) equally valid then (whenever "then" may be) and now. The act of creation, or re-creation, is an essential, even if unconscious, part of the historian's craft, but it is an essentially neutral one. Joined to knowledge and judgment, it illuminates the past; deprived of these, it distorts it. But history written without the aid of the historical imagination inevitably fails, insofar as it prevents the reader, as he discovers the past, from discovering himself.[1] Identification with the past is an intuitive, imaginative process which seeks as its fulfillment a perception not merely of the relevancy of the past, but of its actuality.

The analysis of the early medieval historical imagination is inseparable from the quest for its formative elements. We can be guided in this quest by the well-known fact that all early medieval forms of thought and expression were compellingly influenced by Christianity and by the cultural legacy of Rome.[2] Between the decline of the Roman Empire in the West in the fifth century and the quickening of intellectual pulses in the eleventh and twelfth centuries, the civilization of western Europe was marked by political instability and cultural conservatism, the results of the occupation of *Romania* by the barbarian nations and of the slow process by which those nations received and assimilated the learning, culture, and religion they had inherited from the Christian empire. Among the products of early medieval culture is a corpus of historical writing which stands in an observable relation to the Christian historiography and historical thought of the imperial period, while manifesting its own peculiar qualities.

Three of the four fall of Britain texts—those of Gildas and

Bede, and the *Historia Brittonum*—exemplify early medieval historiography as just described. (The fourth, Geoffrey's *Historia*, was written later and is a product of new attitudes and influences which were part of the twelfth century's revival of learning and expansion of intellectual interests. Geoffrey's work, though pseudohistory rather than history, is still representative in many ways of the historiographical developments of its day.) By examining the origins of the early medieval historical imagination, then, we lay the groundwork both for understanding each fall of Britain text (especially the first three), and for making useful distinctions among them.

The preliminary endeavor of this study, in accordance with the immediately evident characteristics of early medieval historiography as mentioned above, will be to summarize briefly the nature and origins of Christian historical thought and writing, concentrating on those factors and characteristics which seem to me most important for an understanding of the fall of Britain texts. Thus the remainder of this chapter considers two phenomena: the rise of an identifiably Christian attitude toward the past, and the Christian attempt to comprehend the historical fact of Rome and her empire within the framework of the history of salvation—God's providential ordering of the world, as revealed in the Old and New Testaments. Christian views of Roman history are of special interest to this study, since Rome figures importantly in all the works to be discussed, and presents a different profile in each. We need not assume that the writers of the fall of Britain texts were precisely aware of the birth pangs of Christian historical thought; it is enough to recognize in the ideas and problems outlined below circumstances—and men who responded to them—profoundly influential in shaping the attitudes and historical imagination of Gildas, Bede, and the authors of the *Historia Brittonum*.

Christianity and History

At the end of the second chapter of the Acts of the Apostles, we are given a provocative glimpse of the apostolic Christian community in Jerusalem as it was understood and venerated by early Christians:

All the faithful held together, and shared all they had, selling their possessions and their means of livelihood, so as to distribute to all, as each had need. They persevered with one accord, day by day, in the temple worship, and, as they broke bread in this house or that, took their share of food with gladness and simplicity of heart, praising God, and winning favour with all the people. And each day the Lord added to their fellowship others that were to be saved.[3]

The impression of a golden age of gladness and simplicity which this passage so strongly evokes should not obscure the very precise details of the life of the community which are here preserved. The communal society of the first Christians, and the peripatetic breaking of bread, with its reference to a primitive eucharistic liturgy, did not exist in total isolation from the established life of the Jewish community. That the followers of Jesus worshiped daily in the temple should not surprise us, for the first Jewish Christians considered themselves still members of Israel— a belief which was to create difficulties in their relationships with the first gentile Christians.[4]

Furthermore, as members of Israel, the Jewish Christians considered themselves heirs in a special way of the Hebraic tradition, i.e., of the law and the prophets.[5] The peculiar, privileged link between the God and the events of what came to be called the old covenant (as opposed to the new covenant affirmed by the life, death, and resurrection of Jesus) and the members of the new Israel quickly became a central preoccupation of the preaching and theology of the church. More than that, it proved a rich, fertile source of speculation and interpretation which permanently molded and colored the life and self-awareness of the first Christian centuries.

When the early Christians thought or spoke of what we would call history, they thought preeminently of the history revealed in the Hebrew sacred writings. This was no ordinary chronicle of the past, but rather the record of God's dealings with man, and especially with Israel, his chosen nation. The essentially historical nature of Hebrew religious thought and tradition has often been remarked; [6] and those elements of the ritual observances of the Jews which manifested a timeless or semicyclical pattern were kept within the living context of the historically-centered prophetic tradition and of its study.[7] Since the nature of Hebraic historical thought, and the way in which this thought controls and is reflected in the imaginative literature of the Bible, have been the object of thorough and often brilliant consideration in our day, there is no need to discuss the subject here.[8] Suffice it to say that the Hebrews saw history as a dynamic process established and controlled by God, and ratified in a series of covenants made between God and man to guarantee, as it were, the eternal value of a world becoming.[9] The prophetic intuition of Israel broke down distinctions between past and present, present and future, and caught up all history in a long, divinely-ordered arc through which God guided Israel.[10] The prophets not only prophesied, they reminded: to them, what the Lord had done and continued to do was as important as what he could and would do in the future, for the Lord ruled over all time.[11]

It was this historical system—or, more accurately, this apprehension of God in time and history—that the Christians inherited; in fact, as heirs of the system, they believed themselves to have completed it. Christianity presented itself to the world quite early, perhaps even from the very beginning, as a religion of fulfillment of history and prophecy in Christ. Jesus, the "Son of Man" and the "New Adam," [12] gathered together in his life, in his message, and especially in his death and resurrection, the strands of history which had first been woven and spun out by the prophets.[13] Not only did he literally fulfill the prophecies, however (a favorite theme of Matthew, but one observable in all the gospels); his life stood in a further special relation to events of the history and prehistory of Israel, or to the history of salvation, as it is commonly known today. This relationship, whereby an historical person or event of the old dispensation was recognized as the temporal, imperfect prefiguration of the new dispensation of Jesus, was variously called by Christian writers *figura* or typology.[14]

As a way of linking landmarks in the history of Israel to later actions of divine providence, typology was not original with Christian commentators on the Old Testament; but it was quickly adopted by the early ecclesiastical communities as a basis for preaching, teaching, and controversy.[15] The universal popularity of typology (which, as an exegetical device grounded in history, must not be confused with allegory) [16] is easily explicable: it enabled the Christian exegete to establish not only God's control over history, but also the absolute uniqueness of Christ as the center of history. Here was valuable support for the Christian "good news" that God had become man at a specific point in time in order to undo the consequences of the fall, and to establish continually in time the church as a home for each member of the kingdom of the New Israel.[17]

That the method of typological exegesis in combination with the stress on the fulfillment of prophecies in Jesus resulted in a new and peculiarly Christian historical imagination has frequently been noted.[18] To observe this historical imagination at work in the creation of a narrative (the test and index, after all, of the historical imagination), we need look no further than the gospels themselves, the examples par excellence of early Christian beliefs and methodology. It will be possible in the process to demonstrate the flexibility of the concept of *figura* as used by the early Christians.[19]

The Matthean gospel's central concern with the fulfillment of prophecies and of all past history in Jesus manifests itself in the very structure of the narrative. The central hortatory and didactic section of the gospel is subdivided into several discourses, the most detailed of which is the sermon on the mount (Matt. 5–7). Binding together the discourses is the concept of the kingdom of God, the coming of which is announced by John the Baptist (3:2 ff.), and the workings of which are the main subject of the discourses of Jesus. The Matthean presentation of the kingdom is quintessentially historical, not only because the good news of the kingdom is announced via the entrance of the Son of God into history, but because the kingdom itself is conceived as a dynamic entity which grows and matures in time. Hence the persistence in Jesus' parables in Matthew (and, indeed, in Mark and Luke as well) of the image of the seed which ripens or the tree which grows to fruition.[20] The kingdom is to grow by its members' adherence to the precepts and example of Jesus, an obedience based on faith in Jesus and acceptance of his simple yet absolute command, "follow me." [21] Throughout the gospel the disciples, representing the primitive church, manifest themselves or are rebuked by Jesus again and again as "men of little faith," and the evangelist acknowledges the difficulty of obeying but insists on the necessity of a complete response which crosses and destroys traditional bonds and substitutes for the family of man the family of the kingdom.[22]

This, then, is the prescriptive content of the good news announced by Matthew—the *raison d'être* of the gospel. But while the gospels are basically publications of the good news rather than histories or biographies of Jesus, each places its message in an historical-biographical context which supports and validates the message. History—specifically the history of Jesus—is neither mere background nor factual description, but becomes the medium through which God announces his plan for man, and in announcing it brings it to pass. Thus the discourses on the kingdom, with their message of growth unto perfection and their exhortation to follow Jesus, are carefully mounted within the setting of a double process of fulfillment in history.

One process is that of prophetic and typological fulfillment. Completed prophecies and *figurae* mark a path through the forest of history, a path leading finally to the crucifixion and resurrection. The theology of this crucial progression is already quite developed in Matthew and the other synoptic gospels, and rests on the identification of Jesus with the "Son of Man" and the "Suffering Servant of Yahweh," both figures of Old Testament prophecies.[23] The historical imagination which operates to link these two prophecies is basically the same as that which prompts the presentation of Christ as the "New Adam" in Romans. In both instances, the past carries within it the seeds of the fruition which is accomplished by the life and death of Jesus. The movement here is from the implications of the imperfect past to the explication of the perfected present.

The second progression in Matthew, which complements the first, is from present to future, the progression found in the prophetic visions and predictions of the Old Testament. It is apparent in the parables which recount the return of the master or of the bridegroom, parables which are themselves part of Jesus' apocalyptic account of the return of the Son of Man to judge the world (Matt. 24–25). The great moment in which all time is fulfilled and all men are judged is so urgently and explicitly proclaimed in Matthew as to become a second structural center of the work, vying with the crucifixion as the point toward which the gospel moves and around which it is organized.[24] I do not believe this structural tension to be accidental; rather, the text of Matthew enshrines and illustrates the complex attitude of the early Christians toward time and history, perceived as a multiple system of movements synchronized by God in the person and message of Jesus.[25]

The narrative framework of Matthew, with its complementary and interacting movements from past to present and present to future, provides valuable insight into the formative stages of the early Christian historical imagination. In particular, the Matthean infancy narrative presents clearly the approach and interests of the whole work; unconstrained by the necessity to organize narrative material around the kerygmatic corpus of Jesus' sayings and teachings, it offers an artistically conceived preface to the main action (the public ministry of Jesus, beginning with his baptism by John in Chapter 3) which is also an imaginative meditation on that action, and announces with deceptive naïveté the main themes which are to be developed in the sections that follow.[26]

We see first of all in the infancy narrative the establishment of Jesus in the line of the history of Israel by means of the genealogy which shows him to be descended from David (1:1–17). Besides the specific purpose of proving the royal lineage of the Messiah, this genealogy serves to identify the Christian attitude toward history with that of Israel, i.e., that history is good and full of promise because it is presided over by God, who carries out his promises to man over generations. This general statement of "generational providence" prepares the way for an exposition of the greatest particular instance of the concept: the birth of Jesus.

Joseph, the husband of Mary, discovers her pregnant with a child which he knows cannot be his (1:18–19). But an angel tells him in a dream that the child in Mary's womb has been conceived by the power of the Holy Spirit, to the end that the child may later save his nation from its sins (1:20–21). It is a marked and by no means accidental feature of the infancy narrative that Joseph is throughout given insight and warnings into God's plans and providence by means of dreams. Are we intended to see here the typological fulfillment of the Joseph of Genesis, also a dreamer, who led his family, Israel, into Egypt, whence God would bring them forth to freedom? The impression is unavoidable that we are. And Joseph, the fulfillment of the Joseph of Genesis, is (according to the genealogy) also the last generation of the royal line of David before Jesus; he sums up the past and the privileges of Israel, God's chosen nation. But he also looks forward, as the precursor of all those in Matthew to whom Jesus says "follow me"; he is the first of the New Israel, the church, inspired by God to provide a setting and home for Jesus in the world, and destined to go with him into Egypt and then back to the promised land.[27]

Nor is Joseph the only one in the infancy narrative who is led by God and follows gladly. The Magi, representatives of the gentile world, follow the star to Bethlehem, and then, "warned in a dream, they proceeded home by another way" (2:12). They, too, are precursors, but of all those gentiles in Matthew who show themselves stronger in faith than the people of Israel, for whom Jesus' mission is primarily intended.[28] In the infancy narrative the Magi are sharply contrasted to Herod, whose larger identification is made clear when the evangelist says that Herod "was troubled, and all Jerusalem with him" (2:3). Herod, in his attempt to find and destroy Jesus, whom he sees as a rival claimant to his kingdom, announces the opposition to Jesus of much of Israel, and thus prefigures the Jews who will have a hand in killing him, "fulfilling" Herod's attempt.

Only when the risen Jesus appears to the disciples does he definitively announce the nature of his universal kingship (28:18), thereby revealing the irony of Herod's attempt and of the Sanhedrin's success: it is precisely Jesus' death which prepares the way for his final revelation and the assumption (through his church) of his kingship. The course of history is triumphantly acclaimed by the resurrection to be entirely in God's hand; even death is ordained by his providence. In anticipating the interlocked themes of death and the attainment of the kingdom, the figure of Herod projects forcefully and imaginatively the basic Matthean premise of God's control over history through the life of Jesus, and illustrates as well how futile are the efforts of those who, in trying to thwart God's plan for history, only manage to corroborate it. For Herod's enmity (and that of his son Archelaus) enables the prophecies concerning the coming of the Messiah to be fulfilled, as the final enmity of the Jews only results in the fulfillment of the prophecies concerning the Son of Man and the Suffering Servant.[29]

The examples which I have taken from Matthew lend support to the contention that early Christianity had constructed a viable and useful vision of history and its relationship to God's plan for human salvation in Christ. There is, however, much more to the Christian idea of history than what has been said or intimated so far. First, the complex system of development in time and history which we have discussed in its Matthean form applied only to the relationship between the history of Israel and that of the kingdom, or specifically of the life, of Jesus. The Johannine gospel applied typology not only to the earthly life of Christ but to his continuous life in the sacraments of the church;[30] the Pauline conceptions of the church as the body or bride of Christ, and of Christ as the New Adam, provided for "the application of the types of the Old Testament to the interior life of the Christian"; and so on.[31]

But the main purpose of these interpretations of providence lay in the catechetical and apologetic uses to which scriptural exegesis and theological formulations were put by the early church, rather than in the provision of a formulation for historical writing or thinking per se. The only historically oriented book of the New Testament besides the gospels, and the only one to speak historically of the church after Christ, is the Acts of the Apostles, which provides valuable information about the form and practices of the early Christian communities and about their attitude toward the Jews (and vice versa), but which changes in form about half way through from a protoecclesiastical history to something akin to romance, in the account of the career and wanderings of the outcast hero, Paul.[32]

After the Acts, as far as we know, no Christian was to undertake a connected narrative of historical events for at least two hundred years, until in the early fourth century Eusebius' *Ecclesiastical History* inaugurated a new era of Christian record and interpretation of nonbiblical events.[33] The hiatus between Acts and Eusebius, however, does not indicate a complete abandonment of Christian thought on the subject of history. There remain many references to history and its ecclesiastical uses in early Christian writings, and from them it is possible to reconstruct at least the church's pastoral attitude toward the past during those centuries.

R. L. P. Milburn has undertaken the task of reconstruction.[34] He points out that in early Christian pastoral literature we find exhortations to regard the great figures of the gospels, especially the apostles, as examples to be imitated in leading the Christian life.[35] There is precedent in both Old and New Testaments for an exemplary interpretation of history, and it was also to this interpretation that classical historians frequently appealed to justify their labors.[36] Given the popularity of the exemplary use of history in the Roman Empire,[37] there may have been conscious or unconscious borrowing of the device on the part of Christians from non-Christian sources. Such a borrowing would in no way imply a Christian dependence upon classical historical thought. The pastoral context of the exemplary references shows their true function as hortatory rhetorical devices within a specifically Christian world view; rhetoric, always the servant of ideology or system, cannot be judged apart from that which it serves.[38]

A second clue to the working of the historical imagination in the early Christian communities is provided by another kind of reference in Christian writings as early as the second century. Writers—and preachers—began to find in the events of their own times the fulfillment of Old Testament prophecies.[39] Actually, this transference of a characteristic interpretation of the life of Jesus to the life of the church was almost inevitable in the light of the typological interpretation of Old Testament characters and events in terms of the sacraments and life of the church. Typology and the fulfillment of prophecies were not equivalent, exegetically; the latter process traditionally belonged more properly to the literal level of interpretation.[40] But it is easy to understand how the transference was effected, since the same apologists who used typology in their preaching would want to use all the effective scriptural weapons at their disposal. What would be more logical than that prophecies uttered in the sacred books of ancient Israel should find their fulfillment in the life of the New Israel? The hortatory and pastoral use of prophecies represents another step in the consistent expansion of the Christian theology of history into the arena of contemporary affairs— into history in the making.

These developments would seem to have promised early and fruitful full-scale encounters between the Christian historical imagination and the events of the Christian era. Yet, as we know, no such general encounter took place before Eusebius. This is certainly to be related to the fact that, as T. E. Mommsen remarks, "during [this] period the attitude of the Christians toward the Roman empire was divided." [41] The earliest Christian views of the power of Rome, as expressed in the famous passages in the synoptic gospels ("render to Caesar . . ."), the epistle to the Romans, and the first epistle of Peter, were tolerant and respectful of the established (i.e., Roman) civil order of the ancient world.[42] But this attitude gave way in the course of the first century to harsher views of pagan authority, captured in all their scathing fury in the Book of Revelation's portrait of Rome as the beast and the whore of Babylon,[43] and perpetuated in Christian polemical writings of the following centuries.[44] Jean Daniélou distinguishes in the rivalry of church and empire between the obvious "ideological incompatibility" of the two institutions, and the specific ill feeling caused on both sides by the Roman view of Christians as politically subversive, from which issued the intermittent persecutions.[45]

The hostility of Christians to the world order in which the church was born and came of age undoubtedly hindered active Christian interest in secular history, which seemed in many respects alien and irrelevant to the history of salvation.[46] In addition to polemics against Rome, the anti-Roman bias of the church also produced a tendency toward imaginative writings of an antisocial and partly antihistoric nature, the literature of hermits and martyrs.[47] The wanderings of Paul in Acts presages this tradition, which will flower only in the hagiography of later centuries.

To see in the early Christians' discouragement with the concrete workings of society and with secular history an abdication of the historical imagination in favor of a romantic creed of antisocial individualism is, however, to misjudge the temper of the religion. Early Christian literature could not have inhabited the realm of romance, for the same reason that Hebraic biblical literature could not.[48] The Judaeo-Christian world view denies to blind chance any role in shaping human destiny, and therefore implicitly denies human freedom from the providential control of God, who, moreover, makes all men and events in accordance with his nature, which is absolutely good. Even as hagiography glorifies the Christian as isolated from or opposed to his environment (the world, or *saeculum*), it still rests on the notion of the church's corporate personality in Christ. The Christian hero may free himself from the evils of the world by withdrawal to the desert or by death in the arena, but he can never free himself from history, which, like his soul, belongs to God. We may almost say that, in early Christian thought, history controls the individual to the point where the concept of individuality disappears. All human destinies are narrowed to two alternatives—salvation or damnation; all society is divided into two groups—the wheat and the chaff, the wise and foolish virgins.[49]

Furthermore, the concept of typology, and the vivid apprehension of Christ's continued life in the church and all her members, sharply limited, if it did not entirely suppress, the portrayal of individualized character as we know it in the novel, or even in the "generic characters" of Greek literature.[50] This is not to deny to Christian thought, as it developed in patristic writings, any concept of personality, or any use of the concept;[51] but it is important to note that the early Christian historical imagination, as reflected in historical and hagiographical writings, did not explore the uniqueness of the individual as a factor in the church's movement through time toward God. This limited outlook prevented Christianity from opting for the individual at the expense of history, even when the church was least in sympathy with its social and political environment. An apocalyptic vision of the final triumph of the church over the secular world at the end of history was the most extreme Christian reaction to society at large; God, having once fulfilled history by sending Jesus, was now guiding history toward the final triumph of the 144,000—a triumph which would constitute as well the ultimate vindication of his providential control of time.

If the providential Christian view of history, anchored on faith in the historic Jesus, his crucifixion, resurrection, and second coming, prevented any absolute Christian rejection of the worth of history, it also prevented the church from creating an historiography dependent upon the classical tradition.[52] Greek historical thought was always limited in its very concept of history, which tended at one extreme toward a mythical record of the past, however rationalized,[53] and at the other toward a flight from history into philosophical abstraction.[54] Furthermore, the intensely humanistic thought and culture of pre-Hellenic and

Hellenic Greece created its literary heroes as types, whose characters determined their fates,[55] and who showed their greatness not in changing history but either in representing it or in falling prey to it. Those representing history are typified in Thucydides' characters, who are introduced by the historian in terse, almost epigrammatic statements which sum them up without in any way explaining how they came to be the way they were; [56] those who fall prey are exemplified in the tragic protagonists of Sophocles.[57] In both cases, the concept of history is not distinguished from that of fate, but rather shades into it. Herodotus, of course, manifests this confusion, or more properly lack of discrimination, most clearly in those places in his history where he describes the action of heaven against men who, like Croesus or Xerxes, have become too great.[58]

The limited, and primarily pessimistic, Greek sense of history just described is not to be equated with the view that man is a plaything of the wanton gods. The gods do not operate in the histories of Herodotus and Thucydides, who have carefully rationalized the myths they found in their sources. Rather, what illuminates the limits of Greek historiography in its greatest exemplars is an unresolved and irreconcilable conflict between the possibilities of human greatness and the forces of history. These forces are not the forces of progress, nor are they in any way analogous to those forces found in the view of historical progress which underlies the Christian view of salvation history. Rather, they are schematizations of opposites—*hybris* and *nemesis,* fear and power—which may be embodied at a particular moment in history in states or conflicts of varying magnitudes, but which are basically the same in every case.[59] The historian is intrigued, excited, or horrified by the men who are active in times of great historical upheaval; and Western literature is infinitely richer for Herodotus' portrayal of Xerxes, or Thucydides' of Pericles, Alcibiades, and Cleon. But Pericles' greatest moment, a funeral oration in which he assesses the effects of inevitable death on the life of a great *polis,* is juxtaposed to a hair-raising account of the plague which decimates a helpless Athens. Unlike the later account of the revolution at Corcyra and others like it, which reveal the degeneration of Hellenic society under the pressures of war,[60] the plague is an uncontrollable manifestation of chance or fortune to which man can respond but which he cannot control. (Even in the revolution, political development that it is, there are forces at work on human nature which the Corcyraeans are powerless to reverse or resist.)

There is, in short, a duality about Greek historical thought which is apparent from the very first sentence of Herodotus' history: "These are the researches [ἱστορία] of Herodotus of Halicarnassus, which he publishes in the hope of thereby preserving from decay the remembrance of what men have done, and of preventing the great and wonderful actions of the Greeks and the Barbarians from losing their due meed of glory. And withal to put on record what were their grounds of feud." The historian commemorates, on the one hand, man and his deeds, and proposes, on the other, a schematized, more abstract vision of the forces in opposition (Greeks versus barbarians, "east" versus "west") which determine the path of events.[61] The two factors are never welded in Greek historiography into a comprehensive synthesis which explains historical or political development in terms of the dynamic potential for development of the individual.[62] We can see at once the radical dichotomy between this view of history and the Christian theology of history, which encompasses personal salvation within eschatological, prophetic, and typological movements in time. There is almost no common ground.[63]

Roman history owed much to the Greek heritage.[64] But for our purposes the one major difference more than compensates for the network of debts and similarities. That difference is the very fact of Rome, and her rise to greatness. However one interpreted the rise of Rome—the passage from principate to republic to empire—her development to a political place astride the ancient world demanded attention as evidence of an order manifested in or imposed upon history. Polybius early set himself to interpret the evidence; Livy's gigantic *Ab urbe condita libri* faced the same question. The most stirring and intriguing answer of all was offered not by an historian but by a poet. Vergil's *Aeneid* offered a synthesis of Roman history mythically presented, philosophically oriented, and centered on the experiences of the new hero, *pius* Aeneas. The triumph of Aeneas at the very beginning of Rome's history is also the final, lasting triumph of Rome; Jupiter's words in the first book of the epic make this clear.[65] But Aeneas' experiences, and those of other central characters, have universal significance as well for man's eternal struggle to master his own passions and find within himself the foundations of dedication, sacrifice, and self-restraint upon which to erect a stable, enduring political edifice.[66]

Nevertheless, at the heart of the *Aeneid*, as at the center of the works of the great Greek historians, is a bitter, unavoidable, and irreconcilable conflict between the human quest for happiness and the larger demands of life. In seeking to comprehend the *Aeneid*, it is wrong to single out either the majestic sadness—the *lacrimae rerum*—or the triumphant vision of *Roma eterna triumphans* as the key to Vergil's meaning. Both are inextricably interwoven in his epic fabric. The sixth book of the *Aeneid* celebrates the hero's penetration into the spiritual world beyond this life, where he reestablishes contact with the immensely fruitful force of family and national tradition, in the person of Anchises, and perceives both the nature of the universe and the destiny of Rome. Yet even at this climactic moment, Aeneas is confronted with, and recoils at, the sight of the less-than-heroic souls in Book Six, preparing to leave Hades after a thousand years of punishment and forgetfulness, and to enter again the cruel, unending cycle of history.[67] As in the Christian vision of providence, so in the *Aeneid* all is ordained, but even beyond the ken of man; [68]

nor is Vergilian history without its figural typology.[69] Unlike the historical imagination which animates the Christian theology of history, and which sees the Christian caught up in a triumphant movement of the church through time toward God and final judgment, the Vergilian imagination perceives tragedy in the future as well as triumph: the young Marcellus dead, and Turnus, Camilla, and Pallas victims of brutal war.[70]

While Vergil's view of history, therefore, and of human virtue as an historical force, is in many respects similar to that of Christianity, it retains the classical sense of a duality in history. This duality is denied by Christianity's declaration that God entered into history in order to remake and redeem it. Moreover, Vergil's vision of the possibility of human triumph was political, and the *polis* in question was precisely the system with which Christianity found itself intermittently at odds during the first three centuries of its existence. It would seem, then, that the expansion of the historical imagination of Christianity beyond the confines of biblical history to include universal history within its understanding of God's unfolding providence depended upon discovering a way to include Rome directly within the divine plan for man. The struggle to accomplish this final synthesis proved to be long, difficult, surprising, and controversial. Nevertheless, from the conflicting theories and the historical crises which tested them emerged the second main element of the nascent early medieval historical imagination, complementing the Christian theology of history. It is to the stormy courtship and ultimate wedding of Christianity and Rome, and to the consequent process of gestation by which was born the historical thought and expression of the early medieval centuries, that we must now turn.

Christianity and Rome

In the preceding section I spoke of an early hardening of the Christian attitude toward civil power, and specifically the Roman state, into one of disapproval, opposition, and even apocalyptic condemnation. Such a presentation of the available information, while essentially correct, is too one-sided; accordingly, we must now address ourselves to clarifying the relationship between Christianity and Rome by indicating the continued existence of a tradition which, while it did not necessarily approve of Roman actions, found an important place for Rome in the scheme of divine providence. The outlines of the Christian positive view of Rome have been clearly sketched by T. E. Mommsen; we need here only summarize Mommsen's findings, and refer the interested reader to his works for further details and bibliography.[71] Mommsen traces the "affirmative attitude" of Christians who "actually hoped and prayed for the continuance of the Roman empire" to the "pagan and Jewish traditions" of the succession in history of several "universal monarchies." [72] (The Old Testament book of Daniel, by its presentation of the dream of Nebuchadnezzar, provided the *locus classicus* for such speculation on the place of great empires in the providential scheme of history.) [73] From the late second century onward, a line of Christian theologians identified the fourth empire of the Daniel tradition with Rome. The Roman Empire was to exist until the end of the world; its fall would announce the arrival of Antichrist, to be followed by the dreaded final judgment. In this light, it became a logical Christian response to pray for the continuance of Rome's control of the world.[74]

Another approach to the place of Rome in the providential scheme of history emphasized not the interposition of Rome between the church and final judgment, but the role of Christianity in making possible a genuine progress in history and in the human condition, through the agency of Rome. This view, according to Mommsen, grew out of an apologetic concern to prove that the world was visibly and materially a better place since the advent of Christianity.[75] Rome, in this conception, was more powerful and more peaceful in the Christian era than it

had been before. The foundations of the *Pax Romana* under
Augustus and of the church under Christ, events so close in time,
were obviously also linked in God's plan for history: the secular
peace of the empire was ratified and fulfilled by the eternal peace
brought to man by Jesus. Since that time, according to the Christian apologists, Rome had encountered less and less opposition in
her attempted political pacification and integration of the ancient
world. As Mommsen says, "From this assertion there was but a
single step to the expression of the belief that the universal acceptance of the Christian religion by the Roman world would
lead to a still greater degree of security and prosperity." [76] Such
expression was, in fact, forthcoming. [77]

It will be noted that the two positive Christian approaches to
Rome outlined so far do not depend overtly on the typological
understanding of history elaborated earlier in this chapter. One,
to be sure, is exegetical, insofar as it applies material in the book
of Daniel to the Roman Empire; the other is apologetic and designed to controvert pagan accusations that Christianity was a
religion subversive of the Roman imperial idea. Neither, however, engages the complex historical imagination and exegetical
approach readily apparent, for example, in the Matthean infancy
narrative. The fourth kingdom of Nebuchadnezzar's dream was
not a type of Rome; it *was* Rome. The indispensable prelude to
the production of a full-fledged Christian history—a work, that
is, not so much apologetic as exegetical in its approach to extrabiblical happenings and their place in God's plan for history—
was the meeting in one mind of the positive Christian views of
Rome here outlined, of the pastoral application of scriptural exegesis to the postapostolic church, outlined in the first part of this
chapter, and of an articulated vision of divine providence as it
operates throughout the events of the history of salvation. The
mind in which occurred the confluence of these streams of Christian thought and imagination was that of Eusebius of Caesarea,

and the result of his synthesis of them was the *Ecclesiastical History*, a work of great importance for any endeavor to reconstruct the formative process of the early medieval historical imagination.

Eusebius, Bishop of Caesarea (in Palestine), was born *ca.* 263, possibly at Caesarea.[78] He grew up in a time of peace and prosperity for the church, but was also to experience its last great persecution, initiated by the emperor Diocletian in 303.[79] When, in 312, Constantine took control of the western empire (his rule over the entire empire was to begin twelve years later), he inaugurated a new era in the relations between the church and Rome. The nature of Constantine's famous conversion is still open to argument, but the results of his toleration of, and then preference for, Christianity after his accession to the empire are incontrovertible. By 380, some forty years after Constantine's death, Christianity was recognized as the official cult of the Roman Empire.[80] It is of great importance for our study that with Constantine the relations between Christianity and Rome took a sharp and unexpected turn for the better, and even more important that Eusebius was a friend and confidant of Constantine, and eventually his official panegyrist and biographer.

Recent research into the life, work, and influence of Eusebius has established beyond doubt the pivotal nature of his contribution to Christian views of history and especially of Roman history. Relying heavily on the insights and formulations of Mommsen, Wallace-Hadrill, and others, the present discussion seeks only to indicate the facets of Eusebius' varied career and production which were a preparation for his climactic work, the *Ecclesiastical History*, and for the views of Rome and Christianity presented therein. The main facts to be acknowledged include: (1) Eusebius' views on the meaning of the scriptures, specifically in regard to history; (2) his interest and skill in biblical exegesis; (3) his thought on the importance of Rome in the divine scheme;

and (4) the apologetic use of history evident in his universal chronicle, a compilation which complements the *Ecclesiastical History*.

The most striking aspect of Eusebius' scriptural historical thought is the importance in it of the pre-Mosaic patriarchs, with whom God made his first covenants. As Wallace-Hadrill puts it, "For Eusebius the roots of Christianity lay, not in Judaism proper, founded on the law given to Moses, but farther back in the pre-Jewish era of the patriarchs. In this era true religion was known and practiced, whereas Mosaic Judaism constituted a decline from the primitive purity of the patriarchal faith. It is the latter which, according to Eusebius, had recently reemerged victorious with Christ. Christianity was, therefore, substantially identical with the faith of the patriarchs." [81] The immediate result of this belief, which Eusebius expounds throughout his works,[82] was to give Christianity a prehistory at once more ancient and more venerable than that of the Jews or of pagan religions. There was, in short, much apologetic and controversial capital to be made of a direct link between patriarchs and church.[83] There was a further advantage, however, in this view for the eventual founder of Christian historiography: it gave a literal fulness to the history of the church even beyond what could be claimed as a result of typology. The patriarchs did not prefigure the church of Christ; they were its first concrete manifestation, separated from the Christian *ecclesia* by the interlude of Jewish history, when, preparatory to Christ's reestablishment of the full splendor of his kingdom, a less perfect law regulated the life of weak and sinful Israel.[84] Eusebius' understanding of the history of salvation prompted a vigorously literal reading of the Old Testament in which the vicissitudes of the church were set forth in full, rather than in figure and shadow, from the very beginning.

That Eusebius' own scriptural exegesis, in the various biblical commentaries written by him, should stress the literal level, including the literal fulfillment of prophecies in Christ, follows logically from what has just been said.[85] Typology imposes on the text a vision of development in history which, as we shall see, Eusebius in some respects shared and propagated. But his theological view of the identity of patristic religion and Christianity worked against, rather than for, a developmental or progressive understanding of God's providence in history. The developmental part of Eusebius' view of history actually involved the relationship of Rome and the church more than it did the relationship between the Old and the New Israel.

There is more to Eusebius' exegesis than his insistence on literal interpretation, however. As a young man, Eusebius studied in the school of Pamphilus, a learned priest to whom he developed a great attachment.[86] The two men studied the works and tradition of Origen with great devotion, and ultimately produced a work in which they defended his opinions. Origen, the great second- and third-century Christian controversialist and exegete, drew together the various exegetical strands of the Christian theology of history outlined in the first part of this chapter, and attempted to assimilate to them the allegorical methods of the Gnostics and of the school of Alexandria. He stressed in his exegesis the spiritual level of scripture—that level which bears on and should form the inner life of the Christian—and the typological relationship of Old Testament events to the eternal order of the universe.[87] Of these two methods of exegesis we find important instances in Eusebius of the latter. In fact, it is tempting to see in the combination of Origenist spiritual and "static," rather than historical and evolutionary, typology and the literal interpretation of the scriptures, equating the patriarchs and the church, a major key to Eusebius' historiography. For Eusebius tells us in the first chapters of the *Ecclesiastical History* that Christ existed throughout the time of Israel, and interprets the anointed (*christi*) kings of Israel as mystical types of Christ, who reigned in heaven as they did on earth.[88] The historical order, in other words, is always a sign of the eternal order established by God for the universe and supervised by Christ. Such a "vertical" and spatial view of the meaning of history is perhaps more easily universalized to include not only Israel but all nations in a providential relationship with God than is the "horizontal," temporal view of history which binds together Israel and the earthly Christ through an elaborate network of typological correspondances. Here, then, may be one major source of Eusebius' desire and willingness to record postapostolic church history in an orderly fashion: his conviction that it, too, is a sign or type of the eternal order. Specifically, the segment of the order of the universe which Eusebius perceives most clearly in church history is the battle between the devil and Christ, here figured in his church. This struggle, as old as the fall of man, is indicated by Eusebius as one of central importance at the beginning of the *Ecclesiastical History* and in many places throughout the rest of the work.[89]

Eusebius' exegesis and view of history militate against his portraying development in history. Yet his views on Rome and its meaning in providence are certainly developmental or progressive. This inconsistency may not admit of any explanation, nor need we seek one here. Suffice it to say that Eusebius adopted the apologetic view described above of Christianity's beneficent effect on the Roman Empire, and expanded it in two ways. First, he found in the rise of Rome the fulfillment of Old Testament prophecies other than the one found in Daniel.[90] He thereby continued and modified the pastoral practice of seeing the fulfillment of Old Testament prophecies in the life of the church, and applied his predilection for literal-prophetic exegesis of the scriptures to the life of Rome, rather than to the life of Christ. A second innovation in Eusebius' view of Rome was to claim not only that the fortunes of Rome prospered because of the coming of Jesus, but also that the establishment of the *Pax Augusta* was a necessary prelude to the incarnation, since it created a unified political world through which the word of God could be spread by the apostles speedily, safely, and efficiently.[91] By means of these new or expanded interpretations, Eusebius prepared the way for the combination of ecclesiastical and Roman history in one complete, imaginative, exegetical synthesis.

Before turning to the *Ecclesiastical History*, where such a synthesis is attempted, we should mention Eusebius' chronicle, a compilation of events from the history of the Hebrews, Romans, Assyrians, Chaldeans, Egyptians, and Greeks, recounted both in connected prose and in parallel chronological tables.[92] The purpose of this work was at least partly polemic and apologetic. As such it continued a tradition of studies in comparative chronology, stretching back to the second century, whereby Christian apologists proved their religion (through its link with the history of Israel) to be far older than any pagan cult.[93] Pagans had attacked Christianity as an upstart religion, and had to be answered on their own ground. Here was a case where theology alone could not satisfy, and history was summoned to be of aid. Before Eusebius, however, no one had tried to complement a chronicle with a connected narrative incorporating the Christian theology of history. It is a mark of Eusebius' originality and also of his aptitude for synthesizing important traditions of Christian interpretation, that he worked simultaneously on the first seven books of the *Ecclesiastical History* and his chronicle, publishing both *ca.* 303; [94] similarly, while he was formulating the last, all-important books of the history, he was also preparing the *Demonstratio evangelica*, in which his views on the importance of Rome in the historical scheme of divine providence were given their first expression.[95]

Such, in brief, is the varied historical and exegetical activity in which Eusebius was involved prior to and during the composition of his *Ecclesiastical History*, and which is so necessary to the adequate understanding of it. As Wallace-Hadrill says of the narrative of the *Ecclesiastical History*, "Its simplicity is akin to that of the Gospels, a simplicity which conceals certain dogmatic presuppositions of which the story itself is the narrative expression." A further comment is especially useful with regard to the concerns of this study: "Everything Eusebius wrote was historical and everything was biblical. . . . [The interrelationship] is inevitable in view of Eusebius' insistence upon the unity of God's purpose for mankind and the consequent unity of the whole story of mankind from beginning to end." [96] As we have already seen, the "insistence upon the unity of God's purpose for mankind" is at least implicit in much of the Christian historical thought of the centuries preceding Eusebius. His originality lies rather in his attempt to find and embody in the history of the postbiblical church, and especially in the church and empire of his own day, "the . . . unity of the whole story of mankind." The *Ecclesiastical History* is the record of that attempt.

The *Ecclesiastical History* appeared in three separate editions during Eusebius' lifetime. This fact is of no mere scholarly interest but is crucial for our understanding of the work as a whole. [97] The first edition, completed *ca.* 303, included the first seven books of the work and brought the history of the church to the beginning of the persecution of Diocletian. By comparing these books with the concurrently prepared chronicles, we see that Eusebius was primarily interested in the church as an historical phenomenon literally and fully present in the world from the time of the patriarchs (though temporarily concealed during the period when Israel was ruled by the Mosaic law), and typifying in its existence and relationship with the world the eternal struggle between God and the perverse aspects of his creation. In this struggle Eusebius made no specific reference to the role of the Roman Empire in the scheme of providence. [98]

Eusebius reworked the *Ecclesiastical History* after the first stage of the persecution, which ended in the destruction of the main persecutors (*ca.* 311), and again after the persecutions had come to an end and Constantine had established himself on the imperial throne.[99] In the course of revising his work, Eusebius' views of history underwent several major developments. His first decision was to interpret the onset of the persecution of 303 as God's punishment of the church for its laxity and sinfulness during the peaceful era preceding Diocletian; after the church had purified itself by its sufferings and had shown itself alone of all the inhabitants of the empire to be steadfast in the face of all afflictions, it was rewarded by God in the person of Constantine, who liberated it.[100] To buttress his perceptions, Eusebius appealed, in the manner utilized in early Christian preaching, to Old Testament prophecies, which he claimed were fulfilled in the sinful church and its punishments. The novelty of the procedure lay in its placing of the fulfilled prophecy within a narrative, historiographical context.[101] Eusebius' other innovation lay in his treatment of Constantine, who appears after the church's trial and effects her deliverance. To Eusebius, Constantine is more than just a liberator of Christianity; he is also the imperial hero who accomplishes the pacification and unification of the empire after a period of intense civil strife.[102] As Eusebius pondered the climax of the twin crises of church and empire, he formulated for the first time his conception of the empire's place in God's providential scheme for history and for the church in history; that is, he admitted the principle of development or progress into his Christian historiography.[103]

With the triumph of Constantine, who effected the double salvation of church and empire, Eusebius' thought was cast into a final, complex pattern which we can speak of as the first complete Christian view of political and biblical history. This view involved the raising of the empire, and specifically of Constantine, to the status of an instrument of divine providence through which God triumphantly revealed the innermost workings of his plan for history. Constantine becomes "the last of the patriarchs," the new Abraham, in whom the promise made to Abraham is literally fulfilled;[104] the Roman Empire of which

Constantine is head becomes the definitive force of providence in history, and promises to the Christian the prospect of an ever triumphant and ever improving society—i.e., the prospect of endless progress in history.[105]

What we have said so far of Eusebius' mature historical vision pertains to the realm of theory and synthesis. The workings of the historical imagination reveal themselves also in the patterns and devices which organize and intensify the narrative in which the theory and synthesis are contained and propagated. To close this brief survey of Eusebius' historiography, we shall note a few of the characteristic devices by which he vivifies history while revealing graphically the foundations of its meaning.

First of all, we cannot fail to note the increasingly important role of the Bible in regulating and shaping the narrative through its content and manner. When he contemplates and denounces the sins of the church which invited the persecution, Eusebius adopts momentarily the tone of an Old Testament prophet; the language of the prophets and the psalms colors the narrative at this point. Later, in describing the climactic battle between Constantine and Maxentius outside Rome, Eusebius again invokes the Bible, and specifically the Exodus of Israel, to describe how the armies of the righteous warrior defeat those of the tyrant. The passage is worth quoting in its entirety:

> Then, that He might not be forced for the sake of the tyrant to make war on the Romans, God Himself, as if with some bonds dragged the tyrant very far from the gates, and confirmed the ancient threats against the impious, disbelieved by most as being in the nature of myth, but worthy of belief with believers since they were inscribed in the sacred books. He confirmed them, in short, by their very clarity with all, believers and unbelievers, who took in the marvels with their own eyes. For example, as in the time of Moses himself and of that ancient and pious race of the Hebrews, "Pharao's chariots and his army he hath cast into the sea, chosen horsemen and captains; they were sunk in the Red Sea; the depths have covered them," in the same way, also, Maxentius and the

soldiers and armed guards about him "were sunk to the bottom like a stone," [Cf. Exod. 15:4, 5] when, turning his back on God's might that was with Constantine, he crossed the river that lay in his path, which he himself by joining boats had successfully bridged and so formed an instrument of destruction against himself. Therefore it were possible to say, "He hath opened a pit and dug it, and he shall fall into the hole he made. His work shall turn on his own head, and his wickedness shall come down upon his own crown." [Cf. Ps. 7:16, 17]

Thus, then, when the bridge over the river broke, the passage across collapsed, and suddenly the boats, men and all, went down into the deep, and he himself first, the most impious; then, too, the shield-bearers about him, as the divine oracles foretell, "sank as lead in the mighty waters," [Cf. Exod. 15:10] so that fittingly, if not in words, then in deeds, like the followers of the great servant Moses [Cf. Exod. 14:31], those who by God's help won the victory might thus hymn in a manner the very words uttered against the impious tyrant of old and say: "Let us sing to the Lord: for he is gloriously magnified, the horse and the rider he hath thrown into the sea. The Lord is my strength and protecter, he is become salvation to me," and "Who is like to thee, among the gods, O Lord? Who is like thee, glorified among saints, marvelous in praises, doing wonders?" [Cf. Exod. 15:1, 2, 11]

Constantine by his very deeds having sung to God, the Ruler of all and the Author of his victory, these words and such as were akin and resembling these, entered Rome with hymns of triumph.

Constantine is the new Moses; his army, the new Israelites seeking the new promised land, Rome. Maxentius is a new pharaoh whom God defeats. Biblical exegesis provides a model for the Christian interpretation of a climactic event in Roman history.[106]

Eusebius also interprets post-biblical church history according to norms which, in biblical narrative, govern Israel's unique relationship to God. The church, punished for its sins by persecution and rewarded for its reformation by Constantine's leadership, partakes of a new pattern of divine providence. Earlier in his career as ecclesiastical historian, Eusebius saw the life of the church as a constant, earthly type of God's continuing battle

with the devil; however, once he decided that "the culminating
stage of human history had been reached" in Constantine,[107] he
constructed a new, definitive typology of things earthly and
heavenly: the judgments of history reflect and prefigure the
reality of God as judge in heaven.[108] And the relationship of
Constantine and the church in Eusebius' own imagination is also
clarified by this perception: for Eusebius, Constantine is a new
type of hero, whose career catches up and typifies the movement
of history in his own time. For this reason Eusebius portrays the
emperor, both in the *Ecclesiastical History* and in his later pane-
gyric works on Constantine, as an idealized type rather than an
individual—a glorious type in whom is revealed the triumph of
the church.[109] As Wallace-Hadrill says, "the conception here
is not of individual but of corporate salvation, a conception of
a whole people under God dedicated to His service, every aspect
of whose life bears reference to their dedication and calling." [110]
The anti-individualistic tendency of the Christian historical imagination, already remarked in connection with Christian hagiography and typology,[111] finds in Eusebius a new and extremely
influential application: that of the social or political hero, identified with both the providential scheme of history (originating
in the typological exegesis of biblical history in terms of Christ)
and the course of national prosperity and crisis. Like Constantine, many heroes of early medieval historical narratives will
partake of the nature of both Christ and Caesar.

Augustine and Orosius

Eusebius brought a Christian historiography to birth in the
age of Constantine. A century later, as Rome and her empire
slid from the pinnacle of greatness toward the shadowy vale of
barbarian occupation and political fragmentation, two other
Christian writers of very divergent outlook and talent brought
the new genre to adulthood and provided it with an imaginative

breadth and depth of great importance for the centuries to come. The contributions of Augustine, in his *De civitate Dei*, and of Orosius, whose *Septem libri historiarum adversum paganos* was the first universal Christian history, comprise, with one exception, the remaining background material essential to this sketch of the origins of early medieval historical thought and writing. (The exception, Salvian's *De gubernatione Dei*, provides such clear grounds for comparison with the first fall of Britain text— Gildas' *De excidio Britanniae*—that I shall treat it in conjunction with the latter work in the next chapter.)

Augustine's approach to history was in many ways the negation of that of Eusebius. It was, indeed, subversive of the kind of interpretation of past and present events which makes Eusebius' work unique and revolutionary. That is not to say that Augustine's thought and imagination were antihistorical. On the contrary, his powerful intellect and profound spiritual and psychological perceptions were disciplined throughout his Christian life by a highly developed sense of history, which operated within the Judaeo-Christian tradition of an historical divine providence, as developed in the Bible. It is, however, the last phrase which is most crucial; Augustine's is a true and uncompromisingly biblical *theology* of history which makes no concessions to the exigencies or attractiveness of mere political and social ideals, however Christian their expression. Consequently, Augustine combated, particularly in his monumental *De civitate Dei*, both the notion that Roman imperial civilization was a great end in itself which Christianity had subverted,[112] and its converse, that Christianity had saved the empire (and vice versa) and together with the empire held the key to human progress. Rebutting the former contention involved Augustine in an apologetic discourse, comprising the first eleven books of *De civitate Dei*, in the course of which the genius of Rome is weighed in the balance, and, despite Augustine's recognition of the grandeur of the Roman ideal at its finest, is found wanting. The latter claim, clearly the legacy of Eusebius (whom Augustine seems at times to be specifically controverting), was seductive and popular, for its justification of a Romano-Christian alliance possessed all the attractiveness of assimilation.[113] To combat it, Augustine was forced to propose another interpretation of history.

Taking as his starting point and inspiration key biblical texts (e.g., the psalms which sing of Jersusalem, and the story of Cain and Abel in Genesis), and interpreting them typologically (especially in the eschatological sense central to the Matthean tradition), Augustine answered the defenders of Rome, the "eternal city," with a vision of two cities existing side by side, or rather intertwined, in the world,[114] from the days of Cain and Abel until the very end of time. One is the earthly city, inhabited by those whose highest satisfaction lies in complete dedication to and enjoyment of worldly goods, fame, and honor as ends in themselves. The Rome of the senate and the Caesars is not the *civitas terrena;* it is a manifestation of that city.[115]

To the inhabitants of the other city, the *civitas Dei,* all worldly glory (and all worldly suffering) [116] are, in contrast, the means to be used in gaining the supreme End, God. The *civitas terrena* finds its fulfillment in self-contemplation, even if the "self" has been refined into a concept of empire which stands above the merits and desires of any of its members. But the "communion of saints is rooted in a love of God that is ready to trample on self. In a word, this latter relies on the Lord, whereas the other [city] boasts that it can get along by itself." [117] The experiences of this life are to be used, not enjoyed—only God is to be enjoyed, and such enjoyment is only to be had in the heavenly Jerusalem.[118]

The two cities—two societies, each united by love, perpetually divided one from the other by loving different objects— are to be separated only at the final judgment, when the citizens of the *civitas terrena,* having enjoyed their "heaven on earth," will be perpetually barred from God's presence, and those of the *civitas Dei* will be united in the eternal love and adoration of the triune Deity. The final separation and rewards are the subjects of the last three books of Augustine's work, which discuss the eschatological climax of history.

History, in the Augustinian view, moves inexorably toward its divinely ordained end, but it does so through the continuous personal choices of the members of the two cities. The process of choice, furthermore, need not produce spectacular results in the political sphere (although from time to time Augustine pondered the effect on society of the joint actions of a truly devoted *civitas Dei*),[119] and is not at all to be identified with the gains or losses of the empire, or with the victories and defeats of a particular emperor, even if Christian.[120] Only God knows and understands all the actions of the members of the two cities, and can appraise their true worth *sub specie aeternitatis*. Fortunately, he gave to man, in the biblical record of Israel, an account of human actions which also illustrates and explains God's providence, and consequently the purpose of history. Augustine therefore uses the Bible as a key to the meaning of history, by which he explains not only what has happened to the two cities, but what is happening, and what will happen as they move through time toward God.[121] Biblical events, understood literally and typologically, tell man more about the wellsprings and results of his actions—i.e., about his relationship to God—than do the successes or reverses of political and social existence.[122] Augustine did not wish to flee history for ahistorical theology; rather, he wished to penetrate beyond the vicissitudes of history to discover the constant principle of God's providence within history.[123] The history of salvation, in short, liberates man from the tyranny of secular (or imperial) history.[124]

The history of salvation which Augustine finds in the Bible, however, is not a touchstone indicating with precision the manifestation of providence in a given extrabiblical, historical situation. Augustine denies emphatically that man can explicate God's design for him as it appears in history; rather, he must believe in it.[125] He thus strikes at the second major Eusebian premise: that providence operates visibly in the world of Christian Rome, and that rewards and punishments in this life are types of God's judgments in the next. In effect, Augustine denies the applicability of typological exegesis to the public, social life of men, restricting its use to the "classical" Christian tradition of types fulfilled in the continuing life of Christ in Christians. Augustine's historical thought, measuring as it does the importance of individual action by criteria other than the immediate results or social impact of that action, focuses finally on the development of the Christian (or a-Christian) personality as the central phenomenon of history. The crucial fact of history is each man's choice between the two cities, that is, between God and man as the ultimate object of love.[126]

Primarily, then, Augustine can be said to have exerted a negative influence on the development of the Christian historical imagination along the lines laid down by Eusebius. In the Augustinian system, as formulated in *De civitate Dei*, the twin Eusebian principles of the observable progress of God's providence in the history of the empire, and of the figural operation of God's judgment in history, are vigorously and profoundly controverted, and an alternative theory of history is proposed. It can be argued that a system like Augustine's—stressing the uniqueness of the scriptural record, the pilgrim status of the citizen of the *civitas Dei* who is never really at home in the stream of political history,[127] and the shroud, penetrable only by faith, which cloaks God's plan for history—was necessary to save the church from degenerating into a Caesaro-papist system and from going down with the sinking fifth-century imperial ship of state. Our intention is not to judge Augustine's theory vis à vis that of Eusebius (a judgment long since made by history), but to point out that it represented a retreat from the comprehensive claims made by Eusebius for the Christian's ability to find the footprints of God in history. In Augustine's vision, the accent falls more heavily on the individual's inner journey to God than on his outer journey through the world and time.[128] Augustine would shape and control the historical imagination by faith and the message of the scriptures; Eusebius would liberate it through the broad and free application of exegetical methods borrowed from scriptural study.

At another level, however, *De civitate Dei* exerted a great positive influence on historical thought in ages to come, for it ratified beyond doubt the fact that a Christian view of history existed; that the Bible—the Old Testament in its complex and colorful story of Israel, the New in its presentation of Jesus, definer of history's meaning—was its cornerstone; and that typology was a key to its meaning.[129] While Augustine emphatically denied the ends of Eusebian interpretation, he corroborated the worth of the means by appropriating them for his own ends.

Despite Augustine's great stature in the early medieval church, Eusebian freedom triumphed over Augustinian control in the writing of history during the following centuries; indeed it can be argued that, given the alternatives, the outcome was inevitable. For Augustine's system led to Christian belief and action, but not to a Christian historiography. Where God's plan cannot be perceived, it cannot be repeated in an historical narrative. Whatever its intrinsic limits, the Eusebian approach to history proved consistently attractive to the minds and imaginations of early medieval historians; in his duel with the bishop of Hippo, the bishop of Caesarea was undeniably the winner.

Nowhere is the triumph of Eusebius more apparent than in the work of Augustine's own disciple, Paulus Orosius.[130] Orosius wrote his historical defense of Christianity against pagan accusations at the request of Augustine.[131] Ostensibly, he was to document Augustine's contentions that the lives of men were no worse under a Christian empire than they had been under a pagan one, and that the pre-Christian history of Rome had, in fact, had more than its share of disaster and misery, including the injustices perpetrated by the expansion of Rome.[132] In keeping with his faith in divine providence, Augustine felt, nevertheless, that God had permitted the growth of the Roman Empire for his own inscrutable purposes.[133] From these two ideas extracted from his mentor's half-completed work,[134] Orosius constructed a most un-Augustinian history of Rome, in which the city and empire become monuments to God's ordering of history. Orosius' work restates and expands the premises of Eusebian historiography: the role of Rome in the divine scheme is that of a chosen nation progressing toward Christ, and finally enjoying triumphant union with the church; and the continuous process of divine judgment passed figurally on man (especially on sinners) is everywhere apparent in the history of Rome. With Orosius, progress and judgment resume their place at the center of the Christian historical imagination.

At the beginning of the *Historia,* Orosius explains the Christian assumptions on which his interpretation of history is based:

In the first place, we hold that if the world and man are directed by a Divine Providence that is as good as it is just, and if man is both weak and stubborn on account of the changeableness of his nature and his freedom of choice, then it is necessary for man to be guided in the spirit of filial affection when he has need of help; but when he abuses his freedom, he must be reproved in a spirit of strict justice. *Everyone who sees mankind reflected through himself and in himself* perceives that this world has been disciplined since the creation by alternating periods of good and bad times. Next we are taught that sin and punishment began with the very first man. Furthermore, even our opponents . . . have described nothing but wars and calamities. . . . *Those evils which existed* [before Christ], *as to a certain extent they exist now, were doubtless either palpable sins or the hidden punishments for sin. . . .*

I shall, therefore, speak of the period from the creation of the world to the founding of the City, and then of the period extending to the principate of Caesar and the birth of Christ, from which time dominion over the world has remained in the hands of the City down to the present day. . . .[135]

The close connection between divine justice and the condition of mankind here outlined theoretically is exemplified by the history of Rome, as organized around "the principate of Caesar and the birth of Christ"—the twin pinnacles of Roman and biblical history already linked together by Eusebius. Moving beyond what Eusebius or any other predecessor had attempted, Orosius constructed a Roman "history of salvation," modeled on that of the biblical Israel, but with Roman events and development as the central concern. The logic on which such a transfer is based is clearly articulated by the historian at the beginning of Book Two:

There is no person living today, I think, who does not acknowledge that God created man in this world. Hence, whenever man sins, the world also becomes subject to censure, and owing to our failure to control the passions that we ought to restrain, this earth on which we live is punished by having its animal life die out and its crops fail. It follows, too, that if we are the creation of God, we are also properly the object of His concern. For who loves us more than He who made us? Who orders our existence better than He who has created and loves us? Who can order and control our actions more wisely or more firmly than He who foresaw what must be done and then brought to pass what He had foreseen? Hence those who have not read, feel, and those who have read, recognize, that all power and all government come from God.[136]

"All power and all government come from God"—a God whose love for man compels his constant control over man, and his correction of man when human failings make it imperative. This ironclad logic, while illustrated in revelation, does not depend upon it ("those who have not read, feel . . .") and cannot therefore be confined, as Augustine would have it, to the history of Israel. No single conclusion was to be more important for the writers of national history in the early Middle Ages. Orosius provided both precept and example for the imaginative recreation of the national past in biblical times.

In the pre-Christian history of Rome, terrible sins and ter-

rible punishments dominate the narrative. Rome during this period knew no peace; the gates of Janus (closed only when Rome
was at peace) were open during all the years save one before the
Pax Augusta, which prepared the world for Christ.[137] But punishment was not abandonment; [138] God had elected Rome, and
despite her rebelliousness and preference for evil she moved
through history toward Christ, guided by God "that [she]
might accept the faith in the future and yet now be partially
punished for her unbelief." [139] When Christ finally appears,
Orosius proclaims, "It is clear to everyone from his own knowledge, faith, and investigation, that it was by the will of our
Lord Jesus Christ that this City prospered, was protected, and
brought to such heights of power, since to her, in preference to
all others, He chose to belong when He came, thereby making
it certain that He was entitled to be called a Roman citizen." [140]
In the period of the Christian empire, Orosius demonstrates that
serene belief in the complete compatibility of Christianity and
the empire which marked Eusebius' vision as well. The famous
passage at the beginning of Book Five epitomizes the attitude:
"Among Romans, as I have said, I am a Roman; among Christians, a Christian; among men, a man. The state comes to my aid
through its laws, religion through its appeal to conscience, and
nature through its claim of universality." [141] The peace and well-
being of Christian Rome reflects the communion of the Christian with his God: "I have everything when I have with me
Him whom I love; especially since He is the same among all.
. . . Neither does He forsake me when I am in need, because
the earth is His and its fulness, whereof He has ordered all things
to be common to all men. The blessings of our age, which our
ancestors never had in their entirety, are these: the tranquillity
of the present, hope for the future, and possession of a common
place of refuge." [142]

In addition to echoing earlier Christian writers on the theme
of the four great kingdoms of Nebuchadnezzar's dream, with

Rome as the last and lasting one,[143] and reestablishing the traditional parallel between Roman and biblical fulfillment at the time of Augustus and Christ,[144] Orosius in at least one section of his history applies a form of typological exegesis to important Roman events. By doing so, he demonstrates the continuing hold on the Christian historical imagination of the exegetical system, which, like Eusebius, he uses to organize and vivify his narrative.[145] In the twentieth chapter of the sixth book, Caesar, after having subdued Egypt, returns to Rome, now at her greatest moment. He enters the city in triumph on the sixth of January, orders the gates of Janus closed, and is first hailed as Augustus. "This title," say Orosius, ". . . signifies that the assumption of the supreme power to rule the world was legitimate. From that time on the highest power of the state reposed in one man. . . ." That such a reign of universal peace and single authority should come on the sixth of January, "on which we observe the Epiphany, that is, the Feast of the Apparition and Manifestation of the Sacrament of the Lord," is clear indication that "the empire of Caesar . . . in every respect . . . had been prepared for the future advent of Christ." Furthermore, there are signs and portents at the time of Caesar's triumph which Orosius interprets as referring to Caesar's role in preparing the way for Christ. A circle around the sun indicates the earthly power and universality of the emperor, and the coming of him "Who alone had made and ruled the sun itself and the whole world." When Caesar decrees that "all the former debts of the Roman people should be remitted and the records of account books should also be destroyed," a spring of oil comes forth from an inn, during an entire day. Caesar's restoration of slaves to their proper masters, and chastising of those who do not acknowledge a master, is, with the destruction of the debt books, an obvious allegory of Christ freeing man from sin and restoring him to his true master, God. The spring of oil is the anointed one, Christ himself, and all his followers, who flow forth from the church; the whole

day is "the entire duration of the Roman Empire." This allegorical scheme, so reminiscent of scriptural exegesis, confirms
the typological character of Caesar. The signs and miracles which
mark his reign are "very clear to those who did not heed the
voice of the prophets." In other words, Rome's career serves
notice to all the world of the new dispensation, as we look back
on it with Christian eyes. Israel has been succeeded by Rome,
which provides universal evidence, in the peace it brings to
earth, of the role of Christ, whose reign is shortly to begin.[146]

Thus Orosius amply demonstrates the durability of the Eusebian historical system, as well as its continued hold on the imagination of Christendom in surveying the past. Orosius' influence,
in turn, was to reach far forward into the Middle Ages, even as
far as Dante.[147] In the early medieval centuries, Orosius' main
legacy was his synthesis of national history and biblical narrative with its exegetical interpretation. Accounts of the barbaric
past of nations whose conversion to Christ was a social as well as
a religious landmark often fell into an Orosian (or Orosian-
Eusebian) pattern—a national history of salvation organized
around the triumph of Christianity and its beneficent effects,
and realized in the typifying personages of Christian social
heroes. The theology of history had become a multipurpose
garment which Franks and Anglo-Saxons, as new Israelites,
could wear as easily as Romans.

Mention of the barbarian nations brings us to the end of this
consideration of the formative period of early medieval attitudes
toward history. The barbarian invasions and settlements of the
western Roman Empire are the watershed of European cultural
and political history; on one side towers the tattered but still
serviceable edifice of Roman institutions and civilization, on the
other, a world of national migration, political flux, and cultural
transition. The barbarian challenge to Roman (and therefore
Christian) civilization was already a major environmental factor
for Augustine and Orosius; the three-day occupation of Rome

by Alaric's Visigoths in 410, which provided a focal point for pagan objections to the Christian empire, was the proximate cause of Augustine's writing *De civitate Dei*. Both the bishop of Hippo and his Spanish pupil rejected any contention that Christianity was causing the downfall of Rome and exposing her to barbarian encroachments, and Orosius was even confident that the Christian empire would assimilate the barbarians and in the process extend even further the sway of Romano-Christian civilization.[148]

Despite Christian rejoinders to pagan accusations, the threat posed by the barbarians to imperial order became a pressing reality as the fifth century wore on, a reality moreover which permanently affected European history. How then did the barbarian invasions challenge the historical imagination of those who lived through them, and of those who came after them? Or, to approach the problem from a different perspective, how did the early medieval centuries comprehend and represent a "past" which was actually three pasts in one: the Christian past, with its biblical, *heilsgeschichtlich* scheme, the Roman past, as interpreted by Christianity, and the national (i.e., barbarian) past of the various nations of western Europe? It is to this question that the body of this study will direct itself.

CHAPTER 11

Gildas'
De excidio et conquestu Britanniae:
In Britain's Fall They Sinnèd All

The situation in which the inhabitants of the island of Britain found themselves as a result of the crisis precipitated by the barbarian invasions differed from that of any other part of western Europe. Britain had been a Roman colony since 43 A.D., in which year the expedition led by the emperor Claudius landed on the island and easily subdued the Celtic tribes of its southern and eastern sections.[1] Current archaeological explorations are constantly increasing our knowledge of this colonial period,[2] but not challenging the standard facts, viz., that the occupation left a deep impress of Roman civilization and political institutions on the urban and rural areas of lowland Britain, while in the northern highlands and in Wales the Roman hold on land and populace was primarily that of a military occupation. During the third century, the difficulties of the Roman legions and government were compounded by the raids of marauding Germanic pirates, whose activities required vigorous Romano-British military countermeasures, and earned for the coastal areas of southeastern Britain the title of the Saxon Shore (*litus Saxonicum*).[3]

The years of distress and catastrophe which saw Alaric's sack of Rome, and the composition of *De civitate Dei* and Orosius' history, were also the years in which Rome gradually abandoned her British colony. The chronology of Roman and British governments in Britain during the first half of the fifth century remains vague and disputed, but transcending the nocturnal clash of ignorant (or near-ignorant) scholarly armies is the undoubted fact that the departure of the imperial legions created a vacuum which migrating German tribes were soon attempting to fill.[4] The resultant struggle, which lasted more than 150 years, was one between barbarians and a heterogeneous, partly Romanized, partly Romanophilic, and partly quite insular Celtic population, deprived of Roman assistance. It is, of course, incorrect to imagine the period between the end of Roman rule and the stabilization of the Saxon kingdoms in the late sixth century as one of continual and universal war in Britain. The Saxon advance was uneven and discontinuous.[5]

During one of the lulls in the contest for mastery of the island, about the middle of the sixth century, a British monk named Gildas wrote a tract addressed to his nation, and especially to some of its errant rulers, rebuking them for their evil ways, warning against the vengeance of an angry God, and urging immediate, sincere repentance. Gildas' *liber querulus*,[6] which he or his readers called *De excidio et conquestu Britanniae*,[7] is an earnest and hortatory *pièce d'occasion*, a "tract for the times," as many scholars have called it. The body of the work, however, is preceded by a section in which Gildas presents a highly selective and individualized picture of the British past, and interprets its meaning for the present crisis. This idiosyncratic historical section is the earliest extant insular account of the fall of Britain, and accordingly the starting point of our study of the fall of Britain texts.

Of Gildas the man little is known; of Gildas the saint and miracle-worker a considerable legendary literature survives.[8] It is neither of these, but rather Gildas the historian (or, more precisely, Gildas the possessor of an historical imagination used for moral purposes) who concerns us here. The historical task which Gildas set for himself in his *De excidio* was nothing less than an explication of the barbarian invasions. In his approach to the past, he illustrates both his age's understandable concern with the historical and philosophical questions raised by the passing of the Roman world order and its varying interest in the nations which at once terminated and inherited that order. It may therefore be useful at this point to comment briefly on some early historiographical responses to the barbarians, in order to provide a minimal context within which to judge the achievement of Gildas.

One such response which, while it preceded *De excidio* by a century, has often been directly or indirectly compared to the British monk's tract is Salvian's *De gubernatione Dei*. A priest of Marseilles, Salvian wrote his work between the years 439 and 451.[9] Like Gildas, Salvian composed a "tract for the times"; *De gubernatione Dei* is a scathing indictment of an evil and decadent Roman world which, according to Salvian, is suffering for its sins at the hands of the barbarians with the consent, and according to the plan, of God.[10] The accuracy of Salvian's portrait of his own society need not detain us, since it is rather his method we seek to determine. His approach is relatively simple: he was convinced that God constantly governs the world, and being a moral God, governs it justly.[11] Such a contention, which seemed highly debatable to many of Salvian's contemporaries undergoing the hardships of the barbarian incursions,[12] was most easily proven from the biblical history of Israel, with its record of divine intervention and providential guidance. Once granted, Salvian's premise was readily applicable to the calamities of his own day: if, he reasoned, things are going so badly for society, if the empire is about to collapse, then the citizens of the empire must all be sinful, and these universal calamities are a clear indication of God's judgment.[13]

In keeping with this logic, Salvian's method consisted first in mining the Old Testament for *exempla* chosen to demonstrate the activity of providence in man's life through the immediate reward or punishment of holiness or sin, and then in using these *exempla* to explain contemporary happenings.[14] The exemplary use of scripture, which we remarked above as a rhetorical characteristic of some early Christian teaching, here becomes the basis of a simple, unified view of history. The first two books of *De gubernatione Dei* consist almost entirely of scriptural examples, and it is noteworthy that Salvian makes no attempt here to develop a theology of history. He employs typology only once,[15] and minimizes, though he does not deny, the movement of history from Old Testament type to sacramental present and final, eschatological fulfillment.[16]

When Salvian turns from the biblical past to the troubled present, he confines himself to enumerating the sins of his compatriots, to reminding them of the sufferings they have undergone and are undergoing for their misdeeds, and to comparing favorably the barbarians, uncivilized Arians that they are, with the decadent Romans.[17] He also indicates in several places the fulfillment of Old Testament prophecies in the Christian empire of his own day, another traditional Christian application of the Bible to history.[18] The total impression left by Salvian's historical vision is one of narrowness, a narrowness forced upon the writer by the seriousness of the situation, which demanded an immediate response to justify the ways of God to men, and to exhort them to change their own ways. I call Salvian's vision narrow or bounded for these reasons: first, the only past which he uses to explain the present is the biblical past—neither Roman nor barbarian history enter into the scheme of *De gubernatione Dei;* second, his invocation of the biblical past to elucidate the present has little imaginative or narrative complexity. His exemplary and prophetic interpretations of scripture never leave the literal level; there is no exegesis of the text to expound a theology of history. There is, in short, no dynamic principle of historical develop-

ment in Salvian's presentation; there are only the facts of God's
nature and purpose which sit athwart history and render it
equally comprehensible at any time to anyone willing to examine
past and present honestly and with Christian eyes.

Salvian's frame of reference was still that of the late empire;
he selected for his purposes a few elements of Romano-Christian
historical thought, and composed a document redolent of the
attitudes of a dying age. In his indictment of his compatriots as
well as in his celebration of barbarian virtues, Salvian is a true
representative of the old Rome, the last heir of Livy and Tacitus.
Soon, however, a new order of historians was to approach the
barbarian revolution in Europe from a directly opposite point
of view. These were the national historians of the barbarians,
who set out to look beyond *Romania,* spatially and temporally,
and to trace the origins and growth of their ancestral races. In
so doing, they not only recorded the nation's migration to new
homes and accession to new power; they committed themselves
to a new, dynamic view of history, in which the expansion of
barbarian power was inseparably linked to the evolution of a
new, postimperial political order. To claim that the chroniclers
of barbarian history gloated over Rome's decline and fall would
be to overstate and to distort the case, especially since it was only
through contact with surviving Romano-Christian culture (primarily monastic culture) that they became able to write about
the past.[19] But it would be equally naive to imagine that the
educated, historically-minded barbarian (or, like Cassiodorus and
Gregory of Tours, the nonbarbarian inhabitant of barbarian
Europe) saw in the past only the continuity of Roman civilization. What prevented such an attitude above all was the large
body of national legends and traditions which the barbarian nations preserved orally among themselves before and after their
accession to the governance of postimperial Europe. Here was a
national past, neither Roman nor Christian, which could not be
ignored.

In succeeding chapters of this study, we shall have occasion to compare the fall of Britain texts with national histories such as Gregory of Tours' *Historia Francorum*, and Paul the Deacon's *Historia Langobardorum*, and to note the variety of approaches to national history which resulted from the combination of barbarian traditions with classical rhetoric, scriptural exegesis, Orosian narrative structure, and the Eusebian national-ecclesiastical hero. For our present concern, it is sufficient to recognize that by the time Gildas wrote his *liber querulus*, the tradition of national history as an indigenous medieval narrative form had already been established. The earliest example, the Gothic history of Cassiodorus, Italian statesman, educator, and preserver of the Roman heritage, has unfortunately not survived, but its abridgment—the so-called *Getica*—by the Goth Jordanes remains. Cassiodorus' work dates from the first third of the sixth century, the *Getica* from *ca.* 551 A.D., i.e., within a few years of *De excidio*. The original motivation for Cassiodorus' work was national and political: to extol the Goths by glorifying their past, and therefore to establish their right to rule over the Romans in sixth-century Italy.[20] Jordanes added to these intentions a desire for a political union of Gothic and Roman races, in order to assure continued peace and prosperity in Italy.[21] The *Getica*, in short, seeks at once to dignify the national past by means of Roman learning, and to integrate that heroic past with the political present, specifically as a stimulus to racial synthesis and harmony. The aim and method are completely different from those of Salvian, and, as described earlier, typically medieval where Salvian's were typically Roman.

Gildas (and, through the influence of Gildas, the fall of Britain texts generally) offers a third approach to the barbarian invasions. The peculiarities of his approach owe something to the historical situation of Britain, and something to the personal preoccupations of Gildas. Historically, the battle between Christian Britain and her pagan invaders was fought for the control of an island already abandoned by the empire and beyond the reach of reconquest through campaigns such as that of the eastern empire in sixth-century Italy. *Romania* was more a memory, less a political heritage, in Britain than elsewhere in Europe. In the crucible of Gildas' historical imagination, however, the image of Rome burned brightly still, as did the outlines of a biblical theology of history. Consequently, in reviewing the past as a guide to present action, Gildas fused three elements into a complex historical vision: the British nation-*ecclesia*, the Roman presence, and the biblical revelation of divine providence working itself out in the life of the Christian and of the world. Unlike Salvian (whose work *De excidio* overtly resembles), Gildas' laments and exhortations find support in a dynamic sense of history; unlike the first historians of the barbarians, his dynamic sense of history is Christian, not national, his materials biblically, not traditionally oriented. Eschewing heroic and pre-Christian legends, Gildas presented to his nation—and to those who came after—a systematic interpretation of the Christian past of Britain, as judged in the light of Rome, of the Saxons, and of the history of salvation.

The historical section of *De excidio* consists of twenty-six chapters, including two introductory chapters in which Gildas explains how he has come to write the work. (By contrast, the purely hortatory section of *De excidio* comprises Chapters 27 to 110.) After the two chapters of self-justification, which, as we shall see, provide a preliminary key to the work, the historical narrative subdivides itself as follows: Chapters 3 and 4 describe the beautiful island of Britain and its unworthy inhabitants; Chapters 5 through 7, the coming of Roman power to Britain, the revolt of the Britons, and the consequent enslavement of the nation by the Romans; Chapters 8 through 12, the coming of Christianity and the establishment of the British church; Chapters 13 through 18, the expedition from Britain of the usurper Maximus, the first attacks of Picts and Scots on the unprotected

Britons, the rescue missions of Rome, and the final departure of
the Romans from the island; Chapters 19 through 22, the temporary British successes in battle thanks to the aid of God, the
consequent prosperity and sinfulness of the Britons, and divine
punishment through further Pictish and Scottish attacks; Chapters 23 and 24, the invitation extended to the Saxons by the
Britons, and the ensuing destruction of the latter by the former;
Chapter 25, the rallying of the Britons under Ambrosius Aurelianus; and Chapter 26, further battles, including the climactic
encounter at *mons badonicus,* after which peace reigns, but is
accompanied by moral degeneration which promises future evils,
and which elicits from Gildas his "tract for the times."

The structure of *De excidio* is organized basically into blocks
of narrative which alternately delineate the Britons' relationship
with Rome and with God. Gildas exploits in a variety of ways
the possibilities for comparison, contrast, and interaction inherent
in this structure. The Romans—to begin with them—are sym-
pathetically treated in the two "Roman" sections, Chapters 5–7
and 13–18. In the first, they arrive in Britain after having established a universal peace.[22] Gildas, whose expression is imagistic
throughout *De excidio,* here portrays Roman civilization and
order as a flame which cannot be quenched by the sea around
Britain.[23] (Movement across bodies of water will serve as one of
many recurrent narrative devices by which Gildas binds together
the various sections of his history.) The cowardly Britons receive
their new Roman masters docilely, but revolt soon after most of
the Roman occupation force leaves the island. This treachery
results in a harsher Roman subjection of the island, which is no
more than the islanders deserve. The Britons have rebelled against
civil order and have brought the consequences of rebellion on
their heads.[24]

In the second Roman section, the Britons send the tyrant and
usurper Maximus to the continent, where he kills one Roman
emperor and banishes the other before being justly punished

with execution. The troops he takes with him from Britain do
not return, thus rendering the Britons helpless before the attacks
of Picts and Scots. The craven natives appeal to Rome for aid,
and the Romans twice succor them, but finally leave forever
when the cowardice of the Britons proves to be insurmount-
able.[25] Thus the Romans, who represent the best in purely human civilization and achievement,[26] are ultimately unable to save
the Britons from themselves. Gildas depicts rather than explains
the reason for this by consistently referring to the Britons in
metaphors and similes drawn from the animal world. Britain is a
"treacherous lioness"; its inhabitants, "crafty foxes," "lambs,"
and "timid fowl." [27] In later chapters, after the final departure
of Rome, the Britons are compared to lambs, wild animals, foolish beasts; [28] several times their tenuous hold on civilization is
indicated by Gildas in recounting their life in the woods, fleeing
persecution or invasion.[29] The implication is clear: Roman order
lies forever beyond the grasp of the semibestial Britons, whose
vices effectively prevent the firm rooting of civilization in the
island. A striking touch is provided by the contention of the
Britons, pleading for Roman assistance, that the Roman name
stands in danger of becoming a thing to be gnawed at among
nations as a result of the uncurbed barbarian incursions.[30] Nowhere does Gildas evoke more vividly the savage world into
which the Britons' sins have drawn them.

In contrast to the "Roman" sections of *De excidio*, the "Christian" sections stress biblical and exegetical approaches to history.
The coming of the Romans to Britain is paralleled by the advent
of Christianity; its initial reception in Britain is only lukewarm,[31]
and soon the great persecution of Diocletian plunges the infant
British church into crisis and misery which recall the slavery inflicted by Rome in the first section.[32] This "spiritual slavery"
does not last, however, thanks to Alban, the great martyr. Gildas'
account of Alban's martyrdom, in Chapter 11, is allusive and
hagiographical. Imitating Christ, the martyr lays down his life

for a sheep (a fugitive British priest), but before being killed, leads a thousand of his compatriots through the Thames, which miraculously parts for them, and converts his would-be executioner. Gildas has selected and arranged his material here to make Alban not simply a martyr but a national hero.

The climactic moment of this section of the narrative is the crossing of the Thames, which has parted at Alban's prayer. Gildas compares the incident to the Israelites' crossing of the river Jordan into the promised land, carrying the ark and led by Joshua. This biblical allusion provides more than a colorful effect; it has obvious typological references. In the tradition of patristic exegesis, the crossing of the Jordan was a figure of baptism, and Joshua a type of Jesus.[33] Alban's exercise of national-ecclesiastical leadership at a dark moment is a free gift of God to save Britain,[34] and the climactic event of Alban's career is itslf visualized in terms of the "baptism" of the British church, the mark of divine initiation which assures the final victory of the Britons over their persecutors. The first "Christian" section of *De excidio* concludes with the advent and consequences of that victory. Alban's crossing of the water has ultimately liberated Britain, where the Romans' crossing had ultimately enslaved it; in one case the vices of the Britons overcome the civilizing potential of Roman order, while in the other the triumph of the Britons over the enemies of God and his church is implemented by divine grace.

The Alban incident not only looks back to, and comments on, the first Roman section of *De excidio;* it looks forward to the second. The triumph of the British church is short-lived; soon bestial heresy tears at Britain. Then Maximus, a seedling from the thicket of British tyrants, and one planted by Britain herself,[35] crosses to the continent, upsets the imperial order, and is finally destroyed. Like Alban, Maximus leads an army of Britons across the water; like Alban, he is rewarded by death. In all other respects the careers of the two men are completely op-

posed. Maximus is, in fact, a parody, or rather a perverse imitation, of Alban; through Maximus' career Gildas demonstrates the
capacity of the Britons to turn victory into defeat, holiness into
tyranny, national triumph into national disaster. Since Gildas
treats Maximus as an overtly political figure, it is the civil, rather
than the divine, order—i.e., Rome—which is called to the rescue.
As we have noticed, however, Roman virtue is not enough, and
Britain is finally abandoned by Rome. Her attempts to operate
at a political level are foredoomed by her ingrained human failings, which only God can heal and overcome.[36]

In the second Roman section, Gildas introduces further rhetorical imagery to interconnect the sections of his historical
survey. One device is the metaphor of vegetable growth, viz.,
the "thicket of tyrants" from which Maximus springs. Gildas
uses this image with mounting intensity as the work progresses.
In Chapter 21, luxury takes root and grows among the peaceful,
prosperous Britons; in Chapter 23 the Saxons, invited into Britain,
are described as a "seed of iniquity, [a] root of bitterness
[which] grows as a poisonous plant, worthy of our deserts, in
our own soil, furnished with rugged branches and leaves." [37]
Finally, in Chapter 24, Gildas says of sinful Britain, "the vine-
yard, at one time good, had then so far degenerated to bitter
fruit, that rarely could be seen, according to the prophet, any
cluster of grapes or ear of corn, as it were, behind the back of
the vintagers or reapers." [38]

Another image applied by Gildas to political and religious
worlds is the common Christian image of the shepherd, the sheep,
and the wolves. This image is by turns used to describe Alban's
martyrdom, the Britons in the grip of the Picts and Saxons, the
sinful British church, and the relationship between Britain and
Rome.[39] Also noteworthy is the continuation of the animal
imagery already mentioned as an indication of the Britons' lack
of civilization. Arianism and other heresies are "poisonous
snakes" and "wild beasts"; the rampaging Picts are "savage

wolves"; and the Saxons elicit from Gildas a torrent of animal imagery upon their arrival in Britain.[40] The effect of Gildas' persistent rhetorical organization is to emphasize the universal community of sin and vice, and thus, ironically and paradoxically, to associate through imagery the warring nations of Britons and Saxons. According to Gildas, the meanings of history are not exhausted in the recounting of events and enmities; exegetical and rhetorical organization reveal other levels of significance for the moral historian.

If the paired figures of Alban and Maximus provide poles of organization for Gildas in the first half of his historical summary, and focus the attention of the reader on personal holiness and vice as keys to national destiny, equivalent figures are not wanting in the second half of the narrative. These, however, are not as sharply etched, since Gildas employs a cumulative rather than an alternating narrative movement after the departure of the Romans, and therefore does not need to establish a personal dialectic like that between Alban and Maximus. The tone and context of the later chapters of the historical section are increasingly Christian, and Britain's career is described with progressive clarity in terms of the norms and methods of the history of salvation. From Chapter 21 onward, Gildas makes frequent reference to Old Testament prophecies which are fulfilled in British events.[41] At the beginning of Chapter 26, he equates Britain with the *ecclesia*, i.e., with the continuation of the Old Testament Israel in the history of salvation, by explaining the war between Britons and Saxons as a means whereby God tests the devotion of his *praesens Israel*.[42] Whether by design or by accident, this reference, placed at the end of the historical section of *De excidio*, assumes the force of a final explication in the light of which all the preceding events take on their full meaning. That Gildas intended such a progressive elucidation of British history is perhaps indicated by his treatment of the two figures chosen for elaboration in the last, Christian chapters of his summary.

The first, the *tyrannus superbus* who admits the Saxons into Britain (Chapter 23), is, as Gildas' appellation implies, a final example of that British tyranny earlier represented by Maximus. As such, he would seem to belong to the political world of *De excidio;* yet Gildas makes it clear that this ultimate act of folly is the logical result of perseverance in sin. Just as, in the early chapters, the Britons bring Roman repression upon themselves, here they accomplish their own richly earned punishment by ignoring both the precepts and warnings of God. The advent of the Saxons is the third corrective punishment directed by God toward the Britons; the first is a Pictish invasion, the second a terrible pestilence.[43] All result from the overturning of values by a nation swollen with pride and prosperity.[44] The obvious model for this analysis of British history in terms of sin and punishment is the last three books of Eusebius' *Ecclesiastical History*.[45] The *ecclesia* in Britain—for such, finally, is the subject of Gildas' concern—undergoes the same process of trial and deliverance which the earlier writer perceived in the history of his own times.

Just as in Eusebius' history the political and religious worlds are (finally joined in the person of Constantine, the Christian social hero, so Gildas indicates a progressive union of these two worlds, not only in the evil *tyrannus superbus,* but also in Ambrosius Aurelianus, the last identified epic hero of Britain's history, who leads the Britons to their first victory over the Saxons (Chapter 25). The victory is obtained "by the Lord's favor," in answer to the prayers of the few survivors of the Saxon terror. The hero through whom God thus rewards the Britons for their piety is, Gildas tells us, the last survivor of the Roman race in Britain.[46] Scholars have been vexed by the historical import of this rather cryptic statement, but in the light of the structure of *De excidio* it seems clear that Gildas intended through Ambrosius to evoke an image of combined Christian and Roman virtue in recounting this climactic British victory. Ambrosius, we may say, is an historiographic descendant of Constantine, who serves the additional purpose of binding together in his person the main strands of Gildas' historical narrative.

Unlike Constantine, whose reign was characterized by Roman peace and prosperity, Ambrosius is not the precursor of a golden age in Britain. Historical fact prevented this, of course; I suspect, however, that it is rather historical vision than historical fact which prompted Gildas to add that the descendants of Ambrosius have degenerated since the day of their famous forebear.[47] To Gildas, degeneration is the characteristic movement of British history, and not only the achievement but the family of Ambrosius are subject to this iron law of moral decay. Ultimately, Gildas seems to feel, political stability in such a moral climate is ephemeral, if not illusory. The Romans failed to impose it upon Britain, and their last representative has no more success. (Gildas' political pessimism is all the more understandable when we recall that his purpose in writing *De excidio* was to chastise and warn a new generation of tyrants.[48]) Only spiritual criteria provide the basis for judgment and for action in Britain. Gildas exposes the bias of his interpretation of history by identifying his nation-*ecclesia* as the *praesens Israel,* as well as by declaring that, in his own day, when Britain's sins have again brought her to the brink of disaster, only a few holy men—probably the monastic communities are intended [49]—are shoring up the *ecclesia* in Britain.[50]

The aim of the historical chapters of *De excidio,* on the basis of the foregoing analysis, can be said to be the establishment of the British past firmly within the context of the history of salvation, i.e., of the guidance of history by divine providence. Gildas argues for a religious, and against a political, explanation and solution of the problems, past and present, of his countrymen. But, as we have seen in the preceding chapter, the history of salvation as expounded in scriptural exegesis involved a multi-leveled interpretation of the biblical record, concurrently applicable to the life of the Christian and of the church. In bringing ecclesiastical and Roman history within the expanded limits

of typological and exegetical interpretation, Eusebius and Orosius
were in effect exalting the Christian experience to a normative
role in the exploration of all temporal development. It remains
to ask whether Gildas, following as he does in the exegetical
footsteps of Eusebius and Orosius, is fully conscious of the responsibility, not simply of a few heroes and types but of every
Christian, for determining the fate of the nation-*ecclesia* purely
and simply by his relationship to God and God's revelation. An
affirmative answer to this question could be deduced from the
matter of *De excidio* analyzed thus far, but such indirect proof
is unnecessary, since the text supplies sufficient further evidence
to place Gildas' intentions beyond the realm of doubt. I will
mention but two of these in concluding my analysis of *De excidio*.

In the first two chapters of the work, Gildas discusses the personal crisis he has experienced in arriving at his decision to write
his warning to Britain. After having kept silent for ten years
because of a conviction of his own unworthiness to speak to his
countrymen, he is finally led by a consecutive reading of the
Old and New Testaments to question the viability of his conviction. First he finds in the Old Testament many *exempla* of
God's judgment exercised on the sinful Israelites,[51] and concludes
that divine judgment and punishment will fall even more heavily
on the Britons, who are sunken deeper in sin.[52] Gildas' method
here is precisely that of Salvian; both writers use the Old Testament as a storehouse of historical *exempla* to prove the reality of
God's judgment—in Salvian's case, a judgment being exercised,
in Gildas', a judgment threatened.

But Gildas adds that the Old Testament is a mirror of our
life, i.e., that the scriptures must be interpreted figurally and per-
sonally. He proceeds to the New Testament, where he says he
reads clearly what had been in shadow in the Old Testament.[53]
(This too is a reference, borrowed from St. Paul,[54] to a basic
assumption of scriptural exegesis, i.e., that the types of Old Testa-

ment narrative find fulfillment in the New Testament presentation of the historical, sacramental, and ecclesiastical Christ.)
Gildas' reading of the New Testament stresses the eschatological
nature of the kingdom of God and the necessary exclusion from
it, both now and at the final judgment, of sinners—of sheep in
errant flocks, and of unruly branches which must be cut off the
tree of the Lord.[55] Perceived in this way, the New Testament
universalizes God's judgment, formerly exercised only on Israel,
and establishes beyond doubt the inevitable working of divine
providence at the moment of fulfillment of all history.[56]

But where does such an interpretation of the Bible—a literal
one, in other words—leave scope for the action of the individual
Christian such as Gildas? This is the crux of his problem: "I
knew the mercy of the Lord [in governing his ecclesiastical
kingdom], but feared his judgment also [exercised on Britain as
it was on the Israel of old]. . . . Do I say to myself, wretched
one, is such a charge entrusted to thee . . . namely to withstand
the rush of so violent a torrent [of evil in Britain] . . . and keep
the deposit committed to thee, and be silent?" [57]

From this impasse, in which the Christian's sense of divine
omnipotence paradoxically undermines his faith in the possibility
of Christian service, Gildas is rescued by considering the biblical
exemplum of Balaam's ass,[58] who suffered for her testimony to
God's power over evil men, but persisted in pointing out the
truth nevertheless. With those who, in their "zeal for the holy
law of the Lord's house," [59] cry out against national sin leading
to national disaster, Gildas sees himself fulfilling within the
Christian *ecclesia* the function imperfectly performed by the
dumb animal of the Old Testament account.[60] He accordingly
resolves to speak.

Not only does this preface to *De excidio* provide a biblical and
exegetical *apologia* for the work and its author, it also establishes
Gildas as the first hero of his own narrative. These chapters are
the most original of the entire tract, and repay careful study in

any consideration of the early medieval sense of personal involvement in history and society. For our present purposes, they provide an excellent indication of the extent to which Gildas' ensuing recapitulation of the British past is regulated by his Christian
vision, which in turn draws its basic strength from an exegesis of
scriptural and salvation history at both personal and national
levels.

The second, more considerable part of *De excidio* furnishes a
further illustration of the method just described, in revealing
how Gildas intended his audience to apply to their own lives the
national lessons of British history. In Chapters 28 through 36, for
example, he addresses each of five tyrants [61] holding sway over
parts of Britain, and upbraids them for their crimes. Leave your
sins, he warns them, or be prepared to be punished horribly for
them by the eternal torments of hell.[62] Implicit in Gildas' stressing of the horrors of God's eternal punishments is a parallel between them and the punishment God has inflicted on all of
Britain in the past. National history, in other words, prefigures
personal judgment and is therefore understandable in terms of
eschatological typology. Like the Old Testament, the history of
Britain is applicable to the personal level of the history of salvation.[63] Gildas warns the tyrant Cuneglas to repent at once;
"otherwise thou shalt know and see, *even in this world (etiam
in hoc saeculo)*, how evil and bitter it is to have abandoned the
Lord thy God, . . . and that in the world to come thou shalt
be burnt in the hideous mass of eternal fire. . . ." [64]

It is by the examples of national history that the individual
Christian may learn his fate, since the calamities recounted there
are the prefigurations, *etiam in hoc saeculo*, of eternal judgments.

We may close this analysis of *De excidio* with a few remarks
on the importance of the work for the later fall of Britain texts.
As indicated earlier, the originality of Gildas lay in his attempting a history of his nation, up to and including the barbarian

challenge to its existence, from a point of view at once entirely Christian and dynamic. That he was probably not intentionally a historian at all in no way diminishes the reality either of his achievement, or of its legacy to the following centuries. In assessing the nature and value of that legacy, we may begin by noting that Gildas had a triple reputation in early medieval writings and tradition. To some, he was a great saint of the Celtic church, around whose name an elaborate hagiography sprang up in both insular Britain and continental Brittany.[65] To others, he was a prophet whose message of warning to the new Israel had lasting validity.[66] And finally, he had an independent reputation as *historicus*, a reporter of the past.[67] Those who concerned themselves with the saintly author were certainly influenced by the stress placed upon personal holiness as a key to national survival, and by the biblically oriented self-portrait of the first two chapters of *De excidio*. Those most impressed by the prophetic zeal of the text properly identified it with the tradition of Old Testament "warning literature," which stressed God's providential control of history. Finally, those for whom Gildas' tract was primarily a historical work testified to the continuing validity of interpreting national history in terms of the history of salvation.

The combined testimony of these various judgments, taken together with the fact that *De excidio Britanniae* was the only primary source which later writers had for the events in Britain during the Saxon conquest, establish conclusively that the early medieval consciousness of British (and therefore Saxon) history was indelibly stamped with the impress of religious ideas, developed in a typological manner through an exegetical method. By a strange accident of history, Gildas imposed a form upon British history which lived on in the medieval historical imagination for at least the next five hundred years. It was a form typical of early medieval historical thought and writing in that it reflected the general influence of Eusebius and Orosius, and yet peculiar to Britain in the depth of its commitment to Eusebian-Orosian scripturally oriented historiography.

Rather than attempt a more detailed discussion of Gildas' influence at this point, I will consider in each of the next three chapters the individual debts owed him by Bede, the *Historia Brittonum*, and Geoffrey of Monmouth. This procedure is necessitated by the fact that none of the later writers included without modification Gildas' own analyses of the British past and its crises; on the contrary, each one who depended upon *De excidio* as a source did so with more or less reservation, adapting Gildas' narrative matter and manner to his own purposes. The resultant variety of treatments, and the frequent tension between the aims of Gildas and those of his "heirs," form a fascinating and vital chapter in the history of early medieval historical writing in general, and specifically that which treats of the fall of Britain. We shall see that none of his successors was able to escape entirely from the assumptions, however divergent or alien from their own, of the sixth-century British monk whose earnest, urgent *liber querulus* stands as one of the most influential minor achievements of early medieval literature.

CHAPTER III

Bede's
Historia ecclesiastica gentis
Anglorum: *Britannia Renovata*

A gap of nearly two hundred years separates Gildas' *De excidio Britanniae* from Bede's *Historia ecclesiastica gentis Anglorum,* the next work to consider the fall of Britain.[1] In assessing Bede's *Historia,* its debt to Gildas, and its relationship to early medieval historiographical traditions, we must first realize that more than time separates the work and world of Bede from those of Gildas. Between the transitional and often chaotic years of the mid-sixth century in Britain and the first half of the eighth century in Northumbria (a period often called "the Age of Bede")[2] lie not only basic and irreversible political changes, but momentous cultural developments as well. Had Gildas been alive in 731, the year in which Bede finished the historical work that crowned a lifetime of teaching and writing, he would have found the Saxons in control of the greater part of the island of Britain, having pushed the Britons back into Wales and Cornwall. Not only had the invaders abandoned their heathen gods for Christianity, but the Anglo-Saxon church had become the richest, strongest, and most learned in Europe. Gildas would surely have decided that this *praesens Israel,* which worked in close cooperation with the bishop of Rome and received from Rome many excellent prelates, indeed loved God, considering its prosperity at home and the success of its missionary endeavors, the first in centuries, among the Germanic nations of the continent.

Bede, like Gildas, was a monk who became involved in the affairs of his nation by writing about them. Such behavior may at first seem inconsistent with the monastic ideal as it grew up in the Christian world. The first Christian monks were hermits who fled the city life of the Roman Empire, seeking, through withdrawal into the Egyptian desert, the salvation to which they were convinced urban luxury posed a serious threat. Like martyrdom, monastic asceticism celebrated the conflict between the Christian and his world; [3] the monk who chose the desert exhibited a practical, antisocial attitude different in degree but not in kind from the anti-Roman feeling among Christians which, we have already noted, impeded the growth of a Christian historiography. The ideals of this earliest monasticism are reflected in its characteristic literature, the hagiography of the heroic hermits. [4]

In the fourth century Pachomius, an Egyptian monk, began to organize monastic communities in the east. [5] Communal or cenobitic monasticism proved the more popular form of religious withdrawal in the west, and many great figures of the church were involved in the establishment of monastic communities. [6] Ultimately, however, the monks of Europe adopted the rule of monastic living formulated by Benedict of Nursia (*ca.* 480–547) and came to be known by his name. [7] Despite the social nature of Benedictine monasticism, it was still based on a withdrawal from the world, [8] each member of the community seeking God in the company of his fellows, but free from worldly distractions and obligations. [9]

By the eighth century, however, Benedictine monasticism had become the great paradox of Christian Europe. Despite its antisocial origin and intent, the monastery was a continuing institution. As such, it inevitably developed traditions which both reflected and promoted a continuity of records and activities. Gradually, the traditional monastic discipline inculcated in its members an appreciation of the possibilities for corporate action, be it in prayer, in work, or in study. In the Europe of the early Middle Ages, such possibilities were all too rare. The *Völkerwanderung* and its consequences prevented political continuity on a large scale, while the character of Germanic political institutions militated against the survival in the secular world of the idea of the *res publica*.[10] The concept of *ecclesia* had assumed the import of a Christian *res publica* for Eusebius and Orosius, as we have seen; in the "dark ages," the monasteries seemed best to exemplify the *ecclesia* as a social entity.[11]

The peculiar position of the monks as the only purveyors of classical and patristic tradition, and indeed of literacy itself, worked to reinforce the social image of the monastery.[12] On the one hand, the monks became essential to the continuation of civilization in Europe,[13] and on the other, they had the opportunity to study and copy works of Christian history and scriptural exegesis.[14] When the world of Eusebius, Augustine, and Orosius had passed away, the interpretations of history which they had offered it were kept alive in the new world of the monastery, whose inhabitants imbibed the knowledge of the Christian past and applied it to their relations with the outside world as such relations became progressively more frequent and intimate. Gildas' *De excidio Britanniae* was a self-proclaimed, early example of this transfer.

In Bede's *Historia*, and in the work of the English Benedictines of his era, the social involvement of the early medieval monastic *ecclesia* reaches a great peak. That Britain, an island far from the traditional center of European civilization, should witness a vigorous rebirth of Christian social ideals and their artistic expression requires a brief explanation. We must first of all recall the circumstances under which English Christianity evolved.[15]

After the Anglo-Saxons had ousted the Britons from large

parts of Britain, they received the gospel from two different quarters. In the early seventh century, the Celtic church in Ireland sent missionaries who established monasteries on the Scottish (Irish) model—i.e., having little to do with each other or with a central hierarchy—in the north of Britain.[16] Even before that, in 597, Pope Gregory, himself a Benedictine who had been forced into the papacy against his wishes,[17] had dispatched a mission from Rome to evangelize the English. The new English Christians were, accordingly, either directly beholden to Rome for their Christianity, and therefore vigorous supporters of an international *ecclesia* headed by the Pope, or followers of isolated Celtic monasticism. In 664, at the synod of Whitby, partisans of both traditions disputed the preferability of certain rites and usages which differed in the Roman and Celtic churches. The Roman adherents won, and their triumph was not simply on the matter of ecclesiastical practice, but involved the future of the English church. Once and for all, England had cast her lot with Rome.[18]

Gregory's successors in the papacy sent many learned bishops to England in the seventh century, and numerous Englishmen traveled to Rome for instruction in doctrine, ecclesiastical discipline, and the traditions of learning of which the church, especially through the monks, was custodian. One of those Englishmen, Benedict Biscop, founded the monastery at Jarrow, in which Bede was to pass most of his life, and stocked it with manuscripts gathered on his travels.[19] The cultivation of international contacts and learning bore fruit in the late seventh and early eighth centuries when the English church, including its preponderant monastic element, became preeminent in Europe both for its learning and sanctity at home and for its missionary work afield. The heroes of this latter endeavor were often monks who returned to society to spread the gospel in new parts, as Augustine, head of the Gregorian mission and first archbishop of Canterbury, had done for their ancestors.[20]

Bede's works were both contributions to and products of the
English church's golden age. In their breadth and depth of interest, they established him as the glory of the English church,
of Benedictine "social" monasticism, and of early medieval, super-
national Christianity. The reflection of that glory, radiating from
his masterpiece, the *Historia ecclesiastica*, still dazzles us today,
as the universal chorus of praise for Bede the historian testifies.
Most modern tributes to Bede center on his ability as a re-
searcher, but I propose, in keeping with the aims of this study,
to discuss Bede's historical imagination, an approach which
stresses the literary and theological, rather than the scientific,
side of the Northumbrian monk's achievement. Bede's vision of
history, we shall see, owes much to the tradition of Eusebius and
Orosius; fitting British and English history into the history of
salvation, he sets out to record the spiritual progress of a chosen
barbarian nation. As critical acclaim from the most widely divergent quarters indicates, he succeeded admirably in creating a
cohesive record of the Anglo-Saxons in Britain, in which monastic life, political life, and missionary life interact smoothly, rather
than compete for Bede's—and our—attention.

The uniqueness of Bede's achievement becomes readily apparent when we compare his history with a work which he certainly knew, and which may in some respects have inspired his
undertaking: the *Historia Francorum* of Gregory of Tours (538–
594).[21] Gregory was bishop of the church of Tours from the
year 573 until his death, and was actively engaged in writing his
history during much of that time. The bishopric was an office
which, he tells us, had been in his family (he was of Roman, not
of Frankish origin) for some time,[22] and he discharged it with
great zeal and commitment.[23] He also wrote several volumes of
hagiography, in addition to his national history. It has been noted
that Gregory's great work is actually more an ecclesiastical than
a national history;[24] compared to the analogous works of Jordanes and Paul the Deacon, it is markedly wanting in details

from the heroic, preconversion era of the nation it chronicles, and is instead full of episcopal and ecclesiastical details, as well as hagiographical stories unrelated to the main movements of Frankish history.

In fact, Gregory's obvious intention is to record the history of the Franks as a chapter in the history of salvation; his models are clearly Eusebius and Orosius. The first book of the *Historia Francorum* begins with an account of Adam and the fall, and recapitulates the history of Israel, which for Gregory is clearly the normative history.[25] In the famous preface to Book Five, furthermore, in which Gregory laments the civil strife and discord which have diminished Frankish power and caused great misery throughout Gaul,[26] he betrays clearly the close relationship in his mind between national history and Christian behavior [27]—a relationship which may also be deduced from the many stories of miracles and divine punishments scattered through the pages of the work.[28] However, a close relationship in the mind of the author is not to be equated with a cause-and-effect relationship in his historiography. The latter, a feature of the writings of Orosius, Eusebius, and Gildas, is approached by Gregory only in his account of Clovis, first Catholic (as opposed to Arian) king of the Franks,[29] whose career is described along the lines of Eusebius' Constantine, in obvious imitation of the earlier ecclesiastical history.[30] Clovis' conversion to Catholic Christianity, says Gregory, is the secret of his phenomenal success as leader of his nation.[31] A new Constantine (or Moses), Clovis is, in Gregory's presentation, an ideal figure typifying the barbarian nation which, by accepting the true faith, moves to the center stage of history, in accordance with God's providential plan. Thus here, at least, Gregory successfully adopts the exegetical approach to history which has claimed our attention in this study.

Elsewhere Gregory's aims, or at least his results, are different. The central concern for political strife which he reveals in the preface to the fifth book of his history controls and shapes his vision of history throughout;[32] it even determines his modes of expression.[33] The over-all impression left by Gregory's work, therefore, is not one of uniformity of purpose or execution. The attempts at interpretation in the tradition of the Christian theology of history remain in contrast to Gregory's keen awareness of harsh barbarian reality; the miracles of Frankish saints and the feuds of Frankish warriors compete for our attention at every turn.[34] In a brilliant essay on Gregory's narrative style and interests, Erich Auerbach demonstrated that Gregory's main achievement in his history was "to imitate concrete reality," to write a language which "lives in the concrete side of events. . . . What he relates is his own and his only world. He has no other, and he lives in it."[35] Insofar as Gregory attempted—e.g., in the Clovis chapters—to live in another world, the systematized and convention-oriented world of the Christian theology of history, he was an uneven and only partially successful historian.[36] Scholars recognizing this limitation have dealt rather severely with Gregory, especially in comparison with Bede, who accomplished a similar project with much more satisfying results.[37]

Comparisons between Bede and Gregory are not as simple as they may appear, however. Gregory wrote in an age of transition and instability when the barbarian assimilation of Roman and Christian culture was by no means complete, while Bede, writing 150 years later, was the product of a society which had absorbed the best of that culture and had attained a pinnacle of civilization almost unmatched in the Europe of its day. Bede, for all his interest in his world and nation, was a cloistered monk and teacher; Gregory was an embattled bishop who devoted much of his life to the care and defense of his flock, often under the handicap of royal displeasure or of civil chaos.[38] Bede knew peace best, Gregory war. These environmental contrasts undoubtedly determined in large part the differences between the historical thought and presentation of the two men. But there is another factor, I think, which contributed significantly to the greater achievements of Bede, and specifically to the consistency of design and clarity of vision communicated by his ecclesiastical history. I refer to the tradition concerning the fall of Britain inherited by Bede from Gildas.

In turning to Gildas for information on the history of Britain before and during the Saxon conquest, Bede obtained not simply an historical account, but, as we have seen, an historical system of specifically Christian character. By accepting Gildas' testimony on the sinfulness of the Britons, he made possible a depiction of the Saxons not simply as virtuous heathens (like Salvian's estimate of the barbarians in the fifth century), but, from his eighth-century vantage point, as the new Israel, chosen by God to replace the sin-stained Britons in the promised land of Britain. Edmond Faral was the first to recognize that this was precisely the image that Bede created, and to insist on the importance of Bede's dependence upon Gildas for an understanding of his historiography as a whole.[39] I shall discuss Bede's relationship to Gildas in some detail shortly; at this point I wish only to reaffirm Faral's contention that Gildas provided an invaluable starting point for Bede in his portrayal of the national past. That the fall of Britain (which Gildas, of course, did not label as such) was best understood in Christian terms, influenced by the theology of history and scriptural exegesis, was Gildas' proposition; that the Saxons' experience in Britain, propounded in the same terms, proved the converted conquerors to be a people predestined by God's providence to link Britain (and other nations) to the universal Roman church, was Bede's corollary.

Like Gregory of Tours, Bede was an accomplished hagiographer; he brought to the composition of his masterwork a keen sense of the Christian heroic life and how best to portray it. Where Gregory's hagiographical interludes create friction with the realistic and concrete sections of his narrative, Bede's harmonize perfectly with the flow of British history—so perfectly, in fact, that one scholar has seen fit to call the *Historia ecclesi-*

astica gentis Anglorum a "national hagiography." [40] But where else did Bede find the inspiration for interpreting national history in terms of political and ecclesiastical heroes, of saintly leaders and Christian generals, if not in Gildas? We must not underestimate his undoubted genius, nor the influence on him of Eusebius; but the work which obviously affected him most profoundly, and which provided him with much of the matter for the first book of his history was *De excidio.* To a far greater degree than is usually recognized, Gildas was the foster father of the most admired offspring of the early medieval historical imagination.

In the light of my contention that Gildas exerted such an important influence on Bede, it will prove interesting to begin this exploration of the *Historia ecclesiastica* by examining carefully Bede's portrayal of the Britons. The story of English Christianity begins, as mentioned above, with the coming of Augustine and the mission from Rome in 597. Bede prefaces this event with twenty-two chapters summarizing the history of Britain from the first arrival of Julius Caesar (55 B.C.) to that of Augustine. Bede's main sources for these chapters included several Roman histories, foremost among them the *Historia* of Orosius; [41] the life of St. Germanus of Auxerre, written *ca.* 480 by Constantius Lugdunensis; [42] and Gildas. Most scholars have ignored Bede's chapters on Britain, citing their derivative nature.[43] In order to indicate that there is nevertheless much to be learned from Bede's use and arrangement of sources in this section of the *Historia ecclesiastica*, I propose to compare the chapters on Britain with the exposition of British history in Bede's other major historical work, the chronicle incorporated into his great chronological textbook, *De temporum ratione* (*ca.* 725).[44] The historical differences between the two views of Britain, and the generic differences between the two works of which they form a part, shed considerable light on Bede the historiographer.

Of the two chronological treatises which are among the many pedagogical texts written by Bede in his work as a teacher at

Jarrow, *De temporum ratione* is the later and more thorough.[45] It combines a theoretical section which discusses universal and theological aspects of time with a chronicle of events listed according to their place in the scheme of the *aetates mundi*, or ages of the world.[46] The chronicle is a practical illustration of the text's abstract presentation of time; both sections aim to show God's providential management of time and therefore of history. Jones summarizes:

From Hippolytus to Bede, all chronicles, so far as can be judged, were designed as the practical part of a textbook. . . . Bede's great chronicle is Chapter 66 of his text on Times; the first sixty-five chapters move progressively through the theory of time from atoms to eras and Chapters 67–72 treat of the nature of eternity [i.e., as as the fulfillment of time]. The chronicle, then, acts as an illustration of the temporal life.[47]

In attempting to discern precisely how the chronicle of *De temporum ratione* elucidates Bede's theoretical text, we must note three features of the work as a whole: first, in the chronicle itself, the events of the Old Testament form the basis for the first five ages of the world, and are interwoven with secular events in the text; second, Chapters 63 and 64, just before the chronicle, explain how the Jewish Passover prefigures both Christ's resurrection and Christian baptism, and how Easter prefigures the final resurrection of the dead and eternal life with God; and third, the entire work closes with an eschatological summary.[48] Bede's textbook, in other words, rests firmly on the foundation of the Christian theology of history. This is not surprising, since Bede's primary interests were those of a theologian and the great bulk of his works are exegetical studies of scripture.[49] A consideration of these writings is beyond the scope of this study, and it will suffice to point out that Bede approached the scriptures as a disciple of the early Christian fathers and borrowed the methods of his illustrious forebears.[50] He was fond of allegorical interpretations after the manner of Origen and the Alexandrian school, but never forgot historical, eschatological, and spiritual *figurae*.[51] He was, in short, trained and qualified to integrate historical data with the theology of history, as he did in *De temporum ratione*, and, as we shall see, in the *Historia ecclesiastica*.[52] This is not to say that the *Historia* and the *De tempore ratione* chronicle are the same type of work. They are not, as a comparison of the place of the Britons in each makes clear.

For the British entries in the chronicle, Bede depends primarily on Orosius and Gildas. There is, of course, no connected narrative of British or any other history here; the year-by-year recapitulation of universal events makes consecutive exposition impossible. Instead, notices of events in Britain before 597 form part of fourteen separate chronicle entries.[53] Many of these are of the scantiest nature. The first comes in the fifth age of the world (from the Babylonian captivity of the Jews to the birth of Christ), in a laconic mention of Caesar's conquests:

Caesar conquered the Teutons and the Gauls, and having received hostages from the defeated Britons, among whom the Roman name was unknown until his time, made them his tributaries as well.[54]

Bede then gives (mostly from Orosius) some of the steps recounting Britain's inclusion in the Roman Empire; in his "universal" chronicle the accepted frames of reference for all history are the world of the Old Testament, and the Roman world, its successor in the minds of the Christian historians Eusebius and Orosius. Turning to Gildas, he takes from the British writer the outlines of the fall of Britain, omitting passages which give to *De excidio Britanniae* its sense of urgency and lamentation. Also gone is Gildas' rich language of recurring imagery and biblical quotation or reminiscence. The last reference is to Ambrosius and his rallying of his countrymen, who are harried by the marauding Saxons; the loss of Britain is briefly alluded to at this point:

Under the leadership of Ambrosius Aurelianus, an unassuming man who was, by chance, the only survivor of the Saxon slaughter (his noble family having been destroyed), the Britons challenged their conquerors to a battle and defeated them; from that time onward, first one side and then the other held the upper hand, until finally the island was completely controlled by the more powerful invaders.[55]

The only other entries worthy of special note are the description of the usurper Maximus,[56] and the brief mention of the sojourn in Britain of St. Germanus, Bishop of Auxerre.[57] The former is from Orosius,[58] and treats Maximus in much less vitriolic terms than does Gildas. Maximus is not the offshoot of British vice, but

. . . a certain energetic and able man and one worthy of the throne, had he not risen to it by usurpation, contrary to his oath of allegiance.

To this more lenient portrait Bede adds, however, Gildas' story that the Britons, in following Maximus, lost all their fighting men and became targets for the attacks of the Picts and Scots.

The mention of St. Germanus is drawn from the same source Bede uses in the *Historia ecclesiastica*, i.e., Constantius' *Life*. The chronicle says only that the Britons, troubled by the Pelagian heresy, summoned Germanus and his companion, Lupus of Troyes, who by preaching and miracles insured the triumph of the true faith;[59] it continues:

But also at that time [the bishops] beat back by divine power the attack undertaken by the joint forces of the Saxons and the Picts against the Britons. When Germanus himself had been made the commander of the battle, he drove into flight a huge enemy force, not by the sound of trumpets, but by the voices of his entire army, raised to heaven in shouts of "alleluia."

Then, in midsentence, the scene shifts to Ravenna where, after a warm imperial welcome, Germanus passes on to Christ.[60] These events take place twenty-four years before the battles of Ambrosius against the Saxons, according to the chronicle.

The history of Britain as Bede incorporates it into the scheme of his textbook chronicle contains no specific information about a Roman withdrawal from Britain preceding the attacks of the Picts and Scots, or about the appeals of the Britons to Rome for aid. The period from the death of Maximus to the arrival of the Saxons is left vague, and the subject of Britain is dropped abruptly, without mention of the *mons badonicus* or of growing British corruption. The single reference to St. Germanus is included in the same entry which describes the arrival of the Saxons, i.e., at the earliest point possible commensurate with the description of a British victory over them, *Germano belli duce.*

It is clear that Bede does not single out British (or English) history for special consideration in his chronicle. The events in Britain are merely steps in the march of time toward its end, the final judgment; history does not, and must not, distract the reader's attention from eschatology.[61] The pedagogical purpose of *De temporum ratione* is to inculcate theoretical appreciation, not to impart moral edification. Hence Bede borrows the "facts" of Gildas' historical summary without the hortatory tone or interpretations. He also leaves out the bulk of the miraculous material which appear in his sources, i.e., Gildas' account of Alban, and the *Gesta Dei per Germanum*, which fill Constantius' account of St. Germanus' two trips to Britain. The vision of the hagiographer, like that of the prophet, had no place in Bede's textbook.[62]

An entirely different aim inspired the *Historia ecclesiastica.* In his preface, Bede explains to King Ceolwulf of Northumbria that history has distinct moral value for its readers.[63] Throughout the work, he shapes and controls his narrative so that, at both national and personal levels, it extols the good and rejects the evil in keeping with a thoroughly Christian view of divine providence operating in history. Furthermore, God's judging of man ceases in the *Historia* to be a goal toward which all history is moving, and becomes a process carried out in history as a prefiguration of the final reward or punishment awaiting each individual when he passes from this life to the next. The details of the process are clearly visible in Bede's narrative of the Britons, to which we must now turn.

Compared with the skeleton of British history in *De temporum ratione*, it is a detailed and colorful narrative which Bede has compiled from his various sources for presentation in the *Historia ecclesiastica*. That it is a compilation does not, as many have felt, preclude its expressing Bede's own opinions. Like many medievals, Bede was not inclined to redo valuable work already accomplished,[64] and we can, I feel, determine his sympathies and meaning by taking into account the order and bias of the works excerpted.

Chapter 1 gives a description of Britain inspired by, but different from, that of Gildas. It is scientific rather than rhetorical, intended to describe and locate Britain rather than to contrast the *locus amoenus* and its stiff-necked inhabitants. Chapter 2 describes Caesar's exploits in Britain, Chapter 3 those of Claudius in the following century. Chapter 4 is a straightforward account of the coming of Christianity to Britain in the reign of King Lucius. Chapter 5 is devoted to Severus, Chapter 6 to the Diocletian persecution.[65]

So far, the difference between the *Historia*'s account and that of the chronicle is one of order and quantity, not of the type of information utilized. But Chapter 7 recounts the martyrdom of Alban in great detail, much more fully than does Gildas in *De excidio Britanniae*.[66] There follow notices of the Arian heresy, largely copied from Gildas, and of the career of Maximus, drawn from Orosius rather than Gildas, and in Chapter 11 Bede reports Alaric's sack of Rome and the end of Roman rule in Britain. Chapters 12 through 16 are from Gildas, practically *verbatim*, and describe the attacks of the Picts and the Scots, the last Roman aid to the Britons, the island's sins, and the advent of the Saxons. The section ends with the victory of the Britons at *mons badonicus*. Then Bede leaps backward in time to insert five

chapters on the deeds of St. Germanus in Britain before and after
the arrival of the Saxons. Finally, Chapter 22 is of Bede's own
invention and ascribes the downfall of the Britons to all the sins
Gildas reported and especially to their failure to preach the word
of God to the Saxons. The latter, whom God foreknew as his
own nation, are to be saved by the gospel in any case.[67] This idea
marks the point of transition to the arrival of Augustine and his
mission from Rome in 597.

The features of this account which distinguish it from the
notices of Britain in Bede's chronicle on one side, and Gildas'
summary on the other, are the sections on Alban and Germanus,
and the explanation of the transfer of power from the Britons
to the Saxons. The source of Bede's *passio* of Alban is not Gildas,
who, we recall, emphasized those elements in Alban's martyrdom which paralleled the Old Testament and therefore made
Alban a national hero as well as a martyr.[68] Bede avoids Old
Testament parallels and any indication that Britain is a new
Israel or that Alban is a national hero. Instead, the formal episode narrates Alban's conversion, his confrontation with a
Roman judge, his suffering, the conversion of his would-be executioner and the divine punishment of the actual executioner,
the conversion of the judge resulting in the suspension of persecution, and the miracles done at Alban's shrine until the present
day. The tone of the passage is much more hagiographical, and
the great virtue of Alban is not his aid to the nation, but his
ability to convert by his example those who had until then denied
God.

The placing and content of the St. Germanus chapters work
to a similar end. In the chronicle, Germanus is placed in correct
chronological sequence, i.e., before Ambrosius and the fall of the
Britons. But in the *Historia*, Bede puts Gildas' narrative first,
thereby exposing Britain's sins and the heroic efforts of the soldier
Ambrosius, under whom the Britons beat off the Saxons. Following the military succor provided by Ambrosius, the *Historia* re-

lates the spiritual aid provided by Germanus, who attempts to
extirpate heresy from the island and converts many to the true
faith.[69] A highlight of Germanus' visits is his debate with the
Pelagians.[70] Truth conquers falsehood and again the word of God
is spread among the multitudes. In the midst of his other miraculous exploits, Germanus overcomes the Saxons and Picts in a
battle won by faith in God, a battle which avoids the shedding of
blood.[71] It is clear, in other words, that Germanus, a missionary
from beyond the sea, is helping the Britons in a way superior to
the efforts of the military hero Ambrosius, himself a Roman.
Bede puts Germanus' deeds last in order of events, since his mission to the Britons makes the sharpest possible contrast to the
refusal of the Britons to evangelize the Saxons.

Chapter 22 is therefore a culmination of the main theme of
British history: the importance of conversion and of the spreading of the truth of God. The Britons, sinful enough in other respects, are especially sinful in their refusal to preach to the Saxons. God's providence, however, will remedy this failure, for
God has chosen the Saxons; they are, in short, the new Israel.

The problem of evangelization and education is examined in
the first twenty-two chapters through several specific situations:
personal conversion and apostolic activity versus error and isolation, and the passage of authority from the old to the new. The
latter idea is subtly underlined in Chapter 21, where Germanus
leaves Britain and goes to Ravenna, seat of the western empire.
He is honorably received by the emperor and his mother, and
dies soon after. Then the emperor Valentinian is murdered and
the western empire comes to an end.[72] In one stroke Bede emphasizes the passing of the old order at all levels outside Britain, and
immediately following this passage comes the stigmatization of
the Britons and the revelation that the Saxons are the new people
of God. This fact is complemented by their conversion by the
new Rome—papal, not imperial, Rome. Gregory, the pope who
sends Augustine to Britain, is, Bede says, the apostle of the Eng-

lish—a new Paul or a new Germanus—and is responsible for the beginning of their spiritual progress.

We may and ought rightly to call [Gregory] our apostle; because, whereas he bore the pontifical power over all the world, and was placed over the churches already reduced to the faith of truth, he made our nation, till then given up to idols, the church of Christ, so that we may be allowed thus to attribute to him the character of an apostle; for though he is not an apostle to others, yet he is so to us; for we are the seal of his apostleship in our Lord.[73]

Typically, he is a hero not only because of his individual holiness, but also because of his missionary zeal.[74] Augustine, his messenger to the English, is also a social hero. He shares in the newness of English Christianity by living the life of the primitive church all over again,[75] and in his letters to Pope Gregory he asks questions about the maintenance of faith and discipline in the "new church of the English." [76] These, too, fall into the old-new pattern developed by Bede. For instance, Augustine inquires about the purification of the faithful necessary for the reception of the Eucharist. In reply, Gregory contrasts the old and new laws, pointing out that the stress on outward forms and on the specific in the former prefigures the inner, universal applicability of the latter. Those observing the new law, the *populus spiritualis*, will understand that

As in the Old Testament the outward works are observed, so in the New Testament, that which is outwardly done is not so diligently regarded as that which is inwardly thought, in order to punish it by a discerning judgment.[77]

This passage throws Gregory into clear relief as one who understands and propagates the universal message of Christ. Implicitly it contrasts him with the Britons and possibly suggests a parallel between the typology practiced in scriptural exegesis and the transfer of power from the old to the new nation (or *ecclesia*) in Britain. The Britons lose their dominion because they do not follow the new law. In fact, it is their adherence to incorrect observances, Bede emphasizes, that keeps them from enjoying the blessings God pours out on his faithful. Two important, imaginatively treated incidents in the *Historia* make this central point, and in their light the passage just quoted from Gregory's letter assumes thematic importance, especially since it also introduces the theology of history according to which the later incidents are ordered. Augustine is the hero of the first of these two episodes, the parley with the Britons at Augustine's oak.[78] His exploits there also furnish further examples of Bede's interweaving of hagiographical strands and matters of national importance.

Augustine, aided by King Ethelbert of Kent, calls a meeting with the Britons, seeking their aid to convert the Saxons and admonishing them to conform to the customs of the Roman church for the sake of Christian unity.[79] The Britons reject his pleas. Augustine thereupon arranges a test to determine which position is the more just: a blind Englishman is prayed over by the Britons to no avail, and is then restored to sight by the Roman bishop, who prays that the opening of the sightless eyes may result in the light of truth penetrating the souls of the faithful.[80] The Britons who observe the miracle are won over, and take up the question of unification with their countrymen. On the advice of one of their number, a venerable anchorite, the Britons decide that their participation in Augustine's mission will depend upon whether the Roman cleric is sufficiently humble to rise when they come into his presence. As it happens, he does not, and no *rapprochement* is effected. Augustine then warns them that if they refuse to join in unity, they will be destroyed in conflict by the English, receiving physical death for refusing to give spiritual life.[81] Soon after there is a terrible slaughter of the Britons by the English at Chester, and among the victims are many British monks. Augustine's prophecy is fulfilled, and temporal death prefigures for the Britons their eternal punishment for rejecting universal truth.[82]

Bede's imaginative approach to history stands out in this episode. The miracle story brings together the several levels at which the historian operates. At the individual level, the physical cure of the Englishman is a "prefiguration" of his spiritual cure; his eyes are opened that his heart may also be. At a national level, the success of Augustine in healing the blind man where the Britons have failed sums up the passing of God's favor from the old, isolated Christians to the new universal Christians.[83] The fulfillment of Augustine's prophecy proves that God acts in history, and the British disaster at Chester prefigures the disaster of the wicked soul in passing to its final, eternal desert. The social hero and his triumph are for Bede, as for Gildas, an artistic device permitting the interpretation of national history in accordance with the theology of history by means of historical and spiritual *figurae*.

Another obviously imaginative detail of this episode lies in the Britons' ill-advised decision to join Augustine's mission only if he rises when they enter his presence. Augustine's behavior is not a deliberate slight,[84] but the Britons, misled by the anchorite,[85] are carried away by their devotion to form. It is precisely this devotion—which Gregory regarded as characteristic of the old law—that leads the Britons to cling to their time of celebrating Easter, and their ways of tonsuring priests and administering baptism. Forgoing universal Christianity for Old Testament reasons, they suffer accordingly.[86]

The culmination of British (or more properly Celtic) isolationism comes at the synod of Whitby in 664.[87] Here Bede makes the Easter controversy [88] the reason for the collision of the Roman and Celtic factions of the English church, although he admits there were other matters under dispute.[89] Bede's description of the synod is dramatic and revealing. King Oswy of the

Northumbrians, who observes the Celtic Easter, first calls on both sides to agree on one date, since agreement on the ecclesiastical mysteries in this world prefigures the unity of the elect in the next.[90] Then the Scottish bishop Colman defends the Celtic Easter as that practiced by St. John in the first days of the church. Wilfrid, the Roman spokesman, replies that St. John indeed observed the literal Jewish custom at Jerusalem, but that the spread of the gospel soon created a universal community which in turn created new practices to fulfill the law rather than simply observe it. The church has changed from *figura* to sacrament, Wilfrid in effect tells Colman, but your practice has not.[91] Wilfrid also attacks the Scots' dependence upon the Easter tradition of Columba, the Celtic saint and missionary, because of his miracles. Quoting Matthew, he says:

Concerning your father Columba and his followers, whose sanctity you say you imitate . . . I may answer that when many, on the day of judgment, shall say to our Lord, "That in his name they prophesied, and cast out devils, and wrought many wonders," our Lord will reply, "That He never knew them." [92]

The Scots are risking an irrevocable rebuke from God at the final judgment.

After hearing both sides, King Oswy decides for Rome, swayed by another text from Matthew, in which Christ gives to Peter and to Peter alone the keys to the heavenly kingdom.[93] Wilfrid's point, which is Bede's as well, has carried the day. The Roman church founded by Peter is in its universality the type of the kingdom of heaven, and the Scots, in cutting themselves off from the former, prefigure their exclusion from the latter.[94]

The whole progress of this central scene depends upon the methods of scriptural exegesis which underlie it and to which the protagonists, Wilfrid and Oswy, continually refer implicitly or explicitly. Bede applies the theology of history and its method to the main crisis of his nation's Christian past, and manages to convey artistically the important fact that this crisis has universal and personal repercussions. The words of the scriptures, actual or implied, shape the debate at Whitby, and Bede indicates through the central characters how the biblical texts (and consequently the episode) should be interpreted. The exegetical knife cuts two ways: not only is the Roman party vindicated, but the Scots and Britons are equated with the old law. The experience of the English, inheritors of Britain, is presented by Bede as an illustration of divine providence operating in history, a process to be understood in terms of the Christian theology of history.

So much for the place of the Britons in Bede's *Historia ecclesiastica*. It remains for us to see how Bede used the system he had inherited and enlarged from Gildas when he turned to the progress of his own nation, the English. We saw that Gildas based his survey of the British past on the assumption that Christian salvation and national prosperity are two aspects of the same providential process in history. From our analysis of Bede's historiography so far, it is clear that he accepts this principle in his story of the miracle at Augustine's oak and its consequence, and that in Gregory, Germanus, and Augustine he portrays three saints who are also Christian social heroes. A peculiarity of Bede's historical vision, moreover, is that its heroes are closely bound to their nation by their penchant for spreading the gospel. It follows logically from this virtue that some of the great heroes of the English are adopted heroes, men not English themselves, who help the English by teaching them the great truths of the universal church. The duty of the Christian hero is not simply to fight or pray for his society but to educate it. Bede's *Historia ecclesiastica* is the unique chronicle of an empire built on educational principles. As Gildas the prophet is the most intense of Christian historians, Bede the pedagogue is surely the most civilized.

Some examples of the ways in which English heroes work out

their own salvation and contribute to their nation will fulfill the last aim of this chapter. There are several kings of whom Bede speaks approvingly and to whom he applies the technique of historical figuration. References of this nature are infrequent in Bede's recapitulation of British history [95] since Bede did not want to suggest, as Gildas did, that the Britons were the New Israel. His purpose, we have seen, was better served by linking Britons and Scots to the original Israelites. In later chapters, on the other hand, he includes among his documents a letter from Pope Gregory (like Paul, a prolific writer of epistles) to Ethelbert, king of Kent, urging Ethelbert to imitate Constantine in converting his people to Christ so that, like Constantine, he may save himself and win earthly glory as well.[96] That he will also be a historical fulfillment of the kings of Israel is later clarified when Bede calls Ethelbert a new Saul, on the occasion of Ethelbert's overcoming the Scots.[97]

Bede's portrait of King Oswald of the Northumbrians is especially flattering.[98] Oswald, *christianissimus rex*, is first of all a military hero. He rescues his nation from the wicked, impious rule of the British king and antihero, Cadwalla, who is guilty of outrageous tyranny during his brief reign over the Northumbrians. Cadwalla wins rule in Northumbria by killing the apostate English kings Osric and Eanfrid, an act, Bede remarks, of just revenge performed by an impious hand.[99] Then Oswald, a man beloved of God (*vir Deo dilectus*), frees his countrymen from the tyrant's yoke in a battle fought against great odds at Denisesburn, in 634. Bede's account is dramatic:

[Oswald] advanced with an army, small, indeed, in number, but strengthened with the faith of Christ; and the impious commander of the Britons was slain, though he had most numerous forces, which he boasted nothing could withstand.[100]

It is also reminiscent of the triumphs of Constantine and Ambrosius.

From this episode of national significance Bede moves at once to consider the miracles of the martyred king, now St. Oswald—miracles which prove his closeness to God as an individual.[101] The episode closes with an account of the evangelization of all the Northumbrians, thanks to the efforts and initiative of Oswald.[102] This happy ending proves beyond doubt the depth of Oswald's virtue and the magnitude of his contribution to English society.

As a sure sign of his piety Oswald is rewarded with great temporal realms, typifying the heavenly realm which he, first of all his royal line, could hope for.[103] It is under Oswald that all the provinces of the island are first united, and this unity is the ultimate mark of his success: not only does he achieve a height of power but he brings peace and Christianity to the English. The words are the words of Bede but the voice is that of Eusebius, interpreting the climax of Constantine's career over four hundred years before Bede wrote his history. The difference is that while Constantine freed his nation-*ecclesia*, Oswald propagates his.

To Bede, as to Eusebius, the Christian vision is preeminently a social one in the last analysis. Bede includes the monastic life within society, and reports an instance where the demands of the Christian society take precedence over the individual's desire to withdraw from the world. The episcopacy of Lindisfarne (a monastery involved in the affairs of Northumbria) is forced upon the unwilling monk Cuthbert by a synod representing the whole of society. The king, Trumwine the bishop of the Picts, and important lay and clerical figures, agree that Cuthbert is the man needed and persuade him to accept their mandate.[104]

It is in writing of this same Cuthbert that Bede gives his clearest illustration of how the monk must become involved in the life of his society.[105] The passage is notable and worth quoting at length.

Cuthbert was placed over [the monastery of Lindisfarne], where he instructed many in regular life, both by the authority of a master, and the example of his own behavior. Nor did he afford admonitions and an example of a regular life to his monastery alone, but endeavoured to convert the people round about far and near from the life of foolish custom, to the love of heavenly joys; for many profaned the faith which they had received by their wicked actions; and some also, in the time of a mortality, neglecting the sacraments of faith which they had received, had recourse to the false remedies of idolatry, as if they could have put a stop to the plague sent from God, by enchantments, spells, or other secrets of the hellish art. In order to correct the error of both sorts, he often went out of the monastery, sometimes on horseback, but oftener on foot, and repaired to the neighbouring towns, where he preached the way of truth to such as were gone astray; which had been also done by Boisil in his time. It was then the custom of the English people, that when a clerk or priest came into the town, they all, at his command, flocked together to hear the word; willingly heard what was said, and more willingly practised those things that they could hear or understand. But Cuthbert was so skilful an orator, so fond was he of enforcing his subject, and such a brightness appeared in his angelic face, that no man present presumed to conceal from him the most hidden secrets of his heart, but all openly confessed what they had done; because they thought the same guilt could not be concealed from him, and wiped off the guilt of what they had so confessed with worthy fruits of penance, as he commanded. He was wont chiefly to resort to those places, and preach in such villages, as being seated high up amid craggy uncouth mountains, were frightful to others to behold, and whose poverty and barbarity rendered them inaccessible to other teachers; which nevertheless he, having entirely devoted himself to that pious labour, did so industriously apply himself to polish with his doctrine, that when he departed out of his monastery, he would often stay a week, sometimes two or three, and sometimes a whole month, before he returned home, continuing among the mountains to allure that rustic people by his preaching and example to heavenly employments.

To Bede, monastic withdrawal cannot be a selfish act, a turning of one's back on society; if he praises those who give up the world it is because, in addition to looking after their own souls, they provide saintly example for all men to follow. He is keenly alive to the variety of ways in which man can serve God, but in all cases, as in Cuthbert's, this service is inseparable from service to men. A man who uses the monastery as an excuse to avoid fighting for his country is wrong and sinful; Bede makes this point in a letter which he wrote to Ecgberct, bishop of York, toward the end of his life.[106] Much of the letter is devoted to an analysis of how Northumbria can be strengthened by coopera- tion between its bishop and its king, by simultaneous improve- ment on both a personal and national level, and by the bishop's exercising full authority even over monasteries.[107] National, ec- clesiastical, and personal *salus* are complementary, concurrent goals of the historical process; once again the exegetical model for Bede's analysis reveals itself in his exposition.

If English society at its best profits from the involvement of each of its members, then it follows that every member can put his particular skill to good use, viz., to a Christian use and an educative one as well. An interesting and, I think, hitherto un- noticed series of *exempla* and references which demonstrate the consistency and breadth of Bede's historiography deal with music and musicians. One of the great events of English church history is the arrival in Britain in 669 of the eastern-born Theodore of Tarsus, designated by Rome as the new archbishop of Canter- bury.[108] Under him the church in England achieves new great- ness, to the profit of all English society.[109] As a sign of prosper- ous unity, the English begin to learn sacred music all over the island, an art until then confined to Kent. This spreading of music also symbolizes the triumph of Roman Christianity: the Northumbrians learn music from one Eaddi, who is invited to come by Wilfrid, that champion of the universal Roman church.[110] At the same time the bishop of Rochester, Putta, passes on the great skill in the Roman style of music which he had re- ceived from disciples of Pope Gregory.[111]

Further references to the practice of church music in England emphasize its close links to the larger question of social unity. Abbot John, sent by the pope from Rome to teach singing after the Roman manner, is also in charge of a papal commission examining English orthodoxy.[112] Of Bishop Acca, successor to Wilfrid as bishop of Hexham, we are told that his musical competence accords with his scholarship, his orthodoxy, and his ecclesiastical fitness; he develops these qualities by trips to Rome with Wilfrid.[113] Music was to Bede an expression of the church's teaching function and universality, a field to be cultivated by exemplary Christians and propagators of God's word.

It is against this background that we must understand Bede's celebrated account of the Northumbrian poet Caedmon. The story (told in Book Four, Chapter 24) of his miraculous acquisition of powers of composition and song, at the behest of an angel, in order that he might put the message of the scriptures into the form and language of the English, is not simply a delightful tale. C. L. Wrenn recognizes it as a hagiographical episode making the point that Caedmon first turned the forms of Old English heroic poetry into an acceptable vehicle for Christian teaching.[114] Caedmon turns the "old" poetry to new uses, and his discovery is a joy not only to himself but to all his countrymen, who can now be evangelized through music and brought to the true knowledge of Christianity. He sings in his songs the great stories of the Old and New Testaments, and aims through his art to inculcate in all his listeners a love of virtue. Caedmon, too, is a hero of ecclesiastical history.[115]

The most characteristic social heroes of the *Historia ecclesiastica* are not, however, the singers of songs at home, but the preachers of the Word in foreign lands. The Anglo-Saxon missionaries who brought the gospel back to the continent and spread it heroically among the barbarian tribes of northwestern Europe represent the latest and greatest blossoms of the nation-*ecclesia* whose flowering Bede recounted in his history. He presents their story with the attention to imaginative details that marks the *Historia* as a whole. The first would-be preacher to the continental Germans is the priest Ecgberct, who decides on an apostolate to foreign lands as a way of fulfilling his Christian responsibility.[116] God, however, has other plans for Ecgberct and tells him by visions and miracles to preach the faith to the Picts, whose Christianity is not orthodox.[117] His companion Wictberct goes to Frisia, but has no success in two years of preaching; he returns, determined to help his own people toward greater holiness.[118] Bede is saying by means of these *exempla* that the Christian's missionary urge is good, but that he must be ready to exercise it close to home, for the good of his own society first. Only after Ecgberct and Wictberct have been placed by God where they are most needed does a mission to the Frisians, that of Wilbrord,[119] meet with success.

Wilbrord, the first bishop of the Frisians, is shown by the narrative sequence just described to represent the final stage of Bede's view of history on a national and a personal level. The successive attempts of Ecgberct, Wictberct, and Wilbrord present imaginatively the order of the Christian's social responsibilities. With holy men like Ecgberct and Wictberct preaching and giving example closer to home, Wilbrord can indulge in his social heroism at the highest level, i.e., as a successor to the apostles, rendering to the Frisians the same service Gregory and Augustine had rendered to the English. At a national level, the successful *ecclesia* is the one which can spare its heroes to spread Christianity abroad. At a personal level, the highest expression of the individual Christian's holiness is the evangelical urge. In teaching others, the Christian fulfills his salvific potential and insures social prosperity; similarly, the society is at its zenith when it can reenact the evangelical propensities of its individual members and send them forth to begin again the cycle of an ever new, ever recreating *ecclesia*.

The parallelism implicit in the Christian theology of history and exploited by Bede in the *Historia ecclesiastica gentis Anglorum* finds its most compelling and contemporary application in the Anglo-Saxon missions. We are therefore justified in believing that Bede's perception of this particular parallel in the society which had nurtured him resulted in his *magnum opus* taking the form it did. From his insight into the workings of providence in his age, Bede re-created the Christian past of his nation, viewing it as the manifestation of a universal order, so harmoniously adjusted by God that every individual act of conversion or accomplishment, from King Paulinus of Northumbria and his vigorous priest Coifi to Caedmon's music-making, caused sympathetic vibrations on a national scale. This is Bede's vision of God in history—perhaps the finest of all its type.

CHAPTER IV

Historia Brittonum: *Heroes and Villains versus Saints and Sinners*

Discussion of the next fall of Britain text, the *Historia Brittonum*,[1] involves complications of a kind which have not beset our study of Gildas and Bede. These complications stem from the fact that the *Historia Brittonum* is not a continuous narrative by one author, but a compilation of texts whose dates and places of origin are various and often obscure. The work exists in several MSS, the contents of which also vary, thereby multiplying the difficulties of approaching it systematically. Nevertheless, such an approach must be attempted, for lying amid the tangle of divergent and often contradictory documents which make up the *Historia Brittonum* are themes and episodes of great interest for the study of early medieval historiography.

The critical literature surrounding the *Historia Brittonum* is itself a dense and tangled growth, a thorough survey of which lies beyond the scope of this study.[2] The main areas of controversy may be summarized as the problem of dating, the contributions of Nennius and other compilers, and the veracity of the historical traditions woven into the text. A subdivision, or perhaps restatement, of the last category is the purpose, or purposes, of such a composite text. Some of these questions are relevant to the concerns of the present chapter, and deserve a few words. Any discussion must be preceded by a summary of the *Historia*

Brittonum, including the main sections found in some or all of the MSS groups.[3] The best MS is, by scholarly agreement, MS Harleian 3859 (Mommsen's H), copied in the late tenth or early eleventh century.[4]

The work begins in some MSS (but not H) with a preface by Nennius, who identifies himself as a disciple of Elvodugus,[5] and claims to have gathered together material from a variety of domestic and foreign sources in order to preserve a record of the British past. There follow, by chapters:

1–6. A summary of the six ages of the world.

7–9. A description of the island of Britain.

10–11. An origin story, tracing the Britons to an eponymous founder Bruto (or Britto), a descendant of Aeneas, who, having killed his father accidentally, flees his Italian homeland, eventually settles in Britain, and populates it with his progeny.

12. The arrival of the Picts.

13–15. Origin stories of the Scots (Irish).

16. A computation of the arrival date of the Saxons in Britain.

17–18. Origin story and genealogy connecting the Britons with Brito, a descendant of Japheth, son of Noah.

19–30. The career of Rome in Britain and the final departure of the Romans after an intermittent rule of 348 years.

31–49. The career, downfall, and death of the wicked British ruler, Guorthigirn, drawn from several sources; the deeds of Guorthigirn's enemy, St. Germanus; Guorthigirn's dealings with the Saxons; and his encounter with the boy-prophet, Ambrosius.

50–55. The life and deeds of St. Patrick, apostle to the Irish.

56. The battles of Arthur.

57–61. Saxon genealogies.

62–65. The war between the Britons and the Saxons to *ca.* 685.

66. Another computation of the dates of main figures in British history.

66–76. Cities and marvels of Britain; a set of annals containing various events of British history, and a set of Welsh genealogies.

The material just summarized can be dated in its various parts from the seventh century to the mid-ninth century. The earliest MS of the *Historia Brittonum* is the so-called Chartres MS (Mommsen's Z), which was copied *ca.* 900 and contains a much abbreviated text.[6] MS Z is described in its heading as a series of excerpts made by a *filius Urbgen* from a book concerning the deeds of St. Germanus.[7] A Rhun map Urien figures in Chapter 63 of the H text, where he is said to have baptized King Edwin of Northumbria in 627. He may therefore have been a first compiler of British historical and hagiographical material, some time before 650.[8] All recent scholars agree, however, that a main recension of the *Historia Brittonum*, which resulted in a text much like that of MS H, took place sometime between 796 and 801; a new "edition" of this recension followed *ca.* 830.[9]

Nennius, the compiler of the *Historia* according to some MSS, is identifiable from other sources as a clerk active in the early years of the ninth century.[10] In the past, his role in the formation of the fullest version of the work was the subject of much scholarly debate,[11] exacerbated by the fact that no MS with the Nennian preface antedates the twelfth century.[12] But since there is now little doubt that the composition or compilation of important parts of the *Historia* came during Nennius' lifetime, if not from his pen, the question of precise authorship has lost some of its importance. Instead, scholarly interest today centers on questions concerning the historicity and purpose of the work, with results of considerable interest for this study.

Even a cursory inspection of the various sections of the *Historia Brittonum* reveals that much of the matter therein is not what we would consider historical record. The text offers accounts of the arrival of the Saxons, of their struggle for mastery of Britain, and of the sorry career of Guorthigirn, the man responsible for the Saxon advances—but these accounts are often contradictory. For a long time it was customary to seek their origin exclusively in folklore, an origin which would explain the divergencies existing side by side in the compilation. While it is true that popular traditions, passed down orally or in writing through generations, are recorded within the *Historia*,[13] the work as a whole can no longer be considered merely a repository of them. Faral, in his exhaustive study of the text,[14] showed clearly that there is a strong learned element in the *Historia*'s main episodes, and that it is necessary to speak of the work's authors as well as its traditions. Since then, more and more attention has been paid to the role played by clerical compilers and "intellectuals" in fabricating, bringing together, and handing on the matter of the British past. In particular, N. K. Chadwick, the leading student today of the intellectual and political milieu of the *Historia Brittonum*, has reached many important conclusions about the circumstances surrounding the compilation of the work. Two of these, at least, are directly relevant to the study of the fall of Britain texts as works illustrative of the early medieval historical imagination.

Prof. Chadwick demonstrates that the British church loomed large as a literary and intellectual force in the centuries following the departure of the Romans and until the time of Nennius, who was himself an apologist for British culture.[15] In the preceding chapter we saw how Bede chronicled the rise of the English church to a position of scholarly preeminence and attachment to Rome; culture and orthodoxy worked side by side for Bede, as both were necessary to spread the gospel. Now, as long as the English and Britons remained politically hostile, and their churches separated by matters of observance, it was not surprising that the British church should defend not only its own ecclesiastical practices, but national traditions and culture as well. It was, after all, the preserver of that culture in its monasteries and centers of British learning.

This brings us to Prof. Chadwick's second observation, viz., that the early ninth century was a period of national revival among the Britons, especially in northern Wales.[16] An integral part of this revival was the growth of centers of British learning, in touch with Irish and continental scholarship [17] and aware of the traditions of Britain's post-Roman past. The political and intellectual climate of the time prompted what Miss Chadwick calls "antiquarian speculation" about the origins of British ruling houses and of the nation itself. Such scholarly speculation, and the consequent creation of eponymous and other origin stories, was rife throughout the Celtic world at the beginning of the ninth century.[18] Moreover, this century also saw the rise of a British hope that the Saxons might at last be driven from the island of Britain.[19] These appeals to a glorious national past and hopes for a glorious national future were secular in feeling; they stressed national, rather than ecclesiastical, traditions and aspirations.

The cultural situation in Celtic Britain at the time when the *Historia Brittonum* (i.e., the recension preserved in MS H) was taking shape was, then, one of broad contrasts: on the one hand, a strong national-ecclesiastical tradition; on the other, an emergent national, secular consciousness, looking for its inspiration to a refurbished legendary and heroic tradition. Of course, these contrasts existed within one and the same learned, clerical milieu, and the emergence from this milieu of a self-contradictory compilation like the *Historia Brittonum* is *a priori* understandable, if not quite predictable. What does surprise us is the conglomerate nature of the composite narrative, and the overt inconsistencies between different segments of its recapitulation of the British past. I think, however, that at least some of the peculiar features of the *Historia Brittonum* can be explained in large measure by the Gildas tradition of the fall of Britain, which the authors and compilers of the work certainly knew and used. As in the preceding chapter, the question of the *Historia*'s debt to Gildas may best be approached by way of a comparison of the British work with some analogous historical writings. In this case, though, the basis for comparison will be contemporaneity rather than generic similarity or demonstrable influence.

The major work of national history closest in time to the *Historia Brittonum* is the *Historia Langobardorum* of Paul the Deacon.[20] Paul was himself of Langobardic stock, and lived an active life in ecclesiastical and court circles in Italy during the second half of the eighth century.[21] The *Historia Langobardorum*, his last work (he died before he could complete it), was a complimentary account of the nation's past, beginning with the heroic period of Langobardic national migration from northern Europe into the boundaries of the empire and finally into Italy. This early part of the work conforms in content and style to the prevalent early medieval type of barbarian national history: Paul's material is drawn in large part from the common Germanic stock of heroic legend, and is presented through the medium of traditional Roman rhetoric. The heroes and episodes are clearly barbarian; [22] the set speeches, the praise of freedom (the great ideal for which, according to Paul, the Langobards fight so fiercely), and the various rhetorical devices which adorn characters and incidents, are as clearly the legacy of classical culture.[23] What is lacking in Paul's account is a central concern with the importance of national conversion for national history; unlike Gregory or Bede, he does not give special prominence to Christian kings and heroes of the Langobards.

This is not to say that Paul entirely disregarded Christianity in his history, or (what is more important to this study) that his vision of history reveals no formative Christian influences; there is, however, no constant application of the methods used by Eusebius and Orosius to interpret history theologically and exegetically. Comparison with the historical work of Gregory of Tours is enlightening here. We remarked in the preceding chapter that the *Historia Francorum* displays both Gregory's desire to interpret history in a specifically Christian manner and his contradictory tendency to record graphically the human, passionate lives of the barbarian Franks. Paul's work, which borrows extensively from Gregory's, confines its hagiographical interests to a few incidents reproduced from the earlier historian.[24] Completely lacking is any *heilsgeschichtlich* context for the Langobardic nation, such as Gregory provides in his first book. The total effect of Paul's historiography, in short, is much less that of contrary interpretations at war than of national interests occasionally colored by Christian concerns. Both these elements deserve closer attention for the light they shed on the *Historia Brittonum*.

Paul's account of Langobardic history dwells at length on the relations between the Langobard kings in Italy and the Byzantine Empire, the heir of imperial Rome. The complicated history of Byzantine-barbarian relations does not concern us here, but rather the reaction of the late eighth-century historian to the Byzantine Empire, as revealed in his portrayal of past Langobard-Byzantine encounters. The most interesting revelation of Paul's attitude, I think, occurs in the fifth book of the *Historia Langobardorum*.[25] A series of Langobard leaders, notably Grimuald and Romuald, lead their nation against imperial forces intent on bringing Italy under Byzantine sway in order to regain a western empire for the heirs of Constantine.[26] In the tenth chapter of Book Five, an imperial army under the general Saburrus is sent against the Langobards, commanded by Romuald. Paul tells us:

And while both lines were fighting with great obstinacy, a man from the king's army named Amalong, who had been accustomed to carry the royal pike, taking this pike in both hands struck violently with it a certain little Greek and lifted him from the saddle on which he was riding and raised him in the air over his head. When the army of the Greeks saw this, it was terrified by boundless fear and at once betook itself to flight, and overwhelmed with the utmost disaster,

in fleeing it brought death upon itself and victory to Romuald and
the Langobards.

Following the defeat, Constantine, the Byzantine emperor, goes
to Rome and loots the city; soon, says Paul, all Italy groans
under the weight of "the avarice of the Greeks."

Paul's handling of this climactic hour in Langobardic history
makes it unmistakably clear that, for him, the contrast between
Byzantine Greeks and barbarian Langobards is primarily cultural, not political. On one side are the fierce, unspoiled Langobards, fighting for their homeland with devotion and with great
strength; on the other stand the "little Greeks," puny and effete,
easily terrified by the barbarians, and driven on not by valor or
love of freedom, but by blind avarice and lust for power.[27]
Paul's historical consciousness is conditioned in part by a conviction that the barbarians represent new blood, so to speak, and
have rightfully inherited the rule of the west from the older
and less potent rulers of the ancient world.

But the Langobards were not destined always to be victorious;
by the time Paul wrote his history they had ceased to be a vital
force in Italian political life, having been conquered in 774 by
the Frankish army of Charlemagne, who assumed at this time
the title King of the Lombards. In explaining the reverses suffered
by his nation, Paul depended upon the tradition of providential
history whereby God rewards and punishes men and nations in
this life, thereby prefiguring the final judgments of the next. A
passage in the sixth chapter of Book Five illustrates this Christian
strain of Paul's historiography.

In those days the emperor Constantine who was also called Constans,
desiring to pluck Italy out of the hand of the Langobards, left Constantinople and taking his way along the coast, came to Athens, and
from there, having crossed the sea, he landed at Tarentum. Previously, however, he went to a certain hermit who was said to have
the spirit of prophecy, and sought eagerly to know from him whether
he could overcome and conquer the nation of the Langobards which

was dwelling in Italy. The servant of God had asked him for the space of one night that he might supplicate the Lord for this thing, and when morning came he thus answered the emperor: "The people of the Langobards cannot be overcome in any way, because a certain queen coming from another province has built the church of St. John the Baptist in the territories of the Langobards, and for this reason St. John himself continually intercedes for the nation of the Langobards. But a time shall come when this sanctuary will be held in contempt and then the nation itself shall perish." We have proved that this has so occurred, since we have seen that before the fall of the Langobards, this same church of St. John which was established in the place called Modicia (Monza) was managed by vile persons so that this holy spot was bestowed upon the unworthy and adulterous, not for the merit of their lives, but in the giving of spoils.

I mentioned earlier that Paul avoids overt reference to the conversion of the Langobards; I cannot help wondering, however, whether he is not here alluding to national conversion as a key to national success. The building of a church dedicated to the Baptist in the territories of the Langobards by "a certain queen" (*regina quaedam*) typifies the burgeoning of the church on national soil; the monarch and the holy announcer of the true faith cooperate to render the Langobards invincible until by its sins the nation poisons the wellsprings of its own greatness. There can certainly be no doubt that the "vile persons" (*viles personas*) who betrayed the Baptist typify the nation as a whole, since their crimes result in national defeat. We may reasonably see in this brief passage an artistic complexity suggested by, and in the service of, a theology of history, and looking back (through the figure of the Baptist) to the biblical history of salvation.

At approximately the same time that the *Historia Brittonum* came into being, then, Paul the Deacon interpreted the national past of his own nation in terms both of a cultural opposition between old and new civilizations, and of the national price paid for sin, in accordance with the Christian view of divine providence operating in history.[28] But his history is not the only manifestation of the coexistence of Christian and secular interpretations of national events in late eighth-century Europe; the great political fact of the age, the Carolingian empire of Charles, King of the Franks, also inspired many and various attempts to explain its significance.

The Holy Roman Empire came into existence in the year 800, when Pope Leo III crowned the Frankish monarch in St. Peter's basilica on Christmas day. Charles was already the strongest monarch in western Europe, but with the coronation his rule over the territory he had inherited and conquered received the church's sanction as the heir of Roman order in the west. What was the theoretical or providential import of this consecration of a new imperial power by the successor of Peter? Contemporary observers differed as greatly in answering that question as modern scholars have differed in attempting to reconstruct the sequence of events which led to the coronation.[29] There were several attempts to integrate the Holy Roman Empire into a purely Christian interpretation of history: the existing Carolingian concept of the Christian king as a new David, the anointed of the Lord (*christus domini*), was applied to Charles;[30] Alcuin, the English Benedictine monk who was Charles' friend and adviser, spoke often to the monarch of a new Europe, a Christian *imperium* headed by Charles;[31] and Augustine's view of the Christian king as just ruler of a kingdom dedicated to peace and to the salvation of its subjects was also popular.[32]

But there were also more secular interpretations of Charles' power and of the meaning of his coronation. (One recent study has even attempted to assign these interpretations, as well as the Christian analyses, to specific groups or factions at the Carolingian court.)[33] Certainly, a significant factor in secular and nationalistic explanations of the triumph of Charles and the Franks was a rivalry with and animosity toward the Byzantine Empire in Frankish circles.[34] This hostility can perhaps be traced to envy; for, as Norman Cantor points out, Carolingian Europe was still a primitive society compared to the Byzantine world.[35] In any case, the Franks, as a bold, strong, barbarian race, undoubtedly felt much the same cultural superiority toward the overrefined and weak Byzantine "Greeks" that we have seen in the pages of Paul the Deacon's *Historia Langobardorum*.[36]

From this hasty survey of pertinent facts, we see that the concurrent existence in late eighth- and early ninth-century Britain of Christian-ecclesiastical and secular-national views of history was by no means an isolated phenomenon, but rather that it partook of a larger pattern of increased self-awareness and self-confidence on the part of the learned segment of European society. There was no question of a break with the Christian and classical legacies of the ancient world; [37] but there undoubtedly was a genuine and deeply felt desire to establish the independent worth of the post-Roman national experience. An intelligent reading of the *Historia Brittonum* requires that we keep this desire constantly in mind. In addition, the Christian sections of the work make insistent and complex demands upon our attention; more so, for example, than anything in Paul's Langobardic history. Nor are the strands kept separate and confined to different works and traditions, as they generally were in Carolingian circles. For example, the important figure of Guorthigirn is treated in the *Historia Brittonum* in two completely different ways, or rather, in two contrasting historiographical contexts, reflecting two different visions of history. H. M. Chadwick has shown that there are also political factors behind the complicated presentation of Guorthigirn in the *Historia*; [38] since the politics of the present always color views of the past, however, our analyses of the *Historia Brittonum* should not be incompatible with this sense of political complexity which the Chadwicks have so admirably communicated, even though we will not discuss ninth-century politics per se.

It remains, then, to ask if it is possible to account for the

peculiar characteristics assumed by the *Historia Brittonum* entirely within the context of the developments just outlined. The
answer must be negative, for, at least in part, such characteristics
resulted from the existence of the Gildas tradition. Here again,
as with Bede, we must realize that the only extant "historical"
consideration of the fall of Britain assumed great importance for
further writings on the subject, and recall that *De excidio
Britanniae* presented its historical observations from an uncompromisingly Christian point of view. Neither Paul the Deacon,
who had no authoritative Christian Langobardic tradition to
contend with, nor the Carolingian chroniclers, who were faced
with an entirely new and unique situation, encountered the peculiar conditions imposed in Britain upon ecclesiastical and national historians alike by the legacy of Gildas. Thanks to that
legacy, secular historians could not treat the British past as
simply a *tabula rasa* on which to inscribe at will antiquarian or
partisan interpretations; while, on their part, Christian historians
could fuse various traditions which shared an approach based on
the theology of history, and could reinterpret or challenge the
traditions and inventions of those who approached the British
past from a national and secular point of view. To imagine a
literal process of action and reaction in the composition of the
Historia Brittonum is dangerous; we lack supporting evidence
and undoubtedly always will. Nor can we eliminate the obvious
possibility that the same man or men could have written both
ecclesiastical and national history, in much the same way that
Bede could compose his world chronicle and his ecclesiastical
history on different principles. But that there are two different
views of history in the various sections of the *Historia* is indis-
putable, and that the clarity of the distinction between them,
and their enforced coexistence in one compilation, are partially
the result of the Gildas tradition is, I think, almost equally clear.

The first noteworthy feature of the *Historia Brittonum* is its
large number of origin stories. The origin story is an artistic

device employed to explain how a nation, a family, or an institution came into existence. At the same time, it is more than merely mock-history. Implicit in the account of an important beginning (important, that is, for the teller and his audience) are the ideals which underlie the author's view of life or which he feels should animate the institution about which he is writing. The origin story, in other words, may be myth or hortatory *exemplum*, or both. The creation story and the fall of man in Genesis are best viewed as the first, while the *Aeneid* fits to a great extent into the second category. To be sure, origin stories figure in folklore and folk traditions, but usually in the reduced form of genealogies which stretch back to a superhuman hero-founder of the tribe or nation. Tacitus, for example, records such folk genealogies among the Germanic tribes in the first century A.D.[39]

In turning to the *Historia Brittonum*, we find four origin stories of the Britons, two of which are primarily genealogies; two origin stories of the Scots; and one account of the origin of a British royal line.[40] I will first discuss the two accounts of the origin of the Britons which are secular in feeling.[41] There are no similar origin stories in Gildas or Bede. The reason is clear: since Christian ecclesiastical-national history applied the theology of history to national happenings, the events of past and present were adapted to the biblical and exegetical scheme, and the only "origins" that mattered were the origins of Israel, of the New Israel, and of the Christian. Just as national disaster prefigured the final judgment, so national beginnings were important at a personal level, i.e., in terms of conversion. Accordingly, the nation that sought its beginning in history instead of in the theology of history revealed thereby a change in its values.[42]

In MSS MNZ, a section headed *De genealogia Brittonum* begins, "De origine Brittonum De Romanis et Grecis trahunt ethimologiam" (Concerning the origin of the Britons, who derive their origin from the Romans and the Greeks).[43] There

follows a genealogy which links the Romans to Dardanus, father
of Trous, the builder of Troy.[44] Rome is built by the three
brothers Romulus, Remus, and Brutus, sons of Silvius Posthumus.
Brutus, now a consul,[45] engages in wars for Rome and, after subduing Spain to Roman rule, takes Britain, which (depending on
the MSS readings) is inhabited by his own stock or by the
descendants of his father Silvius.[46] The aim of this origin story is
clearly to attach the Britons to the ancient world and make them
the heirs of Roman greatness. This theme recalls the papal interpretation of the Carolingian empire as a *renovatio romani imperii*.
I do not mean to imply that there is a concrete connection between Charles and this type of origin story, but only to point
out that one learned element of early ninth-century Europe
preferred to think of its civilization as the heir of Rome.[47]

Quite different in outlook is the other origin story which turns
to Rome for an eponymous ancestor of the Britons.[48] This account appears in MS H, and its hero is also Brutus (Britto), son
of Silvius. The starting point of the story is Aeneas' flight to Italy
after the Trojan war. Some time later, the wife of his son Silvius
gives birth to Brutus.[49] Before Brutus is born, a *magus* prophesies
that the child will kill his father and mother and be an outcast
among all men.[50] The prediction is fulfilled: Brutus' mother dies
in childbirth, and several years later his father is accidentally
shot by him while hunting. Brutus then flees Italy to the islands
of the Tyrrhenian sea, but is expelled by the Greeks living
there, who recall that his grandfather had slain Turnus. He goes
to Gaul, founds the city of Tours, and comes at last to the island
to which he gives his name, Britain; he fills it with his progeny,
the first Britons.[51]

There appears to be no pro-Roman bias or yearning for the
days of imperial glory in this account. Rather, its hero, Brutus,
finding himself alienated from his home and legacy through no
fault of his own, is forced to flee the proto-Roman world, a
victim of fate and of universal, though unmerited, opprobrium.

His first attempt to find a new home fails, for it takes him among the Greeks, his grandfather's ancient enemies, who blame Brutus, again without guilt on his part, for the death of Turnus. At this point there is a significant bit of wordplay in the text. Brutus finds no refuge "because of the murder of Turnus [*Turni*], whom Aeneas killed. And he traveled as far as Gaul, and there he built the city of the Tournians, which is called Tours [*civitatem Turonorum, quae vocatur Turnis*]." The destruction of Turnus is part of the hateful legacy bequeathed to Brutus, who, as if in atonement, leaves behind his ancestral world and constructs his own Turnis. Then he proceeds to an island home, far from the "old world," and there establishes a new, fertile nation. The implication is, I think, quite clear: the Britons are a new order, free from the traditions of war and vengeance which in effect condemn the individual in the old society before he can help himself. Brutus is a romantic hero vis à vis the world from which he departs in disgrace in quest of a home.[52] He becomes a social hero in Britain, which he founds and fills with his descendants. Again, contemporaneous continental attitudes help in comprehending the intention of this second account of Brutus. Just as the Franks found reason to consider their new society (and their "new Rome" at Aachen) more than a match for the "old Rome" of Constantinople, which they scorned as effete and uncongenial to vigorous, free men, so here there is a similar exaltation of Britain, a nation freed by its founder from the burden of hatred imposed by the old world.

The third and fourth origin stories are more precisely genealogies. They look at the origin of Britain from a very different point of view, that of a Christian trying to connect his nation with the history of salvation. One [53] combines a Germanic tradition with the biblical information that the earth was repopulated after the flood by the sons of Noah. According to the text, which is related to the account of the origins of Europe in a surviving sixth-century Frankish chart,[54] Britto, the eponym of Britain, is the son of Hessitio, who is also the ancestor of the Franks, Romans, and Alamanni.[55] Hessitio, through his father Alanus, is descended from Iafeth, son of Noah, who came to Europe after the flood. The aim of this improbable series of genealogies is simply to emphasize the relationship among all men and connect them all to God.[56] It is the approach of a Christian rather than a nationalist.

The same judgment applies to the second genealogy, which combines the Trojan descent of the Britons with the genealogy of the sons of Noah.[57] This list, missing from some MSS,[58] also retains the Hessitio-Britto genealogy and, coming at the end of the origin story section, seeks to synthesize all the attitudes preceding it in the text.[59] Its inclusion of the Trojan-Roman hypothesis has special significance, for whereas the Germanic folk tradition of the sons of Alan is innocent of political meaning, the conjectures about Rome do involve the formation of an attitude toward an imperial order and toward national goals. The attempt to integrate the secular origin stories into a genealogy stretching back to Noah and God appears to be more than genial "antiquarian speculation"; it is the response of a conservative Christian tradition to the challenge of a new view of history. (The final British origin story [Chapters 33–35] concerns not all the Britons, but one of their royal lines, and will be treated later in its context, the Guorthigirn-St. Germanus section.

In the midst of the origin episodes, the *Historia Brittonum* recounts very briefly the arrival of the Picts in Britain,[60] and at greater length, the origins of the Scots (the inhabitants of Ireland).[61] The Scots come to Ireland from Spain. A first expedition under Partholomus is destroyed except for one survivor by a plague; a second, headed by Nimeth, is at sea for a year and a half, and is shipwrecked upon arrival in Ireland; after several years, Nimeth sails back to Spain. A third colonization is attempted by three brothers, but their attempt meets catastrophe when the Scots attack the inhabitants of a glass tower rising in the sea off Ireland. As the Scots land on the island around the tower, the seas suddenly close on them. All are drowned except for one small group which could not take part in the raid because their ship had been wrecked. From these survivors Ireland is finally peopled.[62]

The difficulties which the Scots face in their attempts to settle in Ireland are in striking contrast to the successful multiplication of the progeny of Brutus in Britain. No explicit reason is given for these reverses, but they are clearly reminiscent of Old Testament situations (the sea inundating the attackers of the glass tower; the few survivors of the destruction by water who people the island), and since the Scots are the enemies of the Britons,[63] it is not surprising to find them described as punished like the Egyptians in Exodus.[64]

On the other hand, the second Scottish origin story traces the nation to a Scythian nobleman living in Egypt at the time of the Exodus. He takes no part in the fatal pursuit of Israel, and is expelled from Egypt by the few survivors, who fear his power. After many long wanderings through Africa and other parts of the Mediterranean world, the Scythian (and his followers, of uncertain provenance) arrive in Spain, where they multiply and fill the land. One thousand and two years later they come to Ireland, when Brutus is consul among the Romans.[65] Again in this narrative, we see an attempt to locate national origins within biblical history—this time to the advantage of the Scots, who, like the Israelites, escape Egypt and after a long journey find a land which they can inhabit and fill with their offspring. There is no way to reconcile these stories; we can only notice that clerical writers and compilers handling national traditions or conjectures fall into the pattern, if not the assumptions, of the scriptures.

The dual nature of the sources preserved in (or composed for) the *Historia Brittonum* should now be clear enough to permit my considering separately a few passages of the work which demonstrate one approach or the other with particular clarity. I will first discuss the largest of the secular sections, the Roman occupation of Britain (Chapters 19–31), and then the encounter between Guorthigirn and Ambrosius (Chapters 40–42), which includes the latter's political prophecy, and is perhaps the most important a-Christian episode in the *Historia Brittonum*. To balance these episodes, I will conclude by analyzing the rest of the Guorthigirn section and the chapters devoted to St. Patrick and to Arthur (Chapters 32–39 and 43–56).

The *Historia*'s account of the Roman occupation of Britain [66] incorporates several references from Gildas' historical summary: the Romans come to Britain after having gained control of the rest of the world; [67] the Britons, proud and tyrannical, refuse to receive the Roman envoys; [68] the sixth Roman emperor to reign in Britain is Maximus, and the seventh is Maximianus, a doublet of Maximus, who usurps the Roman "kingship" from Gratian and drains Britain of her soldiery; [69] the Britons, harassed by the Picts and Scots, periodically send for Roman aid.[70] This is the inescapable basis provided by the Gildas tradition; on it, however, the author of this section has constructed an edifice substantially different in tone and intention.[71] The lamentations and accusations have disappeared, as has their elaborate rhetorical framework. The judgment of God is not invoked to explain national calamity. Most importantly, Rome is not presented in the favorable light with which Gildas suffuses his account of the would-be saviors of Britain. Instead, the mistress of the world is treated as a foreign power who imposes her will on Britain and whose reign is at best a mixed blessing, at worst a cause of national disaster.

The key to the rather confused narrative of the Roman chapters is the author's conception of the emperor. This approach is greatly at variance with Gildas, who seldom mentions an emperor by name,[72] and never considers the role of the emperor in the formation and maintenance of Roman excellence. The *Historia*'s assessment of the emperors who came to or reigned in Britain is hardly adulatory. The first, Julius Caesar, tries twice without success to conquer the Britons before finally defeating them. Claudius, the next, conquers Britain with much depredation and loss, and apparently establishes insular emperors to hold the Britons in subjection.[73] Then comes Severus, who, having built a wall to keep out the Scots and Picts, is slain by the Britons;[74] and Caritius, who avenges Severus by punishing the Britons and becoming their emperor.

The fifth Roman emperor in Britain is Constantine, son of Constantine the Great; the sixth is Maximus and the seventh Maximianus, both of whom reign (continuously?) in Britain instead of having come to it, as their predecessors had.[75] The implication of the different phrase used in the text seems to be that these last two emperors are permanently attached to Britain (in keeping with the idea of specifically British emperors introduced in Chapter 21), without themselves being Britons, since they are the direct successors of Julius Caesar, Claudius, etc. This is an important detail, for it is under Maximianus that Britain suffers her greatest blow: when the emperor sets out to usurp Gratian's imperial throne, he denudes Britain of her soldiery and, reluctant to allow them to return home, he insists that they settle in Armorica, where they are useless to their nation and lost to their families. As a direct result of Maximianus' adventure and its consequences, the Britons are left a prey to foreign nations ("gentibus extraneis"), and lose their land, which they will regain only when God sees fit to aid them.[76]

This passage is climactic as it directly imputes the loss of Britain to Roman interference. Maximianus, far from being an offshoot of British vice, is a Roman creation who brings misery to Britain, thanks ultimately to the Roman conquest of the island. The anti-Roman bias of these chapters is nowhere more apparent, and recalls, though in a much more direct fashion, the anti-Graeco-Roman sentiments of the second *Brutus eponymus* story.

After the author-compiler has related the careers of the emperors in Britain, he ends with a brief recapitulation of what he now openly calls a war between the Britons and the Romans.[77] The salient feature of the war, as he sees it, is that for a period of 348 years the Romans came periodically to renew their hold on Britain and often to protect the inhabitants from the Picts and Scots. Compared to this danger, even the Roman yoke seemed to the Britons preferable,[78] but they soon rebelled against the oppressors and killed the Roman leaders. Rebellion left them free but helpless, and then a new appeal had to be sent to Rome. The Roman occupiers would come again, strip the island of all its wealth, and then depart in great triumph.[79]

This account is not entirely clear, but its import is unmistakable: Rome brings protection at the price of freedom; the Britons do no wrong in revolting since their weakness is a military, not a moral one. Therefore, the fall of Britain is the result of external pressure, not internal disorder and vice; forces beyond the individual's control and not dependent upon his virtue decide national destiny. The theology of history has given way to the artistic presentation of history as an *exemplum* to express a political belief, viz., that imperial tyranny and loss of freedom are ruinous.

When the Christian theology of history no longer serves to interpret national history, Christian eschatology *ipso facto* ceases to be an organizing principle of historical narrative. The nation ceases to move with its members toward a divine judgment prefigured in the daily fortunes of the Christian and the world. If history is still to have a specific goal, therefore, another one must be found for it. Chapter 42 of the *Historia Brittonum* provides just such a substitute: secular eschatology. I do not mean to imply that the episode—the meeting of Guorthigirn and Ambrosius—was added specifically for this reason, although

it is a tempting possibility, as we shall see. It is difficult to consider Chapter 42 separately from the rest of the Guorthigirn
story or from its immediate context of the two preceding chapters, because various narratives have been combined here to present a Christian moral in Guorthigirn's career.[80] Nevertheless, a
secular interpretation of history obtrudes in Chapter 42, despite
its submersion in the Christian flow of the narrative.

In Chapter 40, Guorthigirn appears in conference with his
magi, who advise him to flee the English.[81] Guorthigirn has received the English into Britain, but now realizes that they are
planning to kill him and seize the nation. The *magi* first tell him
to seek a citadel at the far borders of his kingdom, but, when he
does not find it, they advise the king to build one. Materials are
gathered for the labor, but mysteriously disappear. Finally the
magi inform him that the site of the fortress must be sprinkled
with the blood of a child who has no father. Fortuitously, such
a boy is discovered and brought to the king.[82] Before he can
be sacrificed, however, he confronts the *magi* and challenges
them to reveal what lies under the earth where they stand. Their
avowal of ignorance prompts the boy to predict in quick succession that there is a pool beneath the earth, a tent in the pool,
and two dragons fighting within the tent. Each prediction is
verified in turn and all watch the dragons, one red and one white,
do battle, until the red one, which at first seems the weaker,
rallies and drives the white one from the tent. None but the boy
understands what the episode represents, and he explains to
Guorthigirn that the pool is a figure of the world, the tent a
figure of the kingdom, the red dragon the Britons and the white
the English.[83] The final victory of the red dragon prefigures the
time when the Britons will finally rise up against the English, who
now control most of the island, and cast them out of Britain.
Meanwhile, the boy continues, Guorthigirn must continue his
wanderings since he cannot build the citadel. The boy himself,
now revealed as Ambrosius, son of a Roman emperor,[84] will re-

main there, presumably to erect the citadel, from which he will rule western Britain.[85]

As it stands, this episode is intended to emphasize Guorthigirn's impotence (he cannot build the citadel), ignorance (he cannot interpret the allegorical battle of the dragons), and sinfulness (he is ready to kill the boy to save himself from the Saxons). These are allegations made throughout the Guorthigirn chapters, as we shall see. But amidst this moral presentation is the prophecy of Ambrosius, a prophecy of ultimate national victory. Ambrosius is in effect an exegete; he explains the *figurae* of the dragon fight. But his eschatological interpretation is nationalistic, not Christian, and contains no reference to a final judgment which the national victory itself prefigures. Rather the inspiration of the prophecy is the hope of a defeated nation that it will rise up against its oppressors (who are said to control most of the island) and drive them beyond the sea. We may trace this hope to Welsh nationalism of the ninth century, as N. K. Chadwick has shown.[86]

Ambrosius tells Guorthigirn to leave the scene of battle; it will not be for the king who received the invaders to cast them out. The boy here judges the king from a political rather than a moral standpoint, for he makes no mention of Guorthigirn's personal turpitude, which is the hallmark of the other Guorthigirn episodes. Guorthigirn therefore assumes briefly in this episode the stature of an individual, as opposed to a type, an *exemplum*, or a personal level of exegesis.[87] As an evil individual, he is able to be isolated from his national context; his subjects can outlive him, or depose him. Political action, in short, can replace national penitence or divine judgment as a response to royal misrule.[88] Is it illusory to see in one of the two variant versions of Guorthigirn's death (Chapters 47–48) a secular, national solution to the problem of the evil king? I think not. One version [89] is overtly Christian, and we shall return to it shortly. The other simply states that the entire nation rose against Guorthigirn, who wandered from place to place until he died, a pathetic, unwanted figure.[90] The latter account is, it seems to me, much more in keeping with the assumptions of the Roman and Ambrosius episodes, viz., that the nation's history is something apart from that of evil men who happen to rule it, and that evil rule can be overthrown without national repentance. In short, the parallel levels into which individual and society are placed in the theology of history are not considered parallel at all in secular political thought. The nation is greater than any individual, and will survive. This is also the meaning of the Ambrosian secular eschatology of Chapter 42.

All these developments away from the norms of Christian historiography will assume greater importance in the historiographical revolution of the twelfth century, and we shall see in the following chapter how they are specifically used by Geoffrey of Monmouth in his re-creation of the British past. We turn now from the a-Christian sections of the *Historia Brittonum* to consider those sections which reveal an attempt to understand the fall of Britain—and the possibilities for national revitalization—in terms inspired or dictated by the tradition of Gildas. The main attempt to impose upon Britain's past the pattern of salvation history is the presentation of Guorthigirn's career as an *exemplum* of the link between personal sinfulness and national disaster.

Guorthigirn is introduced in Chapter 31, forty years after the Romans have left Britain for the last time. He is presented as a fearful monarch, afraid of the Picts and Scots, afraid of renewed Roman aggression, and afraid of Ambrosius.[91] In this chapter, the Saxons arrive and are welcomed by Guorthigirn. The next four chapters abandon Guorthigirn to recount the arrival in Britain of St. Germanus and his encounter with a British tyrant named Benli, who is punished by the saint. To replace Benli as ruler, Germanus chooses a humble man whom he has just baptized and who becomes the first of the royal line of Powys. This episode is an origin story. Chapter 36 returns to Guorthigirn and parallels Gildas in describing the demands which the Saxons present to their hosts. In Chapter 37 Guorthigirn meets and falls in love with the daughter of Hengist, the Saxon leader. In order to obtain the pagan woman, he betrays another British ruler in promising the kingdom of Kent to the Saxons. The Saxons then invite more of their countrymen to join them in Britain.

Chapter 39 opposes Guorthigirn and St. Germanus over another marital abuse by the former, this time his marriage with his own daughter. In a confrontation between the two men, the saint miraculously outwits Guorthigirn, who flees. The Ambrosius episode follows, and then (Chapters 43–44) an account of the victories of Guorthemir, son of Guorthigirn, over the Saxons. Guorthemir dies, and the Saxons return (Chapters 45–46); they trick the Britons and massacre their leaders at a supposed assembly to discuss peace. Guorthigirn is given his life (and the continued possession of Hengist's daughter) in return for more British lands, this time Essex and Sussex.

In Chapter 47, the death of the unrepentant Guorthigirn comes in answer to the prayers of St. Germanus, who has not been able to make the king forswear his unlawful marriage.[92] Chapter 48 recounts the variant, secular death story already mentioned, and Chapter 49 consists of a genealogy of Guorthigirn's descendants and mentions the return of St. Germanus to his own land.

The main sources for this series of chapters seem to be: a legend of St. Germanus in Britain, different from the *Life of St. Germanus* by Constantius which Bede used; a narrative of Guorthigirn and the Saxons which emphasizes the role of the king's love for Hengist's daughter as a determining factor in the fall of Britain; the prophecy of Ambrosius and perhaps an elaborate context for it, part of which was combined with other material for insertion into Chapters 40–42; and possibly a separate account of Guorthemir's battles against the Saxons and his death.[93] The sources have been unevenly woven into a patchwork narrative which offends aesthetically. Like Bede, the compiler of this section was quite willing to combine past accounts in order to make his own judgments; yet it would be foolish to overlook the point of view discernible in the crudely fashioned narrative.

Originally a separate piece of hagiography, the St. Germanus section has been inserted into the narrative in a way reminiscent of the Alban legends of Bede and Gildas, or of Bede's use of the same St. Germanus.[94] The conflict between Germanus and Benli or Germanus and Guorthigirn is a traditional hagiographic conflict intended to glorify the holy Christian at the expense of the wicked king, himself exemplary of the evils of society.[95] But once again, when a hagiographical account is placed within the framework of national history, its import is changed. Germanus himself becomes a social hero, saving Britain from the sins of its leaders. The Benli episode, which seems at first to have nothing to do with the saint's encounter with Guorthigirn, is in fact inserted to establish the operation of God's providence in British history. Germanus' role in the undoing of the wicked king and in his replacement by a new Christian forces the reader to recognize the importance of holiness in the nation's career, and the inevitable defeat of sin. There are many imaginative touches in the combination of narratives at this point which repay closer attention.

In Chapter 31, Guorthigirn welcomes the Saxons, who arrive in Britain as exiles from their own land.[96] The Saxons, we learn at once, are idol-worshipping pagans;[97] the date of their arrival, however, is reckoned in years from the passion of Christ,[98] a subtle hint of the separation between Christian and pagan which Guorthigirn's love for the heathen princess violates. St. Germanus' arrival in Britain at the beginning of Chapter 32 is thus a parallel to the *adventus Saxonum*. He comes to preach, to save many and damn many more.[99] Whereas the ruler of Britain welcomes the heathen who will ruin the nation in the preceding chapter, the British tyrant Benli refuses to receive Germanus, who is bringing him the good news of the gospel.

In Benli's castle, however, is one good man, a lowly servant who receives the saint into his humble home when the latter has no resting place. In return for his generosity, Germanus performs a miracle, restoring to the servant a calf which he had slaughtered to feed the saint. A second miracle involves prophecy. An unknown man appears before Benli's castle while the saint is waiting there. Germanus baptizes him, and reveals that Benli will have him killed at once, but because of his conversion he will go directly to heaven and enjoy eternal bliss. Now is the time for Germanus to bring God's wrath upon the wicked king. He summons the faithful servant, and tells him to leave the castle with his sons and to pray all night to God without looking back at the citadel.[100] These orders are obeyed, and soon heavenly fire destroys the castle and its inhabitants. Germanus then baptizes the servant, and installs him as the new king and father of kings, thereby fulfilling the psalmist's prophecy that the lowly shall be raised up to sit with princes.[101]

The deeds performed by Germanus before Benli's castle fall into a pattern. The gift of the "resurrected" calf in a sense prefigures the greater gifts to come to the servant, Cadell. The ritual command of the saint that no bones of the calf be broken is a clerical reminiscence of Exodus, where the same command is given concerning the paschal sacrifice, itself a prefiguration of the greater sacrifice to come.[102] The two baptisms are noteworthy: the first is followed by heavenly reward, the second by earthly prosperity. Since the first baptism plays no other part in the episode, it is reasonable to suppose that its insertion was effected to establish the true goal of the Christian and to suggest that the reward given to Cadell prefigures the final reward awaiting him in heaven. Consequently, the destruction of Benli by analogy prefigures eternal destruction for his sins (including the

killing of the innocent man whom Germanus has just baptized).
The *gesta* of St. Germanus, in other words, serve to instruct the
reader in the Christian theology of history, which is applied in
these chapters to Benli and may now be applied to Guorthigirn.

The meetings between Guorthigirn and Germanus work
toward the same end. The king has committed the grievous sin
of incest with his daughter; Germanus unmasks and rebuffs him
by means of the offspring of the unholy union, whom Guorthigirn claims is a bastard of Germanus. The saint has the boy
reveal his true father ("patrem carnalem"), and Guorthigirn
flees in disgrace.[103] Finally, in Chapter 47, Germanus pursues
Guorthigirn, prays for God's vengeance on the evil-doer, and
sees his adversary destroyed, like Benli, by heavenly fire. The
Germanus episodes therefore interpret history in terms of providence, with punishment for sin in this world a consequence of
the power of God vested in his saints.

The narrative of Guorthigirn and the Saxons supplies the
other main assumption of Christian national-ecclesiastical history,
i.e., that personal sin has national consequences. This narrative
does not have a miraculous or figural element, while the Germanus sections are lacking in national or historical context. The
two narratives fit neatly together to form a Christian historical
vision, the link between them provided by Guorthigirn's exces-
sive sexual appetite, which leads him in one story to marry his
daughter and in the other to marry the daughter of a pagan
enemy. Guorthigirn, already unsympathetic for having foolishly
welcomed the first Saxons who arrive in Britain, now allows them
to bring more compatriots.[104] Hengist, himself a crafty and clever
man, perceives that his opponent is the lazy king of a defenseless
people.[105] He suggests a banquet in honor of the newly arrived
Saxons, apparently as part of a plot to trick the Britons by ine-
briating them.[106] The author relates that Satan entered into Guorthigirn's heart while he was drunk, causing him to yearn for the
girl. He bargains with Hengist for her, and the nation suffers:

the kingdom of Kent is given over to the heathen without the knowledge or consent of its rightful lord.[107] The love affair is plainly an artistic device to connect the sins of the king with the national loss of freedom.

The same pattern is repeated in the episode of the massacre of the Britons. Guorthigirn receives the Saxons because of his wife.[108] At the meeting between the two nations ostensibly to discuss peace, the Saxons draw their hidden knives [109] and kill all but Guorthigirn, whom they keep alive for the sake of Hengist's daughter and of the ransom that they expect,[110] and indeed receive, at the further expense of Guorthigirn's nation.[111] The beginning of this episode contains a clear reminiscence of Gildas' explanation of the Saxon success:

And the barbarians returned with a great host. . . . And no one was able boldly to drive them away, because they occupied Britain not through their own valour, but by the will of God. Who shall be able to resist and strive against the will of God? But as the Lord wills he acts and he alone rules and governs all nations.

While not fully explained, these sentences suggest that not only Guorthigirn but all Britain is immersed in sin.[112] They are intended to be read in conjunction with the slaying of all the British leaders, which, in such a context, becomes an act of divine vengeance; they are also probably inspired by the end of the preceding chapter, where the death of the national hero Guorthemir is recounted. Guorthemir asks that his body be placed in a sepulchre in the harbor from which the Saxons left Britain, retreating before him. This deed, he says, will safeguard that part of the island from further harassment.[113] The text continues, "But they defied his command and did not bury him in the place he had ordered." The Britons here display disobedience and a disregard for their own safety, which bring about the return of the Saxons at the beginning of the following chapter. The addition of the explanation that divine favor had turned against the Britons was therefore inserted at this point, since the context seemed to warrant and support it.

I have already mentioned the Christian, contextual (as opposed to the secular, eschatological) meaning of the Ambrosius episode, which in its place in the Guorthigirn section contributes to the picture of the sinful king, a would-be murderer who can neither build himself a fortress nor aid his nation against the English invited by him to the island.[114]

These remarks will suffice to support my allegation that a strong vein of Christian historical interpretation runs through parts of the *Historia Brittonum*. Even without the existence of the Gildas tradition, we would have cause for surprise if the theology of history had given way entirely to new approaches in ninth-century Britain. On the continent, in spite of the newness of Charlemagne's Frankish lordship and the practical politics involved in its relationship with the papacy and Constantinople, men like Alcuin cast Charlemagne as a Christian prince in the Augustinian mold or in the tradition of the Old Testament kings of Israel; they poured the new wine of Carolingian power into the old bottles of Christian historical theology, and in so doing held fast to the principle that God ruled the Christian and the nation-*ecclesia* with the same guiding hand.

A final word on two other sections of the *Historia Brittonum*: Chapters 50–55, concerned with St. Patrick, seem at first glance to have little to do with the history of Britain; Chapter 56, on the other hand, introduces Arthur into British history, and has been the object of an immense amount of critical speculation.[115] My own feeling is that both sections are inserted to shed light on British history from a Christian point of view. St. Patrick converts the Irish, performing many miraculous deeds and great works, twelve of which are listed in Chapter 54.[116] He solicits three favors from God: that the Irish never be conquered by barbarians, that each Irishman repent before dying, and that all the Irish join Patrick in triumph at the last judgment.[117] Finally, in Chapter 55, Patrick is compared to Moses in four ways.[118]

The information selected for this brief account reveals the interests of a Christian historian. Patrick is more than a holy man; he is a new Moses, a social hero of the Irish nation-*ecclesia*, which he protects from invasion and saves for eternal life. Patrick's twelve apostolic works are a parallel to the twelve battles of Arthur, who appears in the next chapter as a holy man in combat with his nation's enemies.[119] Arthur performs great feats of valor in defeating the Saxons twelve times,[120] and his appearance in the *Historia Brittonum* at this point provides an *exemplum* of the combination of social heroism and piety which, in sharp contrast to the turpitude of Guorthigirn, will save Britain. The inclusion of Patrick and Arthur in the narrative following Guorthigirn supports the impression that clerical authors-compilers were attempting to reassert in ninth-century Britain the efficacy of the Christian theology of history as a moral approach to national history.[121]

The *Historia Brittonum* is a dangerous text from which to draw conclusions about actual happenings of British history. It is also, because of its composite nature, treacherous ground for the student of early medieval historiography. I have indicated in this chapter only some of the main strands of historical judgment which have been given artistic form in the *Historia*. As I have said, the work is not easily read for pleasure; the seams of its composition show at every turn and the conflict in sources is often bewildering. But the very confusion of ideas and data is useful in analyzing the intellectual climate of early ninth-century Wales. There, in the age of Charlemagne, the apostolic and patristic legacy of Christian historical thought was challenged by new interpretations of past and present, and the fall of Britain became a crux of the early medieval historical imagination.

CHAPTER V

Geoffrey of Monmouth's
Historia regum Britanniae:
Great Men on a Great Wheel

The secular interpretation of British history brought to birth by at least one of the authors of the *Historia Brittonum* can be said only to have reached a promising youth in that work. Its potential remained unrealized for over three hundred years, until Geoffrey of Monmouth's *Historia regum Britanniae*, appearing suddenly in twelfth-century England, offered to its first, amazed readers a comprehensive and spectacular vision of the British past largely free of Christian assumptions.[1] The work's remarkable reception occupies a special place in the history of medieval literature: almost at once the story and the heroes of the rise and fall of Britain became matters of excitement and controversy, not only on the island itself, but throughout much of western Europe as well. Furthermore, the duration of Geoffrey's success was to equal its magnitude, for his account of British history exercised an enormous influence over historians and chroniclers for centuries to come.[2]

Geoffrey, who lived *ca.* 1100–1155, and spent most of his life as an Augustinian canon in Oxford,[3] must be considered a major literary figure of his day and of the entire medieval period. That he has not always been accorded such recognition is due not so much to his limited output—his only known work besides the

Historia is the *Vita Merlini,* a poem of 1500 Latin hexameter
verses on the legendary Welsh prophet-bard who also figures in
Historia regum Britanniae [4]—as to the unfortunate treatment he
has received at the hands of many critics through the centuries,
beginning practically in his own day.[5] To his detractors, Geoffrey has always seemed a liar pure and simple, the unscrupulous
fabricator of a legendary British past, and as such deserving of
no serious consideration whatsoever. Happily, contemporary
criticism has succeeded almost entirely in abdicating the office
of censor with regard to Geoffrey; [6] he remains, however, often
misjudged if not condemned, and as controversial as ever.

   In this century, scholarly disputes over Geoffrey can generally
be classified under one of two headings: the relationship of the
Historia regum Britanniae to its sources, and Geoffrey's purpose
in writing it. The first of these questions lies outside the scope
of this study and need not detain us; suffice it to say that the eye
of the storm is a passage at the beginning of the *Historia,* where
Geoffrey claims that his account of Britain is a translation of an
old British book ("britannici sermonis librum vetustissimum")
given him by his friend, the archdeacon Walter.[7] Many and
varied have been the attempts to deduce, discover, or defend the
existence of Geoffrey's *vetustissimus liber,* or, as has been the
case more recently, to delineate the nature and extent of the
Welsh traditions, vouched for in works of Geoffrey's contemporaries, which were available to him.[8] While the search has un-
earthed much interesting material and prompted attractive con-
jecture, it must still be considered very much in progress, with
the issue in doubt. Several scholars, preferring not to involve
themselves in it, have simply dismissed the idea of Geoffrey's
single source or coherent tradition, recognized the great originality of the *Historia,* and explained that its author was actually
a romancer, an historical novelist, a shrewd propagandist for
both the Welsh and the Normans, or the writer of a political
tract.[9]

This brings us to the larger question of Geoffrey's purpose in writing the *Historia regum Britanniae*. I have already remarked that a gap of more than three centuries separates the *Historia Brittonum* and Geoffrey's *Historia*,[10] and that the latter takes up the secular strain of the former, systematically amplifying it to dominate the narrative exposition of the British past while reducing to a few scattered references the Christian, ecclesiastical view of history. Geoffrey's specific relationship to the earlier fall of Britain texts will shortly be considered in some detail; however, it is readily apparent that a major change has taken place in the historical imagination of a writer who deliberately removes national history from its traditional context, the history of salvation.[11] The reasons for such a change in historical outlook —and historical writing—may forever be lost in the mists of time, but it is worth the attempt to reconstruct them, however tentatively. Accordingly, the main intention of this, the last chapter of the present study, is to anatomize Geoffrey's historiography, and thereby to lay bare his ultimate aim in reinterpreting the fall of Britain tradition at a point so distant in time from the events (be they true or fictitious) he is narrating.

As the latest, longest, and most celebrated early medieval treatment of the British past, *Historia regum Britanniae* has many obvious claims on our attention. Even more important than these attributes, however, is the fact that Geoffrey's *Historia* captures uniquely the spirit of a major evolution—one might almost say revolution—in historiography which occurred in twelfth-century England and Normandy, and which remains one of the most remarkable landmarks of a century rich in striking cultural and intellectual developments. The Anglo-Norman historians who reexamined and recounted the national pasts of the English and Norman peoples introduced into the tradition of Christian, early medieval historiography new methods, new interests, and new concepts; they approached the human condition, the national past, and divine providence in novel and sometimes startling ways. Without consciously wishing to break with the historical vision of the past centuries—indeed they shared a tremendous admiration for Bede the historian [12]—they modified, and in some respects undermined, that vision fundamentally, if not irrevocably. And what they did unconsciously, even perhaps unwillingly, in treating the recorded history of the Anglo-Norman national past, Geoffrey imitated, or rather parodied with considerable consciousness and purpose, working not with historical material but with legends and with his own fertile imagination, in filling out the great unrecorded gaps in the British past. In his work we have a valuable and absorbing document, a controlled and self-aware testimony to a momentous change in the early medieval historical imagination.

To understand Geoffrey's achievement we must therefore: (1) recapitulate, from a point of view slightly different from any taken so far, the early medieval Christian historiography which Geoffrey is rejecting; (2) outline briefly the new historiography which he parodies in *Historia regum Britanniae;* [13] and (3) examine his relationship to the Gildas tradition which, as we have seen, dominated the fall of Britain literature up to Geoffrey.

With regard first to the national histories of barbarian nations written in the centuries before Geoffrey: [14] the facet of this genre which has here been under scrutiny is its general tendency to treat barbarian history at least in part as ecclesiastical history. The extent to which a nation's heroic traditions and postimperial career were interpreted in terms of the history of salvation varied widely from writer to writer, but it is generally true that an early medieval historian who wished to make the past serve a moral purpose presented it in an identifiably Christian context. In so doing, he was reiterating the conviction, as old as historical writing, that the past is in its very nature instructive to the man who cares to profit from it. I have already mentioned the early appearance among classical historians of the exemplary view of history, and remarked that it was primarily a rhetorical device.[15] But rhetoric, the science of effective expression, must always express something. The oft-repeated dictum, therefore, that history provides us with examples to be imitated and others to be eschewed, and the presentation of history in order to support the dictum, are the rhetorical consequences of the conviction that history is moral.

How is history moral? Rhetoric cannot by itself answer that question; only ideology or belief can. History is moral, and historiography exemplary, in one way for a Stoic, in quite another for a Christian, in yet a third for a Marxist. To put it more concretely, the fact that Livy and Bede, in the prefaces to their histories, declare in practically identical words that history provides good and bad (or paradigmatic and cautionary) *exempla* in no way means that Livy and Bede share similar views on the meaning of history. Rather, the continuous use of such an exemplary formula [16] would seem to indicate that the tradition of historical rhetoric has protected historians from realizing fully how greatly and how distinctively their historical methods and writings have been colored by their ideologies. This should not surprise us; the dominant moral view of a period tends always to be taken for granted, and it is harder to put one's own bias—especially when it is held in common with most of one's contemporaries— in perspective than it is to distinguish the prejudices of the past.[17]

The early medieval Christian historian constantly revealed his moral commitment in his exemplary attitude toward history. Passages in national-ecclesiastical histories that we would call stylized or conventional were inserted specifically for their exemplary value.[18] It is largely these passages which I have analyzed in this study, showing that the ideological beliefs which control the form of the *exempla* were specifically Christian, and operated within the context of the history of salvation, as clarified by scriptural exegesis. The twelfth-century Anglo-Norman historians inherited and propagated the tradition of the exemplary value of history, but we should not automatically assume, as many critics have, that they preserved intact the Christian view of history and providence which has occupied us until now in this study. The rhetoric remained the same,[19] but its flowers now sprang from the rich soil of a new historical outlook. The providential view of history was subtly modified to allow a larger role for purely human causation, and to reflect a lively interest in psychological motivation; complementarily, divine providence was impersonalized to a certain extent, and even at times replaced by the concept of fortune's ruling the affairs of men. Traces of a cyclical view of history appeared, although situated within a larger framework that remained Christian. Most importantly, the exegetical parallel between personal and national levels of history grew markedly weaker, implying a conscious or unconscious revaluation on the part of the historian of the link between the history of salvation and national history. While these changes cannot here be studied in detail, they demand some attention if we are to understand the milieu from which Geoffrey of Monmouth's highly imaginative historiography sprang.

The twelfth century was a period of brisk historiographical revival within the boundaries of the Anglo-Norman empire established in 1066 by William, Duke of Normandy, and inherited after his death in 1087 by his descendants and successors, William Rufus (1087–1100) and Henry I (1100–1135).[20] The main figures of the "new" historiography were Eadmer, who was a monk of Anglo-Saxon origin and a follower of Anselm, archbishop of Canterbury, and who completed his *Historia novorum in Anglia* by 1115;[21] Ordericus Vitalis, an English-born monk of the monastery of St. Evroul in Normandy, where his *Historia ecclesiastica* was written in several recensions from some time after 1109 until 1141;[22] Henry, archdeacon of Huntingdon, whose *Historia Anglorum* was published in successive editions between 1129 and 1154;[23] and William of Malmesbury, a Benedictine monk whose *Gesta regum Anglorum* covered English history until 1125, and was brought up to date by a continuation, the *Historia novella,* in 1135 and 1140.[24] No brief consideration of the large and varied output of these historians can begin to do their work justice; however, some attempt to account for their near-simultaneous activity and to generalize about their historical vision or visions is worth making.

In considering the twelfth-century revival of literary interest in the past, we must locate historiography within a larger context of cultural expansion and renewed intellectual activity, the so-called "twelfth-century renaissance." In its early maturity, this period of European intellectual aggressiveness was marked by a great fascination with the political and literary achievements of the classical past.[25] Evidence of this fascination is especially apparent in the works of the Anglo-Norman historians, and takes a variety of forms: intoxication with the heroes and events of classical literature; [26] awe at the success of classical institutions, especially the political achievements of Rome; [27] and a willingness to apply to new narrative situations the traditional techniques of classical rhetoric.[28] In short, the routine early medieval dependence upon the legacy of Rome has given way in these histories to a fresh awareness of the extent of that legacy, and to an engaging, almost naive eagerness to effect a massive transfusion of classical blood into the veins of a vigorous and exciting, but still culturally anemic civilization.[29]

The factor which more than any other had impressed upon the civilization of the Anglo-Norman historians its peculiar form was the phenomenon of the Normans themselves. These last pagan, barbarian invaders of northern Europe had won control in the tenth century of the part of France which still bears their name; by the middle of the eleventh century their dukes had taken their place among the continent's most powerful rulers, and had established within their domains an ecclesiastical hierarchy and organization that rivaled the wealthiest and best organized of Europe.[30] In 1035, the large and tightly controlled duchy devolved upon William, the bastard son of Duke Robert I, who was to prove himself worthy of his inheritance. When Duke William, already an innovator within his ancestral domain,[31] decided to extend his power by claiming the English throne after the death of Edward the Confessor in January 1066, he embarked upon an undertaking which culminated in his coronation on Christmas day of that year as King of the English, and confirmed him as the greatest political and military figure of his day in Europe.

The remarkable career of the Normans, still fascinating today, enthralled contemporaries as well, and it is certainly the expansion of Norman power, and specifically the spectacle of the Anglo-Norman monarchy established by William, that prompted the rash of historical works now under consideration. William, Henry, and Orderic devote whole sections in their histories to a minute consideration of the reigns of the Anglo-Norman kings.[32] In so doing, they reveal basic assumptions of their views of history. First of all, as Christians, they feel that the phenomenal rise to splendor of the Normans, and especially of William, is a clear indication of God's providence.[33] In keeping with this judgment, they attempt to explain the Norman Conquest in terms reminiscent of those used by Gildas to interpret the ruin of Britain, i.e., as the work of God operating figurally in history to punish sinful men and nations.[34] (Henry even draws a parallel between the Saxon conquest of the Britons and the Norman conquest of the Saxons, an important point to which I shall return shortly.) [35] From one point of view, then, the Normans are God's chosen people—the latest heirs of Israel, and the successors in national-ecclesiastical history of Gregory's Franks, Paul's Langobards, and Bede's Saxons. But this is only one side of the story. From another point of view, one provided by classical history and rhetoric, the Normans are imperial repressors of English liberty.[36] The juxtaposition of this theme to the first creates a tension within the historiography of the Anglo-Norman historians, and reflects the coexistence in the minds of the writers of two mutually distinct views of the past, the legacies of two different moral and rhetorical traditions.

Nor do these two approaches exhaust the Anglo-Norman historians' complicated understanding of their immediate past. The Norman barons, a colorful and tempestuous lot, were continually at war with each other and with their feudal lords. The Anglo-Norman historians present the barons as men of tremendous ambition, bravery, and greed, who are also capable of great cruelty and treachery.[37] Their shortcomings and sins repeatedly result in social disturbance and misery for Normans and English, in the form of national disasters which the historians brand now as punishments inflicted by God, now as exemplary proof of the classical dictum that internal disorder ruins national greatness.[38]

The political world of the Anglo-Norman historians was therefore one of greater complexity than they could compress into one consistent historiographical vision or system. Although any age presents enormous complexities to its chroniclers, in this case the genuine uniqueness of the Norman experience and the divided interests of the Christian but antiquity-loving historians combined to render impossible a unified approach to the past. Nor was this ambivalence the result of conscious choice. In an intriguing and, I think, highly indicative passage of his ecclesiastical history, Orderic complains that in the past history has been full of miracles, examples of God's power among men, but that in this evil age such manifestations of divine intervention are hard if not impossible to find.[39] The historian here reveals, in effect, that despite his allegiance to the tradition of Christian ecclesiastical history (signified by the "old-fashioned" title and overt aim of his work),[40] his sense of the present no longer corresponds to the norms of that tradition.[41] Orderic claims literally to be looking about him for miracles; this procedure, I submit, is essentially foreign to the writers of early medieval ecclesiastical history or hagiography, who sought their miraculous material not in literal experience, but in the norms of the history of salvation (i.e., in the facts which gave real meaning to all history, but which were fully visible only in the revelation of holy scripture).[42]

In addition to political complexity and the coexistence of traditional Christian interpretations with revivals of classical values, there are still other noteworthy features of Anglo-Norman historiography in the twelfth century. Further common traits which strike the modern reader's eye are an interest in new, wider realms of human experience and possibilities (including extremes of behavior and ability), an attempt to give psychological insight into the lives and characters of important men, and an increased awareness of the role played by fortune in the lives of men and nations. The historians are constantly drawn beyond the boundaries of their homeland by events whose oddity or symbolic qualities fascinate them and demand inclusion in even a national history. William describes the occult arts practiced by Pope Sylvester II, and adds stories of visits by magicians to fabulous hidden worlds; [43] he is attracted by stories of men who returned from journeys to hell and told of their experiences; [44] he reports that in Normandy two women shared one body from the waist down, and uses the prodigy as an occasion to lament the union of England and Normandy, which has cost the English their liberty.[45] In addition, William and Henry both describe at length the exploits of the crusaders.[46]

Amid the welter of human activities and experiences, the figures of the Anglo-Norman kings rise like great beacons surveying the world of little men which lies about them. The historian is as sensitive to the ways in which William the Conqueror and his successors tower over their age and kingdom—ordering its life, bringing it misery or prosperity—as he is to the relentless movement of history, which, through fortune, ultimately rules the rulers themselves. In order to provide relief, as it were, from

the self-imposed burden of explaining the stature of great leaders and the events which determine their fate, the Anglo-Norman
historians appeal to the complexity of life as lived at a less exalted level, or long ago and far away. The introduction of
anecdotes and extraneous matter into the histories resembles the
opening of a safety valve in order to prevent the pressure of history from weighing too heavily on the life and destiny of the
ordinary man; [47] for the individual is no longer the architect of
his own salvation within a national context responsive to and dependent upon the aspirations of each Christian. The divergence
of the history of kings and nations from the history of human
experience as a continuing, self-justifying phenomenon marks a
sharp break in the development of medieval historiography.
Analogous in part to the contrast between Christian and classical
interpretations of political and national history described above,
this new distinction separates the work of the Anglo-Norman historians from the tradition of Christian historical writing, in which
personal and national history run on parallel tracks under God's
guidance and toward his chosen end.[48]

We must finally consider the attitude of the Anglo-Norman
historians toward the monarchs who had controlled recent national history, and toward those forces which in turn had controlled the monarchs. I mentioned above that the lives of the
Anglo-Norman kings occupied much of the attention of William,
Henry, and Orderic. The historians consciously attempted to
present balanced pictures of those great men which, while stressing their virtues, did not hide their vices.[49] The portraits are
rich in detail, utilizing characteristic gestures, encounters, and
acts, as well as describing circumstantially the physical and
mental peculiarities of the monarchs.[50] In short, the Anglo-
Norman kings are presented as individuals, not simply as royal
types or ideal Christian monarchs. Unlike Bede's Oswald or
Eusebius' Constantine, the man behind the office matters to the
historian, who probes for precisely those characteristics which

separate one man and one king from another, and which may therefore help to explain the character of each reign.

Although the Anglo-Norman kings and other great men of the kingdom emerge as individuals, they do not, however, exist beyond the control of external forces. Beside the Christian tradition of a divine providence still embraced by the historians, the new force of fortune comes into play—Dame Fortune who strikes down the mighty at the summit of their achievement.[51] Of course, blind fortune and Christian providence make strange bedfellows; nowhere do we see more clearly the peculiar duality of this new historiography than in Orderic's description of the death of William the Conqueror in the seventh book of his *Historia ecclesiastica*.[52] The dying monarch, bedridden at Mantes, is seen justifying his reign and repenting for his sins at great length in a rhetorical, set speech. The Conqueror's words are, on the one hand, full of conventional piety;[53] on the other, they provide a political resumé of English and Norman history during the twenty-one years of his reign in England. The speech betrays William's (and Orderic's) vital and articulate sense of the Normans as a people:

The Normans, when under the rule of a kind but firm master, are a most valiant people, excelling all others in the invincible courage with which they meet difficulties, and strive to conquer every enemy. But under other circumstances they rend in pieces and ruin each other. They are eager for rebellion, ripe for tumults, and ready for for every sort of crime. They must therefore be restrained by the strong hand of justice, and compelled to walk in the right way by the reins of discipline. But if they are allowed to take their own course without any yoke and like an untamed colt, they and their princes will be overwhelmed with poverty, shame, and confusion. I have learnt this by much experience. My nearest friends, my own kindred, who ought to have defended me at all hazards against the whole world, have formed conspiracies, and rebelling against me, nearly stripped me of the inheritance of my fathers.

The beleaguered greatness which was William's is communicated with noble intensity in this passage, as is the historian's response to a mighty and turbulent nation.

In confessing his sins, William reveals eloquently many extremes of human behavior such as fascinated the Anglo-Norman historians. "I was bred to arms from my childhood, and am stained with the rivers of blood I have shed. . . . I wrested [the crown of England] from the perjured king Harold in a desperate battle, with much effusion of human blood, and it was by slaughter and banishment of his adherents, that I have subjugated England to my rule. I have persecuted its native inhabitants beyond all reason. . . . These events inflamed me to the highest pitch of resentment, and I fell on the English of the northern counties like a raving lion." The great, strident voice booms on, alternately imploring and accusing.

Meanwhile, the king's sons are seen to react to their father's dying behavior in highly individual ways. William Rufus, promised the throne of England, rides away at once to secure the crown. Henry, to his chagrin given no land but only five thousand pounds of silver, "was equally prompt in securing the money allotted to him. He had it carefully weighed that there might be no deficiency, and, summoning his intimate friends in whom he could confide, sought a place of safety in which to deposit his treasure."

Finally the king expires, "suddenly and unexpectedly," throwing all the courtiers and retainers present into great confusion. All ride away to look after their own interests in the face of an anarchic interregnum, while "the inferior attendants, observing that their masters had disappeared, laid hands on the arms, the plate, the robes, the linen, and all the royal furniture, and leaving the corpse almost naked on the floor of the house hastened away."

Orderic then describes the funeral services, at which the bishop

of Evreux eulogizes "William's having extended by his valour
the bounds of the Norman dominion, and raised his people to a
pitch of greatness surpassing the times of any of his predecessors." However, an old enemy of William steps forward dra-
matically to claim the land on which the church lies and in which
William is to be buried. He must be bribed into agreeing to the
burial; then, as the body is being placed into the stone sepulchre,
its bowels burst and a terrible stench fills the church. "The
priests therefore hurried the conclusion of the funeral service
and retired as soon as possible, in great alarm, to their respective
abodes." Orderic adds passionately,

A king once potent, and warlike, and the terror of the numberless
inhabitants of many provinces, lay naked on the floor, deserted by
those who owed him their birth, and those he had fed and enriched.
He needed the money of a stranger for the cost of his funeral, and
a coffin and bearers were provided, at the expense of an ordinary
person, for him, who till then had been in the enjoyment of enormous
wealth. He was carried to the church, amidst flaming houses, by
trembling crowds, and a spot of freehold land was wanting for the
grave of one whose princely sway had extended over so many cities,
and towns, and villages. His corpulent stomach, fattened with so
many delicacies, shamefully burst, to give a lesson, both to the prudent and the thoughtless, on what is the end of fleshly glory. Behold-
ing the corruption of that foul corpse, men were taught to strive
earnestly, by the rules of a salutary temperance, after better things
than the delights of the flesh, which is dust, and must return to
dust.

It is impossible not to be struck by the air of disillusionment,
decay, and horror which repeatedly intrudes into the narrative of
the Conqueror's death and burial. The ephemeral nature of
worldly glory and the slenderness of the bonds between a ruler
and his subjects fascinate the historian and are obviously associ-
ated in his mind with the insufficiency of human achievement in
the face of malignant fortune. The lesson to be drawn from this
is that all earthly triumph fades and sours. "His corpulent

stomach, fattened with so many delicacies, shamefully burst, to give a lesson, both to the prudent and the thoughtless, on what is the end of fleshly glory." [54]

Having exposed so graphically the pessimistic, visionary strain of Anglo-Norman historiography, Orderic then hastens to remark on the need to "turn over the pages of the Old and New Testament, and take from thence numberless examples which will instruct you what to avoid and what to desire." In so doing, he reveals his desire to save his highly dramatic vision of the Conqueror's death for the Christian view of history, according to which he has merely been recounting "manifestations of God's providence at the duke's death." But the attempt is not convincing; the Christian theology of history accords ill with Orderic's morbid reflections on the fate of all human achievement. The purely human greatness of the central figure—his violence, his control over an unruly people, and their attainment under him of new heights of glory—impress us more than the historian's overtly Christian reflection on the deathbed and funeral scenes. Orderic is no Bede; his interest is clearly divided, and his narrative at this point vibrates with the tension between his human involvement and his Christian detachment.

Having arrived at a minimal appreciation of the twelfth-century Anglo-Norman historiographical achievement, its complexities and its internal tensions, we are now ready to examine the relationship to this achievement of Geoffrey of Monmouth's *Historia regum Britanniae*. Critical investigations have already demonstrated that the structure of the *Historia* is basically a copy of that of the histories of William and Henry; starting with smaller notices of events in the distant past, the narrative pace broadens as the "present" is reached (the reigns of William, William Rufus, and Henry I in the actual histories, the reign of Arthur in the legendary history), and is followed by a more disconnected, less circumstantial chronicle form (as in the post-Arthurian period of Geoffrey's work) as the historian adds later

recensions to bring his work up to date.[55] The difference between Geoffrey and his structural "sources" lies in his inde-
pendence of factual record, which enables him to integrate into
his narrative greatly expanded key incidents whenever his artistic
conscience dictates. The resultant effect—alternate sections of
tersely recounted, quickly moving events and of thoroughly explored crises—has often been remarked as the chief artistic virtue of the *Historia regum Britanniae*.[56]

To what end, however, has Geoffrey carefully elaborated such
a structure? The answer, I think, insofar as one can ever be
given, is that he felt impelled to create a work in which the interests of the new historiography of his day could have free play
—in which, that is, the innovations in thought and expression of
the Anglo-Norman historical vision, isolated from the Christian
traditions with which they clashed in the works of William,
Henry, and Orderic, could regulate a complete and self-
consistent narrative of the past. If this was Geoffrey's intention,
then it may seem singularly odd that he should choose the history
of Britain as his vehicle, for, as I have attempted to show, the
Gildas tradition exerted all its weight on the side of a strictly
Christian interpretation of the fall of Britain. The key to this
paradox lies in certain passages of Henry of Huntingdon, already
described, in which the historian perceives a divine plan in the
successive rule of Britons, Saxons, and Normans in Britain.[57]
Like so many other judgments by the Anglo-Norman historians,
this one cuts in more ways than Henry perhaps intended. If the
overt regulating factor in the succession of reigns in Britain is
God's providence, there is nonetheless a covert, even unconscious recognition of a cyclic pattern in history, a pattern which
remorselessly regulates the life and death of realms in a manner
analogous to fortune's regulation of the lives and deaths of great
men.

It was this imprecisely articulated perception of Henry's
which, I think, intrigued Geoffrey, and led him to retreat to the

more remote past to reconstruct the *rise and fall* of Britain—an earlier phase still of history's endlessly recurring cycle—as the ideal context within which to work out the implications of the new historiography. The traditional interpretations of Bede and Gildas exercised an honorable tyranny over the end of British history and the beginnings and early maturity of English history, from which no later writer could hope to escape. By leaping backward beyond the fall of Britain, Geoffrey partially avoided the Gildas tradition and landed in *terra incognita* with only the origin stories of the *Historia Brittonum* to guide him. The remaining problem, i.e., Gildas' interpretation of the actual fall of Britain, Geoffrey solved by "translating" a key passage of *De excidio Britanniae* from the prophetic, religious language of Gildas into a stylistically similar, yet thoroughly secular language and inserting it toward the end of his narrative, thereby preserving what we might call the "Gildas tone" and insuring the plausibility of his work, while making a very different point.[58]

In one sense, then, Geoffrey was the first historian of the fall of Britain to escape completely from the Gildas tradition—but in another sense his *Historia* merely testifies to the lasting influence of Gildas. For, while muting the intensely religious voice of the British monk, the Anglo-Welsh canon preserved intact the tradition of a self-caused, catastrophic climax to British history. Even the inventive Geoffrey felt the accumulated weight of the interpretation of British history bequeathed him by Gildas; he could secularize the legacy, but not ignore it.

Geoffrey's carefully constructed historical account makes use of all the fall of Britain texts in ways which continually support the hypothesis that he intended to produce a thoroughly original and primarily secular account of the rise and fall of a nation.[59] He modifies Gildas in other passages besides the one just mentioned,[60] and does even more violence to Bede; where the latter described justifiable English victories over the obstinate Britons, the *Historia* presents the same episodes in precisely the opposite sense, making the Britons heroes and the Saxons villains.[61] The best example of this technique is Cadwaladrus, the last British king, who goes to Rome after fleeing Britain and dies there in the odor of sanctity. The inspiration for this character is partly Bede's portrait of the holy Cadwallo, a Saxon king! [62]

If Geoffrey's rehandling of Bede and Gildas is revealing, equally revealing is his decision to expand certain source material without reinterpreting it. The best examples of this procedure are the Brutus origin story, the advent of Caesar and the Romans, and the encounter between Vortigern and Merlin, culminating in Merlin's prophecies.[63] Each of these episodes is crucial in the structure of *Historia regum Britanniae*. Brutus' adventures state themes which appear throughout the work; the Roman victory over the Britons defines Geoffrey's concept of Roman power and begins a narrative movement toward Arthur's battle with Rome, the climax of British history, and his sudden downfall; and Merlin's entrance into the story marks the beginning of Britain's finest hours, while his prophecies clearly establish a link between the events of the *Historia* and Geoffrey's own day.[64]

Now, it is noteworthy that these three episodes which Geoffrey borrows from *Historia Brittonum*—expanding them greatly, as I have said, but without altering their essential character from the earlier text—are precisely those which were singled out in the last chapter as indicative of the secular strain of national history present in that ninth-century compilation of British historical texts. Comparison with Geoffrey's wholesale reinterpretation of Bede and Gildas leads us to a conclusion which is reinforced by the fact that Geoffrey omits certain Christian features of the *Historia Brittonum* narrative—all the St. Germanus portions of the Vortigern story, for example [65]—viz., that Geoffrey, having found a way to neutralize the Gildas tradition, actually set about constructing a narrative on the basis of the secular chapters of *Historia Brittonum,* adapting his other main sources to conform to this skeletal scheme.

Within this structural and narrative framework Geoffrey also considered separately and in combination themes which he borrowed from the historical works of his contemporaries, and which we may now summarize before examining the *Historia regum Britanniae* in some detail.

One of his central preoccupations is the spectacle of human greatness. In Brutus, Cassibelanus, Ambrosius, Uther, and especially Arthur and his court, Geoffrey presents a cavalcade of national heroes whose careers and achievements he elaborates with obvious pleasure. The inspiration for Geoffrey's concern with secular greatness was undoubtedly the Anglo-Norman historians' presentation of William the Conqueror and other Anglo-Norman monarchs and barons.[66] The same pride in accomplishment, ease in wearing the mantle of authority, and potentiality for a violent greatness, demonstrated continually by these rulers in the pages of William or Orderic, appear as well in Geoffrey's presentation of Brutus, the liberator-founder of his nation, and of Arthur, who, like William the Conqueror, "extended by his valour the bounds of the [British] dominion, and raised his people to a pitch of greatness surpassing the times of any of his predecessors." [67]

Against this near-intoxication with the human greatness of national leaders must be set the cyclical view of history which I have already suggested was extracted by Geoffrey from Henry of Huntingdon. For, if the heroic deeds of men emphasize human control of history, the view of history as an endless series of cycles emphasizes the power of history over men. Operating through Fortune, the inexplicable and fickle force which raises man on her wheel and then throws him off, history tyrannizes over man and mocks his efforts to control his fate and that of his nation.[68] Arthur's career provides the prime instance of Geoffrey's dual historical vision. His reign illustrates the pinnacle of human greatness and at the same time serves as a mighty *exemplum* of Fortune's thrusting greatness down to sudden destruction. The ultimate consequence of Arthur's fall is the fall of Britain and the rise of the Saxons. Personal fortune here mirrors and affects national fortune; the two levels interact in a manner which we may call the secular equivalent of the Christian theology of history working itself out at personal and national levels of exegesis.

Geoffrey elaborately develops and repeatedly underscores the cyclical nature of history. The British nation arises from the ashes of Troy: the first Britons are Trojan captives of the Greeks who unite under Brutus and free themselves from Grecian bondage. Arriving in Britain, the Britons grow strong and prosperous, and, having reached maturity, must face two national enemies, the Romans and the Saxons. In treating the relations among the three nations, Geoffrey establishes the cyclical nature of history by showing the similar effects of recurrent national crises upon each of the three as they pass through the stages of their political existence.[69] Finally, when Britain reaches the end of her cycle and succumbs to the Saxon invaders,[70] Geoffrey invents a vision in which an angel appears to Cadwaladrus, last king of the Britons.[71] The angelic voice tells the king, who is in exile in Brittany, not to contemplate a return to the island of Britain, for God has willed that the Britons will only regain their homeland at some time in the indeterminate future when certain specific (and primarily religious) conditions are met.[72] Cadwaladrus, convinced by the voice, abandons his planned return and goes to Rome, where he dies a holy death. The import of this episode is clearly that the fall of Britain is but another phase in the eternal cycle. At some point, the Britons' turn will come again to mount Fortune's wheel, just as they rose at the beginning of the story from the ruined remnants of a previously prosperous nation.

Beyond all these indications of the cyclic nature of history, Geoffrey also hit upon a rhetorical organization for his narrative which reinforces his cyclic theory at the same time that it fills British history with exciting incidents. In recounting the successive reigns of the British monarchs, he repeatedly inserted variants of several basic situations—feuds among brothers, British expeditions to Rome, the illicit loves of kings, etc.—which have far-reaching national consequences. The inevitable effect upon the reader of this repetition of incidents at various points in British history is a semiconscious realization that "this has happened before"—i.e., that history continually repeats itself. In evoking such a response to his creation, Geoffrey brilliantly gives credence to one of his basic historical theses.

Geoffrey's twin concern with human greatness and historical recurrence (one could almost say determinism), reminiscent as it is of the duality not only of the Anglo-Norman historians but of the historiography of classical antiquity as well,[73] can serve as a transition to other aspects of his historical vision: the use of classical rhetorical themes and the formation of a general outlook more in harmony with classical than with Christian assumptions about history. The constant motivation of the Britons in their dealings with other nations is the desire for liberty and the escape from tyranny. This traditional theme of ancient historiography [74] states rhetorically the way in which history is moral or at least meaningful: when a nation impairs the freedom of others, it encounters resistance and arouses its would-be subjects to great deeds in defense of liberty. Not the least of Geoffrey's achievements is the deftness and plausibility with which he integrates this *topos* into the context of Britain's rise and fall. Like the theory of rise and fall, or of human greatness versus fortune, freedom versus tyranny is an historical abstraction of the kind which the Oxford canon proves himself to be a master at handling and interweaving with other such abstractions.

But is *Historia regum Britanniae* simply a *jeu d'esprit* involving the juggling of historical abstractions? I think not. Geoffrey's profound interest in the human condition can be deduced not only from his keen appreciation of human greatness but also from what is perhaps the most remarkable feature of the *Historia:* a narrative technique whereby he addresses himself to the crucial and concrete problem of personal fulfillment within the march of history. Here Geoffrey seizes upon yet another feature of the historiography of his contemporaries: its division of interest between the great men and events of history and the complexity of human life considered in itself.

I have suggested that the latter fascination resulted in the digressive character of Anglo-Norman historiography, and in its willingness to include stories and reports of prodigies, supernatural experience, and the like. Geoffrey's approach is much more sophisticated, and, as we might expect, carefully integrated into the larger patterns of his historiography. It grows out of his technique, already noted, of casting microcosmic incidents into reiterated narrative patterns whereby similar characters undergo similar crises at various stages of national history. Geoffrey thereby ingeniously supports his cyclical view of history.

This rhetorical device, however, sometimes dramatizes a new and serious tension between individual desires and national welfare, especially when Geoffrey employs it to set at odds the individual's search for happiness (a secular equivalent of salvation) and national order, the keystone of national prosperity.[75] The protagonist of a thematic episode, in other words, seeks a personal *desideratum*—Assaracus the Greek his patrimony,[76] Androgeus the Briton justice for his nephew,[77] Brennius his rightful share of the kingdom,[78] etc.—and in the process brings chaos to his society. In some of these episodes the protagonist is clearly in the wrong: he is a traitor, or an overreacher.[79] But in other cases it is not possible to decide on the guilt or innocence of the destroyer of civil order; the structure or circumstances of the particular incident do not provide criteria. A typical example is the treason of the Greek Anacletus,[80] which ruins his brother Pandrasus, king of the Greeks, but allows the Trojans to escape from slavery and to settle Britain.[81] Anacletus acts to save his life, betrays his nation, and yet strikes a timely, albeit unwilling, blow for the cause of British freedom. How is he to be judged?

In many cases where tension exists in the *Historia regum Britanniae* between personal needs or desires and national stability, the crux of the situation is a special relationship of some kind, i.e., between two brothers, or cousins, or even between father and daughter. Again and again Geoffrey constructs episodes in which one relative is given the diadem of Britain, while the other, convinced he has been cheated, becomes disaffected from the king and the national good. A common development underlies and relates all these fabricated crises: the individual begins to emerge as a person from the pattern of history, a person moreover whose extrapolitical relationships, especially kindred ones, determine his actions, even if the result is national chaos.[82] Again, the duality of history and the resultant historical tension press in upon Geoffrey and upon his reader. The synthetic historical imagination of earlier centuries, when Christian world views determined a harmonious vision of providential history, has vanished and been replaced by an analytic approach leading consistently to the stone wall of irreconcilable tendencies by which history is surrounded.

Far from ignoring the individual in history, then, Geoffrey exalted him to new stature, distinguishing him as a creature with a destiny and desires potentially different from those of his nation, and as an individual involved in a range of relationships not integral to, and even at odds with, the political relationships which determine national history.[83] In the process, Geoffrey opened a Pandora's box which had remained closed during the centuries when Christian thought dominated historical writing, and wrote a final chapter to the literary history of the fall of

Britain which contains developments hardly imaginable in the light of what had gone before it.

Since it is not possible to examine Geoffrey's historiography thoroughly within the limits of this study, I shall choose from *Historia regum Britanniae* episodes and characters which illustrate these three phases of its art:

(1) Geoffrey's treatment of national achievement and disaster. Using exemplary figures and incidents, Geoffrey explores human capacities for greatness or turpitude, specifically as they involve the rule of a nation. The exploits of the Britons and the conduct of good and bad kings serve to illustrate the author's political interests, and to reflect in general the concerns of the Anglo-Norman historians in recording the *res gestae* of the Norman dukes and monarchs of England.

(2) The tension between national and personal interests, and the consequent impairment of national stability or prosperity. As I have suggested, Geoffrey gives eloquent expression through *exempla* to a much less clearly articulated tendency of contemporaneous historiography, which considered human experience at large and the affairs of kings as two different kinds of historical matter.

(3) The presentation of history as a cycle of nations, and of the particular "meaning" of British history. Exemplary incidents and narrative patterns in this category illustrate Geoffrey's creation of a philosophy of history from the hints provided in the new historiography by the role of fortune and by the dim outlines of a cyclic history in the succession of nations ruling in Britain.

The protagonists and antagonists discussed in the following pages exemplify national virtues, vices, and crises—all facets of Geoffrey's central "character," the nation itself.[84] They are, in other words, explanatory and descriptive, rather than hortatory and prescriptive examples. In removing the Christian theology of history almost entirely from his pages,[85] Geoffrey has not substituted a unified political theory of national prosperity to be embraced by his contemporaries,[86] but rather a vision of history linking past and present through an imaginative presentation of human behavior and the patterns into which it tends to fall. His contribution to the fall of Britain tradition is also a major contribution to the history of the early medieval historical imagination.

The extraordinary cohesiveness of Geoffrey's narrative makes it easy to distinguish the large concerns of his historiography, but extremely difficult to illustrate them in isolation. One incident or a related series of incidents presents political, personal, and philosophical *exempla* in a tightly woven, carefully reinforced fabric. An excellent example of this characteristic method is Geoffrey's treatment of those kings of Britain who capture Rome. Brennius, the first, conquers Rome with his brother Belinus.[87] This deed is the culmination of a victorious campaign initiated by the reconciliation of the two brothers, who had contested the throne of Britain for many years, to the detriment of the kingdom.[88] The episode as Geoffrey presents it is exemplary: the end of fraternal strife restores civil harmony and paves the way for the conquest of foreign lands. When the brothers have taken Rome, Brennius, the younger, remains there as emperor while Belinus returns to Britain.

Brennius thereupon passes out of the narrative, but not without supplying Geoffrey with an occasion for irony: as the younger of the royal brothers, he has received a smaller part of the kingdom, a portion he feels to be unjust.[89] After having fought hard and long for his dignity and having finally assumed power in Rome, he proceeds to tyrannize over the Romans with extreme severity.[90] Belinus returns to Britain and reigns with great justice over a peaceful kingdom. The end of Geoffrey's *exemplum* reveals definitively the character of Brennius, whose search for dignity at home and abroad [91] culminates in success—

and tyranny. Of his further career, the *Historia* says nothing; he
has fulfilled his function, not as a person, but as an *exemplum* of
the young nation's "growing pains" and the dangers of restless
ambition. Brennius is also a foil for Belinus, the just king who
realizes that his proper concern at this point in his nation's history is to uphold its new laws.[92] Belinus' attitude issues in his
returning to Britain, as logically as Brennius' issues in his remaining in Rome and becoming a tyrant.[93]

The next Briton to capture Rome is none other than Constantine the Great.[94] Geoffrey makes Constantine a native and king
of Britain, but pays little heed to his imperial career. The reason
for this treatment is provided by the narrative. Constantine wins
a great reputation as a valorous, just, and peace-loving king.[95]
Because of his virtues, Roman refugees who have fled the tyranny
of Maxentius come to him for aid in regaining control of Rome.[96]
At this period in their history the Britons are engaged in an intermittent struggle against Roman domination, and when Constantine leaves to conquer Maxentius they revolt against Roman
authority. But the victorious Constantine is now himself that
authority, and he sends an army to crush the uprising.[97] The
nation which produced a king of Constantine's stature now pro-
duces, in the fictional Octavius, a champion to battle the troops
dispatched by its former king, and the Britons finally drive out
the Romans, thereby gaining freedom for many years.[98]

In this episode, the trip to Rome is again part of a period of
disorder in Britain, but this time the Briton involved is the lawful
king who brings trouble to his nation after, instead of before,
going to Rome. So presented, Constantine's behavior sums up the
dangers of Roman imperialism in Britain (a main theme of this
part of the *Historia*), and reiterates the theme of the harmful
consequences of ambition, here as before closely connected with
the trip to Rome. Constantine, having served Geoffrey in these
two ways, then passes from the narrative; his historic imperial

career, brilliant though it may be, has no further interest for the *Historia.*

Maximianus,[99] who takes the next trip to Rome, is not himself a Briton but becomes king by marriage, and returns to his native Rome to take revenge on his enemies there.[100] The part of Maximianus' career which interests Geoffrey is his colonization of Brittany, which Geoffrey treats as an adventure in ill-conceived imperialism. Maximianus is an unscrupulous politician,[101] who seeks and wins the crown of Britain as a stepping stone to imperial power.[102] In becoming king, he frustrates the claim of Conan, the king's nephew, who is ambitious for the throne and supported by some of the British nobility.[103] Conan at first wars with Maximianus, but is later reconciled with him, and the two leaders go abroad to conquer Gaul.[104] They subdue Armorica with great slaughter and cruelty, and Maximianus offers it to Conan as a compensation for the latter's loss of Britain. The "new Britain," glowingly described by Maximianus,[105] captivates Conan, who receives it from him. To colonize Armorica, Maximianus strips Britain of her soldiery and able-bodied population. He then goes on to Rome and disappears from the narrative.[106] Meanwhile, the savage Huns and Picts, dispatched by the Romans to destroy Maximianus and his partisans, learn that Britain is defenseless and lay waste to it. The chaos thus initiated culminates in the worst of all kings of Britain, Vortigern.

The part played by Maximianus in the founding of the new nation of Brittany, to the detriment of Britain, is symbolic of the destructive effect of imperial ambitions upon the nation.[107] Maximianus' career, so centrally involved with the trip to Rome, is even more disastrous for Britain than was Constantine's. Furthermore, Maximianus anticipates Vortigern in his behavior and prepares the way for that arch-villain by his policies, so that he can be said to partake of both a cycle of ambitious monarchs who lead Britain to Rome, and a progression of "vile politicians"

whose devices bring national disaster upon the Britons. At least
in the latter case, Maximianus is both type and cause of his "fulfillment," Vortigern. Finally, he is useful to Geoffrey as a last
precursor of the most calamitous trip to Rome, undertaken by
Arthur, the best of all kings of Britain.

Arthur is the last British king whom Geoffrey follows to
Rome and back.[108] When Rome challenges the Arthurian empire, Arthur takes a mighty force into Gaul, where he crushes
the Roman armies. But while he is away from Britain, Modred,
his nephew and regent, claims the throne. Arthur rushes back
to destroy the traitor, but is mortally wounded in battle. His
surrender of the throne to his nephew Constantine is the beginning of Britain's fatal decline.[109]

Under Arthur, the Britons achieve their greatest imperial
success and then immediately experience their greatest domestic
crisis, one from which they will never completely recover.[110]
As Geoffrey brings British history to its great climax, he emphasizes the contrast between the political heights which a united
Britain is capable of scaling under a powerful monarch, and the
sudden depths into which monarch and nation alike are suddenly thrown. One moment, it seems, Arthur is alive and Britain
rules the world; the next, the king is dead and the nation divided.

Arthur's career illustrates that fatal opposition between human greatness and the arbitrary power of history which we
have seen in the Anglo-Norman historians; nowhere will Geoffrey present it with greater effect. Yet, because the Arthurian
climax comes during a trip to Rome—that is, during an episode
which has cyclically repeated itself throughout British history—
the immediate response to it which Geoffrey elicits from the
reader is also both prepared and heightened by knowledge of
the earlier segments of British history. At the moment of Arthur's triumph and fall, in other words, we not only experience
the specific exhilaration and then shock which proceed from our
vicarious participation in the events of the narrative at this point;

in addition, we suddenly perceive with greater clarity the entire pattern of British history. This heightened perception is the direct result of the parallels between the earlier trips to Rome and Arthur's expedition. In every case, the trip to Rome contains two contrasting elements: national greatness, permitting the trip to be undertaken and achieved, and the personal failings (of Brennius, of Constantine, of Maximianus, of Modred) inextricably intertwined with or irrevocably released by the venture. In the Arthurian episode the nation is so great and the treason of Modred so heinous that the contrast between the two actually becomes a dialectic governing British history, in conjunction with the other dialectic—human greatness versus fortune—which, reappearing here, seals the fate of Arthur himself and, through him, of Britain as well.[111]

While Geoffrey's handling of Arthur's career within the context of the trip to Rome is a unique achievement, other recurring narrative episodes which place British heroes in a milieu exemplifying the human contribution to national fortunes abound throughout *Historia regum Britanniae*. An interesting pair are the two giant fights, that of Brutus' lieutenant Corineus with Goemagog, and that of Arthur with the giant of Mont-Saint-Michel.[112] The former giant poses a challenge to a nation colonizing a new land, while the latter lies athwart the path of a mighty empire *en route* to its greatest battle. Corineus' destruction of Goemagog is the last event in the settlement of Britain,[113] and represents the triumph of the young civilization over the savage forces of nature. Geoffrey underlines the importance of this epoch by inserting two eponymous details into the text: the naming of the place where the giant is thrown into the sea "Goemagog's Leap," and the naming of the area of Britain in which the fight takes place "Corinea." One name commemorates the passing of the old order (or disorder), the other consecrates the role of the hero in establishing a new order.

Arthur's battle occurs on his learning that the niece of his nephew, King Hoel of Brittany, has been carried off to the top of Mont-Saint-Michel by a lustful giant. Arthur arrives to find the girl, Helena, dead, and dispatches the giant after a fierce struggle. Pähler has pointed out that Geoffrey placed the incident here to establish Arthur's personal bravery and strength on the eve of his—and his nation's—greatest battle.[114] The episode comments on Arthur's national role in other ways as well. The king receives general praise after the fight for having freed Armorica from the giant's lust;[115] we are surely intended to recall that, in his recent wars, Arthur has also freed much of Europe from Rome's lust for power.[116] Furthermore, Arthur himself is reminded of an earlier battle with the giant Ritho in Britain. Ritho had demanded Arthur's beard as tribute, to add to a coat the giant had made of the beards of conquered kings. Instead, Arthur killed Ritho and won the grotesque coat. This folk tale[117] is probably alluded to here in order to mock Rome's request for tribute from Arthur, and to predict the victory of the Britons. The episode manages to sum up the strength, capability, and, in the rollicking tone of Arthur's account of his battle with Ritho, the high spirits of the nation on the eve of its great trial[118]—all qualities which Geoffrey has developed in his triumphant account of Arthur's reign preceding this incident.

Geoffrey does not confine himself to exploring the parts played by ambition and valor in national history. Sexual passion, for example, comes in for scrutiny as well. The *Historia's* first consideration of the effect of passion on the national good involves Locrine, the eldest son of Brutus.[119] Locrine falls in love with the captive daughter of the king of Germany, and wishes to marry her. He is, however, betrothed to Guendoloena, the daughter of Brutus' formidable companion Corineus. Corineus compels Locrine to keep his word, but the young king, his passions not to be denied, secretly takes the foreign princess, Estrildis, as his mistress. When Corineus dies, Locrine deserts his wife and makes his mistress queen. Civil strife between Cornwall and Loegria (later England; named after Locrine) follows, and Locrine is killed. The incident sets the tone for the period between Brutus and the coming of the Romans, a period encompassing many reigns and almost continually disturbed by civil wars and bickering over the government of the island.[120] Locrine, because of his passion, is a social antihero, who loses his life and costs Britain her peace. Geoffrey here draws a purely secular parallel between individual shortcomings and national calamity; analysis, not judgment, is his aim.

With the love of Vortigern for Renwein, the daughter of Hengist the Saxon leader, the theme recurs.[121] Vortigern, already guilty of murder and treacherous usurpation of the throne,[122] sees the beautiful pagan at a feast celebrating the Saxons' arrival. Drunk with wine and with lust, he asks her father for her hand. Hengist agrees, and receives in return the province of Kent, which is not rightly Vortigern's to give.[123] The Britons are astonished at Vortigern's dealings with the pagans, and when he will not heed their objections, they choose his son Vortimer as their leader and rise against him. Vortimer is finally poisoned by Renwein, the revolt fails, and Vortigern is reinstated.[124]

Geoffrey's additions to this episode as he found it in *Historia Brittonum* work in part to emphasize the national effects of Vortigern's passion. Geoffrey is responsible for the rebellion of the Britons with Vortimer as leader, and for Renwein's murder of Vortimer. Lust for the Saxon princess therefore costs Vortigern his son, and the Britons their chosen ruler. But there is another, contrasting side to the story of Vortigern's Britain: the nation rises up against its ruler and dissociates itself from his crime; the tyrant does not sum up the faults of those he rules. At this point in his historiography, Geoffrey plainly demonstrates the separation of individual and nation, in a manner suggested by the secular account of Vortigern's death in *Historia Brittonum*.[125] The rehandling of the treacherous massacre of the Britons by the Saxons provides corroboration for such a reading.[126] In *Historia Brittonum,* the Britons do not resist when the Saxons draw their hidden knives at the supposed peace parley. In *Historia regum Britanniae,* the unarmed and outnumbered Britons present a stout defense, rallied by Eldol, Duke of Gloucester, who dispatches many of the enemy with only a club for a weapon. Vortigern's passion is ultimately responsible for this catastrophe,[127] which is nonetheless the occasion for a notable show of British valor quite unthinkable before the treacherous accession of Vortigern to the throne.[128]

Vortigern's passion, like the ambition of Brennius, is an *exemplum* of the kind of human weakness which, embodied in a national leader, invites political disaster. Vortigern differs from earlier antiheroes, however, in that his nation, for all his catastrophic effect upon it, stands on the brink of a period of unequaled greatness—i.e., the Arthurian age. The nation, ready to climb history's cyclic path higher than ever before, unites against Vortigern and finally excises the cancer. As the *Historia* moves toward Britain's golden age, the ordinary formulation of political cause and effect in which a wicked or weak king creates a disordered kingdom undergoes modification by the superpolitical force of national destiny. It is not coincidental, for example, that Vortigern's attempt at cruel murder should result in Merlin's prophecies,[129] and that the massacre at Kaercaradoc, also Vortigern's responsibility, should inspire Merlin's miraculous transfer of the Giants' Dance from Ireland to Kaercaradoc as a monument to national heroism.[130] In both cases the destructive desire, far from bringing national collapse, ultimately exalts the Britons.

Geoffrey nowhere reveals more clearly the strength of his structural art than in the rich complex of narrative threads that binds together the careers of Vortigern, Merlin, and Arthur.[131] Merlin, who first appears in Vortigern's reign, and whose prophecies and miracles oppose him to the wicked monarch, also figures centrally in the third *exemplum* of passion and its effects,

the love of Uther for Ygerna, which results in the conception of
Arthur.[132] Ygerna is the wife of Gorlois, Duke of Cornwall and
one of the king's first barons. Like Estrildis and Renwein, she
is a paragon of beauty,[133] and Uther, seeing her at a great banquet, instantly falls in love with her. Gorlois perceives his sover-
eign's reaction and quickly leaves the court, rejecting Uther's
summons to return with Ygerna; soon king and duke are at war.
News of Uther's grievous desire for Ygerna reaches Merlin,
who promises to fulfill the king's desire by means of new arts.[134]
He metamorphoses Uther into Gorlois' shape, by which strata-
gem the king penetrates the duke's castle and enjoys Ygerna.
On that night, Arthur is conceived.[135]

Gorlois is slain in battle and Uther weds Ygerna, making
Arthur legitimate heir to the throne. Meanwhile Uther falls
sick, but his great energy is such, in war as in love, that he rises
from his sickbed to snatch victory over the Saxons from the
jaws of defeat.[136] Finally he is treacherously slain by Saxon
spies, who poison a clear spring which alone satisfies the ailing
monarch's thirst. Thus Uther, who loved by deceit, dies by
deceit.[137]

Vortigern's passion does no irreparable harm to the nation, and
Uther's is positively salutary, for it gives to the Britons their
greatest leader, Arthur. Despite the injustice involved in the
wooing of Ygerna, and the suggestion of retribution in Uther's
death, the episode of Arthur's conception manages to sum up in
one act the great energy and passion which is driving Britain
forward toward the zenith of her power. The differences between the passion of Vortigern and the love of Uther are that
the latter is a desire of a Briton for a Briton instead of for a pagan
alien, and—much more importantly—that Merlin was Vortigern's
enemy, whereas he is Uther's ally.[138]

Merlin's inimical confrontation with Vortigern results in his
assuming for the first time the prophetic office which is one-half
of his role in *Historia regum Brittaniae;* it is, he later declares, a

gift available to him only in times of great need and distress.[139] His other function is as a performer of marvelous deeds, a talent which he places at the service of the good kings Aurelius and Uther, who lead the nation in the fight against the Saxons. Merlin's insistence that his prophecy is a special, occasional art places him under the control of history, which determines the circumstances of his utterances, and thereby makes of him an exemplary creature of historical destiny or fortune.[140] His use of his special power to perform magic deeds, however, reverses this relationship, and puts him temporarily in control of national progress, as with Arthur's conception. At such moments, Merlin exemplifies human greatness creating history and its own destiny. Since, however, he has predicted Arthur's coming in his vatic seizure, he acts here too as an agent of inexhorable history, bringing to fruition that which he knows must happen. It might be said that Merlin is Geoffrey's symbol for the artist-historian, whose insight into predetermined history gives him some control over the historical process.[141] But he is also to be equated with the androgynous, passive-active form of history itself, and, as a crucial figure in a specific part of the *Historia*, with the British *regnum*, or with that part of its career which he oversees, viz., its rise to greatest eminence.[142]

The character of Modred deserves consideration in our examination of figures used by Geoffrey primarily to characterize national rather than human experience. As Merlin's life has no ending in the narrative, so Modred's has no beginning. We first hear of him when Arthur places the kingdom in his hands, prior to leaving for his war with Rome.[143] Nothing is said of Modred's character; his treason comes as a great shock, surely so intended by Geoffrey.[144] Yet it is possible to discern something more about Modred's structural importance from the information Geoffrey does give. First of all, Modred's role as destroyer of Britain's glory contains elements from several reiterated narrative situations. The unfortunate imperialism of the trip to

Rome, as we have seen, sets the stage for national difficulties. The theme of treason has also been sounded many times at crucial points before Modred's appearance.[145] A third theme is the disastrous result of inviting foreign soldiers into Britain, a policy Modred follows in order to have a force with which to challenge Arthur on his return.[146] Then the fact that Arthur's queen Ganhumara, whom Modred claims with the throne, flees to a convent and vows to lead a chaste life on hearing of her husband's return, suggests an illicit love affair as well as an illegal marriage between her and Modred.[147] Such an affair would in turn link Modred to Locrine and Vortigern and perhaps provide a motive for his treason. The text does not allow certainty but does permit speculation.

More important than these allusions is Modred's function as the initiator of the disorder which grips Britain after Arthur's death.[148] In this sequence we perceive that Geoffrey used Modred to epitomize and to propel the rapid passage of the "over-reaching" state into the grasp of its archenemy, internal strife. When Arthur and Modred are dead, their enmity lives on in the next generation. Modred's sons rebel against Constantine, Arthur's nephew and successor. In order to pursue and finally kill the rebels, Constantine violates the law of sanctuary established long ago in the reign of the great lawgiver Dunwallo Molmutius.[149] Constantine is punished by God for this trespass. His nephew Conan slays him and reintroduces civil war into the island. Shortly afterward comes Geoffrey's apostrophe to the Britons, berating them, in the *persona* of a political Gildas, for the civil discord which will cost them their homeland.[150]

The crucial link in this chain of catastrophes is the breaking of the Molmutine law of sanctuary which, instituted when Britain was young, had marked a step forward in the establishment of an ordered civilization.[151] Now Britain's retrograde motion propels her into collision with her laws; Geoffrey makes us realize with a start that the peak of national achievement has

passed, and that national decline has begun. His adoption at this
point of the unaccustomed role of a Christian national-ecclesiastical historian seems to serve a double purpose: he responds to
an appropriate situation in a way typical of his contemporaries,
who still find God judging in this life the acts of men who make
history; [152] and he also reminds us again of the superior forces
controlling history over and above the efforts of national leaders
and heroes. The grouping of these themes around Modred, and
the importance of his "moment" for Geoffrey's exposition of
national history, demonstrate that the relevance of the "incom-
plete" exemplary character in *Historia regum Britanniae* is rarely
as univocal as it looks at first glance.

The first book of the *Historia*, with its hero Brutus, the
founder of Britain, serves as a useful transition from Geoffrey's
political *exempla* to those which epitomize the tension in history
between personal desires and national goals. The second category, we recall, includes protagonists who seek their happiness
by moving counter to the order or demands of society and yet
are not obviously presented by Geoffrey as villains. Brutus begins his career as an exile, continues it as a rebel, but ends as the
first ruler of Britain and a true social hero.[153] The adventures
which Geoffrey invents for him [154] expose main themes of the
Historia and also present the author at his highest peak of
originality.

Brutus is modeled on the Brutus of the second Roman origin
story of *Historia Brittonum*. Like his namesake, he is born of
Trojan stock, the son of Silvius, and is innocently responsible
for the death of his parents. Driven from Italy, he finds in
Greece a colony of Trojans living in captivity among the Greek
nation of King Pandrasus. Brutus rallies his countrymen and
leads them into the forest, whence they issue an appeal for freedom to King Pandrasus, who rejects it. In the war that follows,
the resourceful Trojans rout their captors and take the king

prisoner, aided by the treason of his brother Anacletus, and the support of Assaracus, a disaffected Greek noble. To save his life, Pandrasus gives Brutus his daughter for a bride and allows the Trojans to depart by sea. The exiles sail westward and arrive at an island temple of Diana, who prophesies a great future for them in their new nation. Other Trojans, commanded by Corineus, join them, and they fight a series of battles with the twelve kings of Gaul. From Gaul they come to the island of Albion and colonize it with little difficulty. Brutus names the land Britain after himself and British history proper begins.

This exciting, Vergilian narrative introduces Brutus as a romance hero, driven by fate from his Italian homeland. In Greece, Brutus discovers a tyrannical nation oppressing its ancient enemies, his countrymen, out of a desire for revenge.[155] The sack of Troy, barely alluded to in *Historia Brittonum,* is here elevated to the role of a major factor in the origin of Britain. The new Britons are Trojans reborn; a nation rises from the wreckage of a preexisting nation. The conditions for rebirth as Geoffrey presents them are the desire for freedom and a leader to implement this desire. Geoffrey could easily have found a model for his opening section in the book of Exodus,[156] but at no point does he intimate a parallel between his own narrative and salvation history. Instead, he links the personal qualifications of Brutus as leader with the unanimous Trojan wish for liberty.[157]

The other unusual feature of Geoffrey's origin story is that its exaltation of freedom takes new, antisocial forms. The traditional defiance of tyranny by a freedom-loving nation was a social act, and Geoffrey evokes it in this form later in the *Historia.*[158] But when Brutus sends a letter of defiance to Pandrasus, he casts the choice of the Trojans in a different form: they can either live in society, enslaved but enjoying the refinements of civilization, or in the woods, with liberty but like savages.[159] As an alternative to the forest life which the Trojans are leading at Brutus' orders, Brutus requests that they be allowed to depart to other nations of the world. But the Trojans are clearly ready to live outside society indefinitely, if necessary. Brutus threatens no uprising against Greek society; the war is initiated by Pandrasus, who orders that the Trojans be hunted down.[160] Geoffrey, in short, raises a disturbing question about the relationship, so basic to the Christian tradition of early medieval historiography, between the quest for personal *salus* and the maintenance of national *salus:* can man always find his happiness within society? His inspiration for this idea may have been Gildas, who described the Britons' flight to the woods as a result of oppression. For Gildas, however, this movement from society was unnatural—a punishment from God—and not a state to be endured.[161]

Geoffrey's use of the woods as a historiographical and thematic device has important implications. The forest is a touchstone by which to judge the romantic tendencies of a literary vision. It is a *locus classicus* of romanticism; within the forest, the rules and forms of normal society are suspended or defied. The individual may live a full life as his own ruler and seek personal fulfillment as he sees fit, unfettered by other obligations. Shakespeare opposes forest and city in his romantic comedies, *Two Gentlemen of Verona, Midsummer Night's Dream,* and (most subtly) *As You Like It.* Medieval Arthurian romance sets most of its marvelous adventures in the forest. An even closer analogy to *Historia regum Britanniae* is the fourteenth-century English alliterative romance, *Gamelyn.*[162] In it a younger brother is cheated and tyrannized over by an elder one, who denies him his rightful inheritance. Gamelyn, the younger, flees to the woods and gathers an outlaw band around him after his appeals for justice to the organs of society have shown him that society is hopelessly corrupt. This romance is also in the Robin Hood tradition, which opposes forest freedom to society's restrictions.

The plot of *Gamelyn* contains a second parallel to Geoffrey's narration of the birth of Britain, viz., the feud between brothers.

Assaracus, the young Greek noble who takes the Trojans' part, turns against his nation because his inheritance is threatened by his brother with the support of the Greeks. Assaracus' mother was a Trojan concubine, whereas both parents of his brother (actually, his half-brother) were Greek. The Greeks favor the latter in the contention, and Assaracus is faced with the loss of three castles conferred upon him by his dying father.[163] The young man, confronted by an unjust society, must betray his nation to retain his rights. Here is the first instance, and by no means the last, in *Historia regum Britanniae* of tension between the individual seeking his happiness or just deserts and the society which acts in accordance with its view of the right.[164]

The feud between brothers becomes another cyclic theme for Geoffrey;[165] at times, the situation he recounts is almost a literal duplication of the Assaracus story.[166] The reiterated narratives betray a drawing apart of personal interests and national order, and illustrate the historian's concern for his characters as individuals whose lives take shape around crucial relationships not themselves political, but of great political import.

Victory comes to the Trojans thanks to the cunning of Brutus, and also to the treason of Anacletus, the brother of King Pandrasus. Anacletus is captured by the Trojans during their first battle with the Greeks, and Brutus threatens him with death if he does not betray the Greek camp at night, allowing the Trojans to infiltrate and destroy the enemy host.[167] Anacletus agrees in order to save his life, and the plot works. Pandrasus is captured and forced to grant the former slaves permission to leave Greece, supplies for their journey, and his daughter as a bride for Brutus. At this point the cyclical "relativism" of Geoffrey's historical outlook becomes evident. The treason of Anacletus is as disastrous to the Greeks as it is helpful to the Trojans. The older, oppressive society has brought itself down, partly by alienating Assaracus, and partly by Anacletus' irrepressible urge for survival. The proto-nation (actually the remnant of a former *regnum*) profits from these collisions of individual desire and national welfare in coming to birth.

Later, Britain in turn feels the negative results of such conflicts. The complaint of Assaracus is echoed by Androgeus, and the treason of Anacletus is "fulfilled" in Modred. Androgeus is a British noble whose nephew runs afoul of Cassibelanus, King of Britain and twice victor over Julius Caesar.[168] The nephew, Cuelinus, participates in national games proclaimed by Cassibelanus to celebrate the repulse of the Romans.[169] He wrestles with Hirelglas, the king's nephew, and, in an argument over the decision, kills him. The king seeks trial for the offender, but Androgeus suspects his nephew will be treated unjustly and refuses to surrender him. Soon the forces of Cassibelanus lay waste to Androgeus' duchy, and the duke, in a desperate bid to defend himself, secretly invites Caesar into Britain to succor him. Cassibelanus had defeated Caesar thanks to the aid of Androgeus;[170] with the latter now helping the Romans, the Britons cannot withstand the assault, and Britain enters into the Roman orbit, surrendering some of her freedom for the first time. For the Britons as for the Greeks, the individual's search for justice at a climactic moment results in damage to the nation.

The obvious parallel between Anacletus and Modred is not developed by Geoffrey, but in both cases treason by a relative of the king ruins one nation and works to the advantage of another at the beginning of its cycle. Britons rise at Greek expense, Saxons at British expense.

Two other antipolitical elements of *Historia regum Britanniae* receive their first mention in the Brutus episode. One is Geoffrey's attitude toward law; the other is his occasional use of pathos to introduce a note of individual helplessness into a narrative of clashing societies. The matter of restrictive law comes up when the proto-Britons are *en route* to Albion.[171] Upon landing in Gaul, Corineus takes a party into the woods to seek food for the fleet. The hunters are accosted by envoys of Goffarius Pictus, King of Aquitania, and are upbraided for trespassing in the king's forest.[172] Corineus denies that they need permission to hunt, and a scuffle ensues, which soon leads to all-out war on the new arrivals by a league of the twelve kings of Gaul, who seek to enslave them.[173]

Geoffrey's mention of the forest laws is one of three revealing references to laws and customs which were a feature of Geoffrey's England or of Anglo-Norman policy. The forest laws here serve to exemplify the tyranny of the kings of Gaul, the would-be enslavers of the newly free Britons.[174] Later, the custom of primogeniture provokes the rebellion of Brennius and its disastrous civil consequences,[175] and the violation of sanctuary by King Constantine is made a part of the decline of Britain after Arthur. The law of sanctuary was not new in the twelfth century; it is an ancient reflection of religious awe.[176] But Geoffrey attaches it to the Molmutine laws, which include many edicts reflecting new legislation of the twelfth century.[177] The pattern which emerges from these specific invocations of law might best be described as a cynicism about the ultimate salubrity of law. This is not to imply that Geoffrey was an anarchist, but simply that he recognized in contemporary historiography a note of alarm at the ability of the supremely powerful Anglo-Norman monarchs to oppress their subjects behind a facade of legality.[178] Laws which serve as an excuse for tyranny may become a stimulus to rebellion—or may, as with Constantine, bring disorder, rather than order, to the nation.[179]

As for pathos, it is a quality largely lacking in Christian historiography, since it usually proceeds from helplessness, and in a providential order a helpless protagonist is almost a contradiction in terms. God helps the good man and his nation. Geoffrey, however, in his probing of society's flaws, finds place for a few brief allusions to the occasions on which the individual is a helpless bystander or victim of national crises. In all cases the protagonists are women. The first is Innogen, the daughter of King Pandrasus, who weeps piteously when forced to leave her homeland with her father's conqueror.[180] The passage bears quoting, for it interrupts the flow of epic sentiments and rhetorical speeches, which dominate the narrative up to this point.

But Innogen, standing in the highest part of the ship, swooned repeatedly into the arms of Brutus; she was prostrate with grief and shed many tears over having to leave behind her family and nation, and would not turn her eyes from the shore as long as she could distinguish it. Brutus comforted her with sweet words and kisses, and continued his ministrations until, worn out with crying, she was overcome by sleep.

For a moment the issues of national birth and freedom are forgotten; history itself is forgotten, and attention is focused on the timeless problems of wives and lovers. This is but a momentary departure, however; Innogen is not spoken of again, except as the mother of Brutus' children.[181]

A similar moment of pathos comes amid the description of the founding of Brittany by Conan, already discussed.[182] As part of his plan for colonization, Conan sends to Britain for women who will be wives for his troops. Seventy-one thousand women are assembled and take passage for Brittany, and Geoffrey adds that most of them would have preferred to stay at home.[183] But they are pawns of Conan's ambition, and suffer accordingly. A storm scatters their ships, and those who are not drowned are driven upon the coasts of Gaul, and there killed by savage Huns and Picts.[184] Again, the affairs of a nation incidentally bring disaster to innocent victims. These two passing details of larger episodes typify Geoffrey's expansion of the boundaries of early medieval historiography toward attitudes foreign to the genre which determined the form of previous fall of Britain narratives.

From characters and incidents exemplary of Geoffrey's political and experiential concerns, we may turn now to a closer scrutiny of his striking involvement with a cyclic theory of history. The rise and fall of Britain is Geoffrey's primary consideration, but he creates a cyclic context for his national "protagonist" by expanding the place of Rome and that of the Saxons far beyond any notices he found of them in his known sources. I propose to conclude this chapter with a brief discussion of some of the incidents involving the Romans and the Saxons, in order to demonstrate that *Historia regum Britanniae* transmitted to the remainder of the Middle Ages a view of Britain and its decline substantially different from that conveyed by the earlier fall of Britain texts, thanks to Geoffrey's subscription to a new vision of history.

The Brutus story just discussed contributes the first data for an understanding of Geoffrey's outlook on history. I have already noted the emphasis Geoffrey places on the Trojan ancestry of the Britons, and on their slavery to the Greeks after the war which destroyed Troy. I have also indicated that the Trojans benefit from Greek difficulties—the rebellion of an unjustly treated noble, the treason of a desperate man—which later beset the Britons themselves and cause similar national setbacks once their own nation is settled in its new home. The nation with which the Britons have the most substantial dealings in the *Historia* is Rome, and accordingly something must be said of Geoffrey's presentation of Rome.

The *Historia* communicates a uniquely adverse judgment of the great empire; practically nowhere else in twelfth-century historical, philosophical, and legal works can we find a denigrating response to the enormous prestige of classical Rome's achievement.[185] The contemporary inhabitants of the city of Rome and the attitudes of the eastern Roman Empire were criticized,[186] but to the men of the twelfth-century "renaissance" the tradition of Roman power and policy was sacrosanct.[187]

One source of Geoffrey's attitude is the summary of Roman dealings with Britain contained in Chapters 19–31 of *Historia*

Brittonum. The bald outline given there furnished Geoffrey with the basis for his extended account of the first Roman attempts to conquer Britain, and of the conflict between Arthurian Britain and Rome at the high point of *Historia regum Britanniae.* The developed, continuous anti-Roman bias of the work, however, reflects Geoffrey's adaptation and expansion of those moments in the works of the Anglo-Norman historians in which the freedom-tyranny *topos* is turned against the Norman conquerors of Anglo-Saxon England. The divided interests of Geoffrey's contemporaries resulted in their now glorifying Norman greatness, now vilifying Norman oppression; but the author of *Historia regum Britanniae* chose instead to divide the attributes of the dominant nation of his time between the two dominant nations of his created past. In consequence, he gained both increased clarity for his presentation of historical forces and an ideal national rivalry around which to construct the central episodes of his narrative.

The first crucial moment of confrontation between Rome and Britain is reached with the arrival of Julius Caesar in Britain.[188] In reworking the standard sources for this episode,[189] Geoffrey pits the Roman leader against Cassibelanus, the virtuous king of Britain; their characters are compared by their words and actions, and from these can be drawn conclusions which reveal Geoffrey's opinion of Roman power.

Cassibelanus assumes the crown of Britain on the death of his righteous brother, Lud. The realm is prosperous and in good order; the new king, Cassibelanus, soon establishes a glowing reputation among many nations by virtue of his prowess and generosity, while concurrently controlling all of Britain.[190] The attributes for which Cassibelanus is distinguished recall those of Brutus and anticipate those of Arthur, the two kings to whom he is most comparable as a leader of the Britons.[191] During his reign, the Britons receive a letter from Julius Caesar asking that they pay tribute to Rome, mistress of the world. Cassibelanus refuses, and rallies the Britons to defeat the forces of Caesar twice. Then come the celebrations, the fatal wrestling match, and the treason of Androgeus, which lead to a third, successful attempt by Caesar to subdue the Britons and make them tributaries of Rome.[192]

Geoffrey's richly thematic portrait of Caesar is the most carefully drawn of any he attempted of an enemy of Britain. Caesar's entrance into the narrative is pompous, but not without wry humor. He appears on the coast of Flanders and contemplates Britain; ascertaining its identity, he declares that its inhabitants are, like the Romans, offspring of Trojan stock, but that they must undoubtedly be a degenerate, unwarlike race because of their isolation from the rest of the world. Now Geoffrey has remarked immediately before Caesar's appearance that Cassibelanus' fame resounds far and wide and that Britain's reputation is anything but unwarlike at that moment. In the light of his ignorance, Caesar's letter to Cassibelanus takes on a ludicrous aspect. The Roman proposes condescendingly that the Britons submit peacefully to Rome in order that her dignity and the noble memory of Priam, common father of Rome and Britain, may not be offended.[193] The pompous antiquarianism of the request stimulates Cassibelanus to a brave reply, in the tradition of the rhetorical speech defending freedom.[194] Speaking for the Britons, whom Geoffrey has been engaged in describing as builders of a new society, not degenerates of an old one, Cassibelanus tells Caesar that his nation desires only to enjoy its accomplishments in tranquillity. If the Romans sue for anything, it should be for friendship, since both races descend from the great Aeneas. The difference in ancestors mentioned by the two leaders is not accidental; Caesar chooses the venerable patriarch destroyed with his Troy, Cassibelanus, the valiant hero who presided over the birth of a new nation.

Cassibelanus defies Caesar and his demands, and assures the Roman that the Britons are ready to die for their liberty and their land. This letter, recalling Brutus' letter to Pandrasus, serves as an indication of the development of British society, which now must repel would-be conquerors from its own homeland, where earlier it sought to regain its liberty in an alien nation. The narrative at this point, with its reminiscences of Brutus and its presentation of Caesar as the spokesman of a tyrannical, established, backward-looking order, is so developed as to suggest the progress and repetitiousness of national history, and to distinguish between the essential newness of the British nation and the traditionally oriented Roman outlook, which does not comprehend Britain and seeks to oppress her.

After Caesar's first defeat by the Britons, he returns to Gaul, where he suppresses a rebellion by the subject Gauls and wins back their allegiance by bribery and by promises of restitution to the disinherited and freedom to the enslaved.[195] These promises, which the machiavellian Caesar has no intention of keeping, recall the grievances of the Trojans and Assaracus which led to the birth of Britain. Geoffrey suggests that the policies of tyrannical nations provide a continuing stimulus for rebellion and therefore aid the cyclic forces of history in the task of producing new nations. (By contrast with Caesar, Cassibelanus observes his victory by rewarding his followers with gold, not with words, and by observing the correct rites for the dead.) A further detail of Caesar's behavior, after his second defeat in Britain, directs our gaze forward along the cyclic path of history. No longer trusting the Gauls, he retires to a tower to be safe from future rebellions. His action anticipates Vortigern's retirement to the tower, which epitomizes his isolation from the nation united against him by his own evil.[196]

The period between Caesar and Maximianus is one of continued struggle against Roman tyranny on the part of the Britons.[197] They are successful until Maximianus is invited to possess the British crown. This misguided decision again involves Britain in Roman politics, brings her to the edge of ruin, and results in the birth of Brittany. Once more the alienation of an individual from what he regards as his inheritance is crucial to the foundation of a new nation, since Conan, to whom Maximianus gives Brittany, was frustrated by Maximianus in his bid for the crown of Britain. Founded by the best soldiers of Britain, Brittany moves in and out of the affairs of her "parent" throughout the remainder of the *Historia.* With Breton help, the British are usually victorious; without it, they are often defeated.[198] The pattern of Breton involvement in British history has led some scholars to decide that Geoffrey's sympathies are pro-Breton and anti-Welsh, and to account for this bias they postulate Breton ancestry for Geoffrey.[199] My own feeling is that the ascendancy of Brittany over Britain in the latter part of the *Historia* does not stem from racial sympathy, but is part of Geoffrey's cyclical view of history. Tension between individual desires and national welfare (on both Conan's and Maximianus' parts) brings about the birth of a nation whose establishment results in the decline of the parent nation. Geoffrey subtly points out that the success of Brittany, which the Bretons attribute to their freedom from the Roman bondage enslaving Britain,[200] is at least as much a consequence of the tensions which activate the cycle of history.

The greatest conflict between Britain and Rome comes in Arthur's day.[201] Britain is now a fully mature, imperial power, and her king a great hero.[202] Arthur, who loves and rewards knightly virtue, and is reciprocally loved by bold men everywhere, orders a glorious celebration to coincide with his crown-wearing in Kaerleon on Pentecost.[203] Arthur's vassals come from all over Europe to rejoice with him, but their enjoyment of ceremonies and sports is interrupted by an embassy sent from Rome to claim the ancient tribute owed by Britain and to protest Arthur's annexation of much of Rome's empire. Arthur is summoned to Rome to answer for his tyranny before the Senate. The festivities are suddenly forgotten and the Britons, in a council resembling those of the contemporary *chansons de*

geste,[204] decide to make war on Rome. Arthur promptly sets out
at the head of a mighty army; the fight with the giant of Mont-
Saint-Michel follows, and finally the two armies confront each
other. Arthur is supported by allies and vassals from all Europe;
Lucius, the Roman emperor, has enlisted the aid of the nations
of the east, pagan hordes with mighty Saracen kings.[205] The
fighting starts unexpectedly, prompted by the inflammatory behavior of an embassy sent by Arthur to the Roman camp. After
a series of fierce encounters, the Britons and their allies carry the
day, and the power of Rome is smashed. Arthur is on his way to
Rome to enjoy the fruits of his triumph when he receives the
news of Modred's treason and must return to Britain.

The Arthurian empire is Britain's highest achievement. Geoffrey chronicles its successes with verve, and creates in Arthur a
great monarch of unequalled prowess and munificence.[206] Arthur's conquest of the Saxons, the Scots, and the Irish bring him
such fame, and his largesse such an international following, that
the kings of Europe come to fear him,[207] and he conceives the
desire to subdue the entire continent to his rule. The campaigns
by which Arthur satisfies his monumental ambition are not
prosecuted without British excesses,[208] but they result ultimately
in an admirable goal: after subduing a foreign land, Arthur insures that justice and peace reign within it.[209] The Christian
alliance which Arthur creates receives Geoffrey's further appro-
bation by its "holy war" against the pagan-supported Romans.
In short, Geoffrey gives us every reason to believe that, by the
standards of political and moral judgment, Britain is in the right
and Rome in the wrong at their final confrontation—and thus
makes the decline which follows Arthur's death all the more
painful in its irrevocability, and exemplary of the tensions always
implicit in the pageant of history.

In the struggle of Arthurian Britain against Rome, Geoffrey
again differentiates between the position of the antagonists in
their respective cycles of existence. Britain has now attained

virile maturity while Rome has passed into decrepitude. This relationship is clarified by several details of the narrative. The embassy from Rome, which interrupts the Pentecost celebration at Kaerleon, consists of aged men who enter with solemn dignity.[210] The letter they bear claims an ancient tribute and registers Rome's objection to Arthur's usurpation of territory previously under her rule. Arthur is even accused of tyranny—until now the Roman vice *par excellence*. The letter, in other words, embodies the reaction of an aged society to its supplanter.[211] In contrast, the embassy Arthur sends to the Romans in Gaul is sparked by the reckless Gawain, Arthur's young cousin.[212] Urged on by the hot-headed, youthful members of Arthur's entourage, Gawain kills a Roman who sneered at British valor. The pitched battle that follows soon engages large numbers of troops on both sides. Roman discipline seems about to gain a victory over British impulsiveness when Count Boso of Oxford urges the Britons to avoid disgracing Arthur by the results of their impetuosity.[213] The youthful energy of the Britons then proceeds to turn potential defeat into victory.

Later, when the emperor Lucius addresses his barons just before the climactic battle at Siesia,[214] he appeals to the past greatness of Rome, retraces the rise of the ancient commonwealth, and seeks to arouse in the venerable fathers ("patres venerandi") the ancient greatness ("avitam bonitatem") of their heritage. This speech of Lucius is a splendid evocation of the Roman golden age, much as Livy extolled it. Its aim, at least in part, is to round out the portrait of Rome as a nation in old age.

Arthur's view of Britain's past is very different. He sees only a history of discord and dissension which gave the Romans their first foothold on the island.[215] The time to redress the grievance is now, in the glorious present. To be sure, Cador, Duke of Cornwall, greets the Roman challenge as an opportunity to refurbish British valor, dulled by a long period of easy, peaceful existence; but this return to the "good old days" looks back only five years.[216] Furthermore, Arthur, in his speech at Siesia paralleling that of Lucius, recalls only the accomplishments of his own reign to spur the Britons on.[217] The purpose of these references becomes clear in Geoffrey's own comment on the battle at Siesia: by their victory, the Britons repay Rome for the slavery imposed on their forefathers.[218] The wheel has come full circle and the two powers have changed places in the historical pattern of rise and fall.

The Saxons, the supplanters of the Britons, are less fully realized in the text, but Geoffrey imparts to their coming a note of significance quite in keeping with the pattern under discussion. He puts the revelation into the mouth of Hengist, the Saxon leader.[219] It is, says Hengist, a custom of his race to banish from the nation at periodic intervals the surplus male population. Able-bodied men are chosen to go forth seeking new realms, led by the noblest born among them. He and his brother Horsus command such a band, in accordance with the old custom.[220]

The point of Hengist's explanation is that the Saxons are not simply adventurers, but, like the Trojans of long ago, follow a national and human dictate in their voyage. The Saxon conquest will be the result of another cycle, this one prompted by the periodic overcrowding of society and the dispatch of groups to start anew. Hengist is another Brutus (or perhaps an "anti-Brutus"), doing what is best for his society. For Geoffrey, the Saxons cease to be a scourge of God and take their place as part of the great cycle (or cycles) upon which Geoffrey's history is based.

The reference Geoffrey makes to the Saxons at the very end of the *Historia*—they hold the island of Britain, live in harmony, and begin to rebuild civilization—indicates that they are on the side of the wheel which is rising, and hence are moving toward national greatness.[221] The implication is, I suspect, that the Saxons shall fall too, and be supplanted by the Normans, a succession already narrated in the historical works of Geoffrey's contemporaries.[222]

The "meaning" of British history for Geoffrey, based on this analysis, is simply that Britain, like other nations, rises, flourishes, and falls. The human-political desire for freedom motivates the nation at great moments in her history, but the wish to be free of Roman domination once and for all also leads Arthurian Britain to undertake the imperial expedition that exposes her to Fortune, exemplified in Modred's mortal blow. Britain's fate does not unravel in isolation, but intersects those of other nations at various points in their histories. Meanwhile, within the limits of Britain, recurrent dramas of human greatness and of the clash between personal and national interests play themselves out before our eyes.

Geoffrey's contribution to the imaginative historiography of the early Middle Ages may be summed up as a removal from history of the idea of eschatological fulfillment, in both its national and personal manifestations. In the *Historia*, the regulation of history by repetitive patterns of personal behavior and national progress has replaced the Christian system of movement toward a final happiness or reward. Geoffrey's story of the fall of Britain lacks, in short, the moral dimension provided in the versions of Gildas and Bede by the theology of history.

It is, then, no accident that the great eschatological moment of *Historia regum Britanniae*, the end of Merlin's prophecy, takes the form it does.[223] Merlin, who can see into the processes of history and aid them to their fruition but cannot change them, is, I have suggested, a singularly significant inhabitant of Geoffrey's historiographical universe; he embodies, as it were, the self-awareness of his creator's historical imagination. When he has finished prophesying events through Geoffrey's day—in other words, when he has stated Geoffrey's claim that his analysis of British history is valid for all history to date—Merlin describes a terrifying apocalypse in which all the elements of heaven and earth are set free from their order and go whirling into chaos. Here is no triumph of divine providence, no judgment which will reward the good, punish the bad, and reveal the forces moving all history; instead, the impersonal universe which has presided over the rise and fall of kingdoms will lose control of itself and history will dissolve into nothingness.[224] There is no clearer indication in all of *Historia regum Britanniae* that its author's vision of past and present has bolted free of the Christian theology of history. The fatal and conflicting forces ruling man and society partake less of the Christian historical imagination of the early medieval centuries than of the classical historiography which it supplanted. With Geoffrey, the wheel has indeed come full circle, and we are absolved from following it further.

CHAPTER VI

Conclusion: Metamorphosis of the Vision

The period of efflorescence of the new Anglo-Norman historiography was as short as it was brilliant. The school (if one may call
it that) whose pioneering efforts found a unique imitator, epito-
mizer, and commentator in Geoffrey of Monmouth did not survive much past the middle of the twelfth century.[1] A categorization of the factors which militated against the continuation of the
work of William, Henry, and Orderic lies outside the scope of
this study, and perhaps of modern scholarship. Certainly, one
factor conducive to new modes of historiography in Angevin
England was a change in literary taste which, in an age that did
not make sharp distinctions between history and literature, affected ways of thinking and writing about the past. The new line
of monarchs which succeeded the Anglo-Norman dynasty on the
throne of England in 1154 was, at least in the person of its first
representative, Henry II, less interested in historical accounts
written in Latin prose than in the literature of the newly respectable French vernacular. The popular "historiographical" achievement of Henry's reign is Wace's *Le Roman de Brut*, an expanded rendering of Geoffrey's *Historia* into octosyllabic "romance" couplets.[2]

This is not to imply that the achievements of the Anglo-
Norman historians, and especially of Geoffrey, were without
influence. The very fact that Geoffrey was being translated into
a more accessible language—and style—soon after his death
argues against any such implication.[3] Geoffrey's influence on the

following centuries was, as indicated in the preceding chapter, both enormous and normative. Until the sixteenth (and in some quarters the seventeenth) century, British history *was* Geoffrey's *Historia*, expanded, excerpted, rhymed, combined, or glossed. Of course, it was one thing to copy Geoffrey's narrative, and quite another to understand or emulate the premises of his historiography. Of the latter phenomenon there are few, if any, examples in the later medieval centuries. Instead, Geoffrey's "facts" were reabsorbed into the over-all Christian and patriotic interpretations of history which (with inevitable changes and developments) reasserted themselves, apparently without difficulty, in the work of most medieval historians who cast their nets widely enough to include the pre-Saxon history of Britain.[4]

In closing this study of the fall of Britain texts and the early medieval historical imagination, I wish to indicate briefly a development in twelfth-century literature which the *Historia regum Britanniae* does not so much cause or influence as it does illustrate, at a particularly valuable moment of transition. That development is the rise of romance.

In the preceding chapter I pointed to the inclusion in Geoffrey's imaginative history of a recurring series of incidents and figures illustrative of a tension between personal desires (partly the result of nonpolitical personal relationships) and national goals or progress. These exemplary moments, I stressed, were basically foreign to the synthetic, multileveled view of history common to the Christian national-ecclesiastical historiography of earlier centuries. Within Geoffrey's own system, moreover, they proved repeatedly damaging to or subversive of national achievement and political order. The "antipolitical" and almost "antihistorical" elements in Geoffrey's *Historia* contribute to its peculiar atmosphere, and ultimately to its singular greatness. But, I suggest, they did not prove to be viable elements of an historical literature in the twelfth century.[5] Instead, there grew up spontaneously and with great, immediate success a narrative genre which, vernacular in language and poetic in form, presented and

examined personal destiny in a deliberately ahistorical context—
not at the Christian exegetical level of national and personal
providence, nor as a factor in political evolution, but as an index
of the human condition considered as a unique, continuous,
ethical phenomenon. This genre is now called romance.

The hero of the romance-adventure, whatever the social characteristics of his world,[6] is actually the fully matured heir of
Geoffrey's "preromantic" heroes such as Assyracus and Androgeus. The identifying characteristics do not lie in the deeds or
adventures, but rather in the status of the hero as an *individual*,
whose needs and their satisfaction, whose conflicts and their
resolution, demand the undivided attention of writer and reader.
At no point in a romance of Chrétien de Troyes or a *lai* of Marie
de France can we speak of an historical level, or point to a
protagonist who symbolizes or exemplifies a national virtue.[7]
Ironically enough, the social context of the romance hero is often
the court of King Arthur—an Arthur borrowed from Geoffrey,
but one from whom all British historical associations have been
carefully pruned.[8] In a romance, moreover, even the most glitter-
ing social setting provides only a beginning and ending point for
adventure, a meeting place of equals wherein the honor gained
in the forest can be ratified and savored.[9] The proving ground of
the romance world is the forest, the *terre de pesme aventure*,
where the specifically individual virtues of the hero are tested.

There is much more to the genre of romance in theory and
practice than the few fundamentals here mentioned. The tremendous expansion (and internalization) of the range of human
relationships beyond that presented in Geoffrey's *Historia*, made
possible by the introduction of love as a motivating force, is
perhaps the greatest innovation of the French courtly romance;
neither scope nor space permit consideration of it here. My aim
is simply to underscore the trend in twelfth-century imaginative
literature toward a concern with the individual (in one sense of
that word) as, if not a free agent, one liberated from the tyranny
of history. Geoffrey of Monmouth, historiographically and

imaginatively committed to the tyranny of history, nevertheless indicates unmistakably (from our perspective-giving twentieth-century vantage point) in some sections of his history the course of future development. Geoffrey's imposing, creative attempt to synthesize, if not to reconcile, the new interest in individual human behavior and the incipient fascination with secular, political history proved to be a *hapax legomenon;* even Geoffrey did not try to duplicate it.[10] The *Historia regum Britanniae* remained in splendid isolation while the disciplines of history took the path to Wace's popular courtly narrative, or toward the more austere and imposing documents of the St. Albans school, and the literary romance opted for the path into the forest.

Geoffrey's *Historia* stands, then, not simply as the culminating work of the early medieval fall of Britain tradition, subversive of that tradition's Christian assumptions although respectful of its basic interpretation of British history. It also claims our attention and even affection as a curious and inspiring monument to a time in medieval literary history when men were grappling simultaneously with the meaning of history and the nature of human achievement, and were attempting to establish to their satisfaction a valid and viable connection between the two. *Historia regum Britanniae* testifies in all its order and complexity to the fact that the historical imagination of the early medieval centuries had been jolted off its eschatological track long enough for new alternatives to its old assumptions to be discovered. The consequent exploration of human autonomy in the face of history, begun in literature in the twelfth century, effected permanent changes in literary expression the impact of which can still be felt today. The passing of Geoffrey's generation signaled the disappearance of an all-inclusive medieval historical imagination; thereafter we must make an important and unequivocal distinction between two separate traditions: the *historical* vision, and the *romantic* vision.

Notes

ABBREVIATIONS

ALMA	*Arthurian Literature in the Middle Ages*
CHEL	*Cambridge History of English Literature*
De civ.	Augustine, *De civitate Dei*
De exc.	Gildas, *De excidio et conquestu Britanniae*
De gub.	Salvian, *De gubernatione Dei*
EH	Eusebius, *Ecclesiastical History*
EHR	*English Historical Review*
HB	*Historia Brittonum*
HE	Bede, *Historia ecclesiastica*
HRB	Geoffrey of Monmouth, *Historia regum Britanniae*
Hist. Zeit.	*Historische Zeitschrift*
MGH	*Monumenta Germaniae historica*
PQ	*Philological Quarterly*
Proc. Brit. Acad.	*Proceedings of the British Academy*
RS	*Rolls Series* (Chronicles and Memorials of Great Britain and Ireland during the Middle Ages)
TRHS	*Transactions of the Royal Historical Society*
Z.f.d.Ph.	*Zeitschrift für deutsche Philologie*

Chapter I. The Formation of the Early Medieval Historical Imagination

1. Cf. R. G. Collingwood's classic statement in *The Idea of History*, p. 10, that "the value of history is that it teaches us what man has done and thus what man is."

2. Among the many works in which are examined the social and cultural background and inheritance of early medieval Europe, the following are accessible and stimulating: W. C. Bark, *Origins of the Medieval World;* M. L. W. Laistner, *Thought and Letters in Europe, A.D. 500–900,* and *The Intellectual Heritage of the Early Middle Ages;* Jean Décarreaux, *Les moines et la civilisation* (translated as *Monks and Civilization*); and a collection of essays, *The Legacy of Rome,* edited by Cyril Bailey. Also useful are the relevant chapters in Norman F. Cantor, *Medieval History: The Life and Death of a Civilization;* and in Jean Daniélou and Henri Marrou, *The First Six Hundred Years,* Vol. I of *The Christian Centuries: A New History of the Catholic Church.*

3. Acts 2:44–47. (In those few places where I have quoted from the Bible I have used the translation of Ronald Knox. The fact that the Knox translation is primarily a rendering of the Latin Vulgate, the version in which most medievals (though by no means all—Gildas was one exception) knew the scriptures, has decided my practice in this matter.)

4. See the record of the council held in Jerusalem to decide whether gentile Christians should be bound to observe all the restrictions of Mosaic law, including circumcision (Acts 15); and Daniélou and Marrou, pp. 29–39.

5. Jean Daniélou, *From Shadows to Reality,* pp. 161–62, points out passages in the Acts which reflect a very early Christian belief that the apostolic community of Jerusalem was a fulfillment of the desert community of the Exodus.

6. The distinguished historian of the Jews, Salo W. Baron, notes on p. 4 of the first volume of his *Social and Religious History of the Jews* that "the Jewish religion has been from the very beginning, and in the progress of time has increasingly become, an *historical* religion, in permanent contrast to all *natural* religions."

7. See Tom F. Driver, *The Sense of History in Greek and Shakespearean Drama,* pp. 53–55. The chapter on the "Judaeo-Christian Historical Consciousness" (pp. 39–66) from which this reference is

taken is an excellent introduction to Hebrew views of history and providence, both for the perceptivity of its insights and for the helpfulness of its bibliographical references.

8. In addition to Driver and the more specialized studies mentioned by him, see Erich Auerbach's brilliant essay, "Odysseus' Scar," in *Mimesis*.

9. See Driver, pp. 40–42. The Old Testament's very first covenant (not so-called in the text but actually such), the first creation story in the book of Genesis, illustrates with unmistakable clarity the importance of the covenant for the order and form of future events. In creating man, God crowns the cosmos; he then tenders authority over the world to man, who is to use it in order that he may thrive. The goodness of the creation is, in effect, to be proven by the goodness and continuity of history. See Genesis 1:28–30, and the sections on Hebrew conceptions of God the creator of history in the essay "God and Nature in the Old Testament," in John L. McKenzie, *Myths and Realities*, pp. 91–99.

10. See Driver, pp. 41, 42, 49, 52–53. As he puts it, "besides seeing the possibilities of newness in history, [the Hebrew view of time] had also a persistent tendency to mingle present and past. Even its visions of the future make constant use of images drawn from the past" and "the Hebrew tended to bring events out of the remoteness of the past and to adopt them into present existence. . . . The event which *was*, meaningfully enters the *now*."

11. See Daniélou, *Shadows*, p. 12; according to him, "All the work of the Prophets . . . rests on a twofold movement. . . . It is at the same time both commemorative and prophetic."

12. The "Son of Man" is a prophetic term; see Daniel, and the gospels, *passim*. On Christ the "New Adam" see Romans 5. Daniélou, *Shadows*, Chapter One, explores thoroughly the Adam-Christ typological pair in scriptural and postscriptural Christian writings, and discovers its initial roots in Old Testament messianic prophecy.

13. See Driver, pp. 63–64; whereas "the future, especially, was open in Hebraism," Christianity in effect closed the future by discovering the literal entrance of God into history to save man. "By identifying Christ as the new Adam, and by seeing him as the one who will return to judge the world at the Last Day, the beginning, middle, and end of a dramatic history were constituted."

14. See Erich Auerbach's essay, "Figura," in *Scenes from the Drama of European Literature*, pp. 11–76, an exhaustive study of

the changing meaning and use of the word *figura* in antiquity; for a series of investigations exploring the history of various popular types in early Christian writings, see Daniélou, *Shadows*.

15. On the Old Testament roots of typology in eschatological prophecies, see Daniélou, *Shadows*, pp. 13, 22–24, and 287, Conclusion no. 1: "Patristic exegesis is founded on the extension of the Messianic typology of the Old Testament Prophets, which described the future Kingdom as a new Paradise, a new Exodus, a new Flood." See *ibid.*, pp. 1–7, for a survey of the catechetical and polemical uses of typology in the early church; it was not until the third century, under the influence of Origen, that scholarly commentaries on scripture, discussing a text exegetically in order, from beginning to end, began to appear.

16. The best consideration of the distinction between typology and allegory is that of Jean Daniélou, *Origen*, pp. 139–99. On the historicity of both members of a typological pair see Auerbach, "Figura," pp. 30 ff.

17. The typological argument is central to the catechesis of the epistle to the Romans, and even more so to that of the epistle to the Hebrews. Daniélou, *Shadows*, p. 19, points out that in these epistles typology "is not limited" in application "to the person of Christ; it equally applies to the life of the Christian. . . . The Old Testament gave us an eschatological typology, while the Gospel shows how all has been fulfilled in Christ: St. Paul will show us its continual fulfillment in each Christian life."

18. Driver, pp. 60–61, refers to Augustine's discussion of the nature of time in Book xi. of the *Confessions* as a product of peculiarly Christian biblical thought in paradoxical combination with Hellenic philosophy. "In it is present the biblical emphasis upon history and what I have called the Bible's 'principle of contemporaneity.' Past and future are drawn into the present, animating it." Note the similarity between this formulation and the general definition of the historical imagination given at the beginning of this chapter. We are today still the heirs of the early Christians in many of our assumptions about history.

19. As Daniélou puts it in his *Shadows*, p. 287, Conclusion no. 3: "The writings of the New Testament show us that [the] Apostolic typology had developed to that stage in which particular traits become marked. One, exemplified by the Gospel of St. Matthew, sees the types fulfilled in the details of the earthly life of Christ—

the other, represented by the Gospel of St. John, sees these types fulfilled in the Sacraments of the Church." On Johannine typology, see below, note 30 and corresponding text.

20. See Matt. 13, 20, 24, etc.

21. *Ibid.*, 4; these are the words with which Jesus first summons those who will be his disciples.

22. See *ibid.*, 10:34–40, 12:46–50.

23. See Myles M. Bourke, *Passion, Death and Resurrection of Christ*, pp. 6–16; Benjamin Willaert, "Jesus as the 'Suffering Servant,'" *Theology Digest*, X (1962), 25–30.

24. The other synoptic gospels also contain apocalyptic passages, but in Matthew the account is longer and more complex, and only there does it include the illustrative parables.

25. An example of the sophistication of this attitude is provided by the figure of John the Baptist who comes before Jesus as the last of the prophets (see Matt. 3:3; 11:7–9), looking backward to the prophetic voice of the Old Israel (11:13) and in a sense fulfilling it (11:14). Yet John is also a precursor who looks forward to Jesus (3:11; 11:10); indeed, Herod calls Jesus the resurrected John the Baptist (14:2—with obvious irony intended by the evangelist). Certainly John's death at Herod's hands prefigures the death of Jesus.

26. By comparison, the Lucan infancy narrative has completely different narrative and theological aims, emphasizing as it does the role of Mary in the history of salvation and the marvelous wisdom already displayed by Jesus in his youth.

27. The flight into Egypt and the return to Israel may also be a reference forward, both to the crucifixion and resurrection, and to the baptismal rite by which each Christian joins the church as a new child of Christ. The crossing of the Red Sea in the flight from Egypt was a standard type of both the crucifixion and baptism. See I Corinthians 10:6 and, on the wide diffusion of the baptismal typology of the Red Sea passage, Daniélou, *Shadows*, pp. 175–201.

28. See, for example, Jesus' saying regarding the centurion whose servant he cures, "I have not found faith like this, even in Israel" (Matt. 8:5–13).

29. See Matt. 2:16, 23; 27:35 (cf. John 19:36).

30. See, for example, John 6:30 ff. (on the Eucharist), 4:5–15 (on Baptism). Daniélou, *Shadows*, p. 161, suggests, "The Johannine Gospel appears as a kind of Paschal catechetical instruction, to show

to those baptized on the night of Holy Saturday that the Sacraments they then received were divine interventions which continued the *magnalia* of Yahweh at the time of the Exodus and also at the time of the Passion and resurrection of Christ."

31. *Ibid.*, p. 287, "Conclusion no. 5." See also pp. 19–21 on the Apocalypse, in which typology becomes the fulfillment of types in the church. Cf. n. 17, above.

32. As R. L. P. Milburn points out in *Early Christian Interpretations of History*, p. 25, the Jews are the real villains of the Acts in that they persecute and pursue Paul, as they have earlier murdered Stephen.

33. Daniélou and Marrou, p. 94, distinguish the late second-century writer Hegesippus with the title, "the first historian of the Church" since, "wherever he happens to be, [he] notes the list of bishops and their dates of office." On Hegesippus see also Milburn, p. 36.

34. See Milburn, *Early Christian Interpretations*, pp. 21–37; esp. p. 28, where he characterizes the writers from whom he draws his examples as "early churchmen who were primarily concerned with practical apologetic rather than with history as a subject of formal study."

35. *Ibid.*, pp. 28–29.

36. See Exodus 9:16; 10:1–2, and I Peter 2:20–22; of the many classical references, the most famous are undoubtedly Livy's formulation in the Preface to the first decade of his *Libri ab urbe condita*, and Thucydides' explanation of the usefulness of his work in Book i. of his history. The latter passage has sometimes been taken as evidence of a cyclic view of history on the part of Thucydides and the Greeks, but as M. L. W. Laistner (*The Greater Roman Historians*, p. 13) points out, such a statement—he quotes a parallel one from Aristotle's *Rhetoric*—is simply a variant form of the traditional justification: "The man of affairs must study the past in order to have a guide for his own public conduct, to profit by the wisdom and to avoid the mistakes of statesmen in the past." On history and *exempla*, see also E. R. Curtius, *European Literature and the Latin Middle Ages*, pp. 59–61.

37. See H. W. Litchfield, "National *Exempla Virtutis* in Roman Literature," *Harvard Studies in Classical Philology*, XXV (1914), 1–71.

38. The whole tradition of the organization of historiography to provide the reader with examples to be imitated or avoided is a fascinating one, and I shall return to it in Chapter Five.

39. See Milburn, p. 29.

40. D. S. Wallace-Hadrill, *Eusebius of Caesarea*, pp. 82–83; Beryl Smalley, *The Study of the Bible in the Middle Ages*, pp. 14–15.

41. T. E. Mommsen, *Medieval and Renaissance Studies*, p. 267. See also J. W. Thompson, *A History of Historical Writing*, I, 125–27 for other suggested reasons.

42. See Matt. 12:21, Romans 13:1–7, I Peter.

43. See Daniélou and Marrou, pp. 83–84, 87; and M. S. Enslin, *The Literature of the Christian Movement*, pp. 357–72. On the Old Testament background of the apocalyptic genre, see C. K. Barrett, *The New Testament Background*, pp. 227–55 (an annotated collection of Old Testament apocalyptic passages), and Enslin, pp. 351–56.

44. See C. N. Cochrane, *Christianity and Classical Culture*, pp. 113–76, 213–14, for a survey of Christian views on the subject, "regnum Caesaris regnum diaboli."

45. On the ideology of the *pax Augusta* and "the deification of imperial fortune," see Cochrane, pp. 1–112; E. Barker, "The Conception of Empire," in *The Legacy of Rome*, pp. 59–65, discusses "the empire as salvation." Daniélou (*Origen*, pp. 113 ff.) examines the political persecution of Christians in connection with the discussion of it in Origen's polemical *Contra Celsum*. As Daniélou comments elsewhere (*The Salvation of the Nations*, p. 44): "Why did the Roman emperors persecute the Christians? It was not for metaphysical reasons, but because religion was identified with the state and was one with it. Consequently, he who turned away from the state religion became a stranger to society. From one point of view, this placed society in danger of disintegration."

46. But see below on a contemporary apologetic strain which sought to find a place for Rome in the history of salvation.

47. See, for example, the famous narrative of the martyrdom of Polycarp, bishop of Smyrna, included in the fourth book of Eusebius' *Ecclesiastical History*, but apparently written soon after the event (156 A.D.).

48. James J. Shotwell, *The Story of Ancient History*, p. 107, is thus incorrect in calling the story of Joseph in Genesis a romance; it represents an adaptation of romance to the Hebrew view of God's providential control of history.

49. Matt. 25:1–13; 13:24–30.

50. On Greek typical characters, see John H. Finley, *Thucydides,* pp. 38–40; Erich Auerbach, *Dante,* pp. 1–4.

51. Cochrane, pp. 399–455, makes much of "the discovery of personality" in the mature Christian speculation of Augustine.

52. But see Daniélou and Marrou, pp. 90–95, on the use of the classical tradition in Christian apologetics, rhetoric, and philosophy in the late second century. On the other hand, J. W. Thompson, p. 126, quotes a third-century Christian text which exclaims, "What dost thou miss in God's word that thou dost plunge into these pagan histories? If thou wilt read history, there are the books of Kings."

53. See the opening pages of Herodotus' history for examples, and J. B. Bury, *Ancient Greek Historians,* pp. 17 ff., and the brilliant, controversial study of F. M. Cornford, *Thucydides Mythhistoricus,* for comment.

54. See R. G. Collingwood, *The Idea of History,* pp. 20–28; Driver, pp. 19–38.

55. Auerbach, *Dante,* pp. 1–2.

56. The most famous examples are Pericles ("the son of Xanthippus, the leading man of his time among the Athenians and the most powerful both in action and in debate") and Cleon ("He was remarkable among the Athenians for the violence of his character, and at this time he exercised far the greatest influence over the people").

57. See Cedric Whitman, *Sophocles: A Study in Heroic Humanism.*

58. See *Histories,* i. 30–34, for the famous exchange between Solon and Croesus on human happiness and the jealous god. Cochrane, pp. 461–68, analyzes the historiography of Herodotus in this light.

59. See Cochrane, pp. 460–61: "To Herodotus the law of balance or compensation is the law to which all physical processes are ultimately subject; and its tendency is to restrict or check the growth of those things which tend to exceed the norm." Thucydides sees political processes in an analogous light.

60. Thuc., iii. 70–84.

61. See Cochrane, p. 463: "To Herodotus the struggle between Greece and Persia presents itself as a supreme example of the working of [the] principle [of equilibrium between opposite forces]. Accordingly, as an incident in human history, it is not unique or abnormal; it is merely one of an endless succession of events which

may be taken to illustrate the eternal dialectic of time, space, and matter."

62. As Shotwell says (p. 191) of Herodotus, "He sought only to keep the motives [for human action] psychologically true and left events to shape themselves under the hand of fate or by the chastening justice of the gods."

63. Interestingly enough, Eusebius of Caesarea recognized this distinction and commented upon the disunity of pagan historiography, wherein man is subject to fate or necessity and history loses its divine purpose, which is, among other things, that man should rule the world in freedom under God. D. S. Wallace-Hadrill, in *Eusebius* (p. 191; see also pp. 183–85), summarizes, "The error of the polytheist, [Eusebius] writes . . . , is that of the immature mind: he fails to see a piece of work in its totality, and can only wonder at each detail separately. The Christian sees the universe whole, and consequently sees it in the over-all design and purpose which knits the individual parts together."

64. See Laistner, *Roman Historians,* Chapter One, and Bury, Chapter Seven.

65. Aeneid, i. 278 ff. Mommsen, pp. 266–67, comments on the belief, almost universally held among non-Christians in the first Christian centuries, that the Augustan achievement had resulted in an eternal *imperium* for Rome.

66. See Cochrane, pp. 61–73.

67. *Aeneid,* vi. 719–21. My attention was directed to this passage by a lecture of Prof. Gilbert Highet.

68. The celestial armor which Aeneas receives in Book viii. includes a shield on which has been illustrated the history of Rome, up to and including the Augustan triumph; but Aeneas, we are told, puts on the armor ignorant of its meaning (viii. 730).

69. The elder and younger Marcellus (Book vi. 854–86) form a "typological pair" in the underworld, as do Iulus and Julius Caesar (789–90).

70. See the illuminating discussion of Turnus, a figure of great human stature who runs afoul of providence and history, in Viktor Pöschl, *The Art of Vergil,* pp. 91–138. As Pöschl says (p. 138), "The impact of the tragic force [of the last half of the *Aeneid*] is insolubly connected with the figure of Turnus."

71. Mommsen, pp. 265–301, "St. Augustine and the Idea of Progress."

72. *Ibid.,* pp. 267–68.

73. Daniel 2:31 ff. See also Daniel's dream of the four beasts, 7:1 ff., which was similarly interpreted.

74. Mommsen, pp. 268–71, discusses various types of early Christian millenarianism which preceded and prompted Augustine's contention that man has no way of knowing when God will bring the world to an end.

75. Mommsen, pp. 277 ff., and the bibliography cited in n. 17, p. 277.

76. *Ibid.,* p. 279.

77. For examples, see *ibid.,* pp. 280 ff.

78. For biographical information on Eusebius see D. S. Wallace-Hadrill, pp. 11–38.

79. Eusebius characterizes the church in which he grew up in the last chapters of the seventh book and first chapter of the eighth book of his *Ecclesiastical History (EH).* All references to *EH* in this chapter are to the translation of R. J. Deferrari.

80. Such was the effect of the Edict of Thessalonica issued in that year.

81. D. S. Wallace-Hadrill, p. 169.

82. See especially *EH,* i. 4, and other examples given by D. S. Wallace-Hadrill, pp. 169–71.

83. *Ibid.,* p. 172.

84. *Ibid.,* pp. 171, 182–83.

85. On these works, and criticism of them, see J. Quasten, *Patrology,* III, 309 ff., and D. S. Wallace-Hadrill, pp. 72–99.

86. Eusebius called himself Eusebius Pamphili in honor of his friend and teacher.

87. See Daniélou, *Origen,* pp. 165, 178–99.

88. See *EH,* i. 3.

89. Christian commentators interpreted Genesis 3:18 as a *proto-evangelium,* or first announcement of the coming of Jesus to provide restitution for the fall. See D. S. Wallace-Hadrill, pp. 191–92, for a summary of Eusebius' mature formulation in his *Theophany* of the war between God (through Christ) and the devils who tempt man into "the childish state of polytheism."

90. Mommsen, p. 282, recognizes as original and important Eusebius' application of the prophetic verses of Psalm 72 to Rome.

91. This view is expressed in the *Demonstratio evangelica,* discussed and quoted by D. S. Wallace-Hadrill, pp. 173–74.

92. Discussed by D. S. Wallace-Hadrill, pp. 155–58, and (with bibliography) by Quasten, III, 311–14.

93. Quasten, II, 138, mentions some of the older Christian chronicles, especially that of Africanus.

94. D. S. Wallace-Hadrill, p. 43. His chapter on "questions of dating" (pp. 39–58) summarizes that extremely complicated and controversial problem, providing adequate references to earlier scholarship.

95. *Ibid.*, p. 175.

96. *Ibid.*, p. 168.

97. I follow the theory of R. Laqueur, as recounted by D. S. Wallace-Hadrill, pp. 40–44.

98. The progressive importance of Rome in Eusebius' historical thought is the subject of a study by H. Eger (summarized by D. S. Wallace-Hadrill, p. 175).

99. D. S. Wallace-Hadrill, p. 41.

100. Eusebius first outlines the sinfulness of the prepersecution church in *EH*, viii. 1, and, after the account of the persecution in the remaining chapters of that book, he narrates its return to worthiness in ix. 8 (the description of a plague in which only the Christians were not reduced to bestiality and despair), and introduces the liberation by Constantine in the following chapter.

101. See *EH*, viii. 1–2.

102. See *EH*, ix. 8, viii. 13–14.

103. See Mommsen's analysis of the meaning and novelty of Eusebius' achievement, pp. 281–85.

104. On the patriarchs and the Constantinian *ecclesia*, see D. S. Wallace-Hadrill, pp. 172–78. The relationship involved is not typology; cf. below on Constantine as a new Moses.

105. Mommsen (pp. 284–85) and D. S. Wallace-Hadrill (pp. 185–89) agree that for Eusebius, continuous political fulfillment replaces eschatological triumph as the end of history. The concept of constant progress, adumbrated in *EH*, is openly stated in the *Laus Constantini*. See also Norman Cantor, *Medieval History*, p. 51.

106. *EH*, ix. 9. Cf. the use of biblical exegesis in interpreting Constantine's life in the *Vita Constantini* of Eusebius, written *ca.* 337. Besides incorporating the passage just quoted and others from *EH* into the text of the *Vita*, Eusebius also declares that the honors granted Constantine on earth prefigure his rewards in heaven, and resulted from his conversion. See E. C. Richardson, *Life of Constantine*, pp. 489–93, 559.

107. D. S. Wallace-Hadrill, p. 189.

108. But the judgment is not an eschatological judgment on all the world. This strain remains lacking in Eusebius' writings. See D. S. Wallace-Hadrill, pp. 188–89, and H. Lietzmann, *From Constantine to Julian*, pp. 164–65.

109. See Cantor's extremely perceptive remarks on the form of the early medieval lives of kings, and how Eusebius established it, pp. 50–51.

110. D. S. Wallace-Hadrill, p. 172.

111. See above, pp. 15–16.

112. This was the charge brought against the Christians by pagan Romans who blamed the sack of Rome by the Visigoths in 410 on the Christianization of the empire and its consequent abandonment by the gods under whom Rome attained imperial greatness. See. E. Hardy, "The City of God," in *A Companion to the Study of St. Augustine*, pp. 260 ff.; Mommsen, p. 272; and Cantor, pp. 92–93.

113. W. C. Bark, pp. 82–84, remarks on the widespread identification of church and empire among Christians of Augustine's day.

114. *De civitate Dei* (*De civ.*), xiv. 28.

115. Augustine analyzes the history of Rome as a quest for goals which generally motivate the earthly city (*De civ.*, v. 12–21, esp. 15), and notes that, like the earthly city as a whole, Rome began its history with a fratricide (xv. 5).

116. *De civ.*, i. 10–11.

117. *Ibid.*, xiv. 28. The translation is that of D. Honan, D. Zema, and G. Walsh.

118. *Ibid.*, iv. 34, xv. 7, xix. 17.

119. See letter no. 138. Christopher Dawson, in *A Monument to St. Augustine*, p. 77, suggests that Augustine's theory of history "first made possible the ideal of a social order resting upon the free personality and a common effort toward moral ends." Cochrane's analysis of Augustine's historical thought (pp. 456–516) tends to the same conclusion.

120. See his discussion of the duties and rewards of a Christian emperor, v. 23–26, and Hardy, p. 264.

121. Cochrane, p. 516, emphasizes that Augustine's eschatology is the key to the Augustinian view of "history as prophecy."

122. See *De civ.*, xv. 7–xviii., the central exegetical section of the work. On the importance of scriptural history for Augustine's philosophy, see E. Gilson, *The Christian Philosophy of St. Augustine*, pp. 183 ff.; M. Ritter, "Studien über die Entwicklung der Ges-

chichtswissenschaft," *Hist. Zeit.*, CVII (1911), pp. 237–63; and Cochrane, pp. 474–77.

123. In concrete terms, Augustine is presented with the familiar problem of understanding God's providence at work in the career of pagan Rome. See *De civ.*, iii.–v. for his consideration of the problem.

124. Augustine was surely stimulated by his sense of the impending collapse of the empire and by his desire to extricate Christianity from the imperial ideal before it was too late. M. Versfeld (*A Guide to the City of God*, p. 2) says, "One may say that [Augustine's] life work was to kindle the light of things eternal in human hearts no longer supported by temporal institutions which had seemed eternal but which were crashing on all sides." Cf. Gordon Leff, *Medieval Thought from Saint Augustine to Ockham*, p. 46: "In a world where hope seemed to reside in personal salvation alone, St. Augustine provided the grounds for that hope," and Cantor, p. 51, who speaks of Augustine's "socially conditioned pessimism."

125. *De civ.*, v. 21–22. It is, he declares, impossible to separate mankind into its two groups except in the Old Testament, where God revealed the origin and early progress of the two cities (xi. 1).

126. See Cochrane, p. 456: Augustine's "discovery of personality was, at the same time, the discovery of history. For, by giving significance to individual experience, it gave significance also to the experience of the race, thereby providing a clue to the meaning and direction of the historical process."

127. *De civ.*, xv. 18, 1. 29, v. 18, xix. 5–7, 20, etc. The inhabitant of the heavenly city is a *peregrinus;* herein lies the importance of the biblical information that Abel built no city (xv. 1).

128. This is, of course, also the message and form of Augustine's *Confessions*.

129. Hardy, pp. 269–70, speaks of "Augustine's conviction that the Old Testament is both a real historical story and also the record of a promise that finds its fulfillment only in Christ." Augustine defends typological exegesis in *De civ.*, xv. 27.

130. On Orosius' life and work see: I. W. Raymond's translation, *History against the Pagans*, pp. 1–25; W. M. T. Gamble, in *Church Historians*, pp. 30–70; and Mommsen, pp. 326–28. (References here to *History against the Pagans* are to Zangenmeister's edition, *Historiarum adversum paganos libri VII*. Translations are Raymond's.)

131. *Historiarum*, dedication (p. 30).

132. *De civ.,* iv. 2–6.

133. *Ibid.,* iv, rubric; v. 16–18.

134. Mommsen, p. 329, emphasizes the importance of Orosius' admission, in his dedicatory preface, that Augustine had completed the first ten books of *De civ.*

135. *Historiarum,* i. 1. 9–14 (italics mine).

136. *Ibid.,* ii. 1. 1–3.

137. See *ibid.,* iii. 8, iv. 12, vi. 20, on the gates of Janus.

138. See *ibid.,* ii. 3: "It is only because of His mercy that we live at all, and that if we live in misery it is because of our own uncontrolled passions," and vi. 1: "Rightly, therefore, does God reprove the ungrateful, the unbelieving, and also the disobedient with various chastisements. Such, we must agree, has always been the case."

139. *Ibid.,* iv. 17.

140. *Ibid.,* vi. 22.

141. *Ibid.,* v. 2.

142. *Ibid.*

143. *Ibid.,* ii. 1.

144. *Ibid.,* vi. 11. He speaks, almost certainly with typological intent, of the "shepherd of the humblest station" who founded the empire.

145. On the other hand, Orosius' overt references to biblical history are less than thorough. Even in Book i., in summarizing Old Testament events, he dates all happenings *ab urbe condita,* and avoids typology for purely exemplary interpretations of figures and incidents. See i. 6, i. 10, etc.

146. See further on this incident Mommsen, pp. 299–324, "Orosius and Aponius on the Significance of the Epiphany."

147. See C. T. Davis, *Dante and the Idea of Rome,* Chapter Two.

148. See the famous story of Athaulf, king of the Visigoths, who first decided to transform *Romania* into *Gothia,* but later realized that far greater glory lay in reestablishing peace within *Romania.*

Chapter II. Gildas' De excidio et conquestu Britanniae: *In Britain's Fall They Sinnèd All*

1. See Peter Hunter Blair, *Roman Britain and Early England,* p. 36, on the extent of the first stage of the Claudian expedition, and Collingwood and Myres, *Roman Britain and the English Settlements,*

pp. 85–87, on the political organization established by Claudius for his new province.

2. See the brilliant methodological summary, "The Nature of the Sources," Blair, *Roman Britain*, pp. 1–31, for an introduction to the contemporary means of gathering information on Roman Britain. R. L. S. Bruce-Mitford has edited a volume of reports on specific "digs," *Recent Archaeological Excavations in Britain*.

3. See Collingwood, *Roman Britain*, pp. 278–79.

4. Blair, *Roman Britain*, pp. 161–63, points out that Germanic tribes had been introduced into Britain as *foederati* by the Romans at least as early as the fourth century.

5. See J. N. L. Myres, "The English Settlements," *Roman Britain*, pp. 425–56, on "the character of the conquest."

6. On the origin of this appellation, by which Gildas' work was widely known in the Middle Ages, see *De excidio et conquestu Britanniae (De exc.)*, ed. T. Mommsen in *MGH*, pp. 10–11.

7. All references in this chapter are to chapter numbers in the edition of H. Williams (Mommsen's text and an English translation); translations cited are those of Williams.

8. See E. S. Duckett, *Gateway to the Middle Ages*, II, 121–39, for a summary of the hagiographical traditions concerning Gildas. The two hagiographical *vitae* of Gildas are printed in Williams' edition, II, 317–413.

9. I follow the dating of E. M. Sanford, to whose translation, *On the Governance of God*, I refer (as *De gub.*) throughout. See her introduction, pp. 18–19.

10. See the persuasive analysis of Salvian's world in W. C. Bark, *Origins of the Medieval World*, pp. 83–158; and, on Salvian's response to that world: R. L. P. Milburn, *Early Christian Interpretations of History*, pp. 92–95; Bark, pp. 76–82; and Sanford's introduction.

11. See *De gub.*, i. 4: "He who devised [the universe's] elements will himself be their governor. He will guide all things by a providence and reason consistent with the majestic power by which he founded them." This logic recalls the similar conclusions of Orosius cited above in Chapter I, notes 135–36.

12. See P. de Labriolle, *The History and Literature of Latin Christianity*, p. 439: "[The barbarians] held the greater part of Gaul, Spain, and Africa; every year the independent territories were be-

coming more shrunk. In the face of all these calamities the Christians themselves were murmuring vehemently against Providence which was allowing the arms of the orthodox to be defeated by Arian or pagan invaders, and seemed to be heedless of the fate of the Christian Empire." Salvian himself tells us in Book vii. of *De gub.* that "the very people who, as pagans, conquered and ruled the world are being conquered and enslaved now that they have become Christians. Is this not clear evidence of God's neglect of human affairs?" His answer, of course, is an emphatic "no."

13. As Sanford says, p. 23, "He undertook, at a time when the task was as difficult as at any period of the world's history, to justify the ways of God to man, to prove His constant government of the world and His immediate judgment."

14. *De gub.*, ii. 1, "The [biblical] examples . . . are sufficient proof, therefore, that our God acts constantly as a most anxious watcher, a most tender ruler, and a most just judge."

15. In the case of Sodom and Gomorrah (i. 8).

16. Speaking of the evils which the good suffer while the bad seem to prosper, he does ask in i. 4 if Christians think that "God neglects everything that happens in this life and reserves his whole care for the judgment to come . . . ?" and replies, "This idea does not seem to be that of an unbeliever, especially as it admits the future judgment of God. But we say that the human race is to be judged by Christ, while yet maintaining that now also God rules and ordains all things in accordance with his reason. While we declare that he will judge in the future, we also teach that he always has judged us in this life. As God always governs, so too he always judges, for his government is in itself judgment."

17. Such odious comparisons are not original with Salvian, of course; Tacitus, in his *Germania*, found some of the barbarian virtues to be in admirable contrast to the Roman customs of his day. Salvian, however, actually considers the barbarian invaders deserving of their conquest because of their moral superiority. See *De gub.*, vi. 2, vii. 9–11, and, on the virtues of the barbarians, vii. 20.

18. See, for example, *De gub.*, vi. 13. Like the exemplary reading of the Bible, this exegetical device remains at the literal level of interpretations. See above, Chapter I, notes 39–40 and corresponding text.

19. See above, Chapter I, note 2, for a list of works in which

may be studied the fascinating story of the conversion and civilizing of the barbarians. Jordanes calls himself in his *Gothic History* (1. 266) "an unlearned man before my conversion."

20. See C. C. Mierow's translation of Jordanes, Introduction, p. 15. M. L. W. Laistner (*Thought and Letters in Western Europe, 500–900*, pp. 95–96) says of Cassiodorus, "Eminently practical as he was, he had a genuine admiration for the new masters of Rome, and loyally promoted the policy of the Ostrogothic rulers so to harmonize Gothic and Roman interests as to form an inwardly united body politic."

21. See Mierow, p. 16; the eastern emperor, Justinian, had conquered the Goths in 540 A.D., and Jordanes tactfully concludes his history (Conc., Sec. 315) with lavish praise both for the Goths and for their conqueror, who shall now be called "Vandalicus, Africanus and Geticus."

22. Williams (tr., *De exc.*, p. 19) points out that the details of the narrative here correspond neither to the expeditions of Caesar nor to those of Claudius, and he suggests that Gildas had in mind the arrival in Britain of Hadrian in 122 A.D., after the Parthian peace in 117. It is quite possible, however, that the British monk is simply introducing the Romans in a manner which immediately exemplifies their relationship to the Britons, i.e., as bringers of a universal *human* order to an island that refuses to receive it.

23. See p. 18: "Non acies flammae quodammodo rigidi tenoris ad occidentem caeruleo oceani torrente potuit vel cohiberi vel extingui . . ."

24. Gildas, applying to Britain a quotation from Vergil, summarizes the episode as proving that the Britons are neither strong in war nor trustworthy in peace ("Britanni nec in bello fortes sint nec in pace fideles").

25. *De exc.*, 18 (p. 36): "The Romans, therefore, declare to our country that they could not be troubled too frequently by arduous expeditions of that kind, nor could the marks of Roman power, that is an army of such size and character, be harassed by land and sea on account of unwarlike, roving, thieving fellows [imbelles erraticosque latrunculos]."

26. When they rescue the Britons for the second time, for example, Gildas says (p. 35) that they were "moved, as far as was possible for human nature, by the tale of such a tragedy [quantum humanae naturae possibile est, commodi tantae historia tragoediae]."

27. *De exc.*, 6, 16, 17.

28. *Ibid.*, 19, 22, 23.

29. *Ibid.*, 11, 19, 25. In the latter chapter, for example, Gildas speaks of those who, "trusting their lives, always with apprehension of mind, to high hills, overhanging, precipitous, and fortified, and to dense forests and rocks of the sea, remained in their native land" despite the Saxon conquest (pp. 59–61). This picture of the natural world of Britain contrasts with the presentation of Britain both as a *locus amoenus* defiled by its sinful inhabitants (Chap. 3) and as an icebound land in grave need of the warming sun of Christ (Chap. 8). Nature for Gildas is a flexible rhetorical concept, usable in a variety of ways to fit a variety of narrative needs.

30. *Ibid.*, 17 (p. 34): "nomenque Romanorum, quod verbis tantum apud eos auribus resultabat, vel exterarum gentium opprobrio obrosum vilesceret."

31. *Ibid.*, 9 (p. 22): "[praecepta Christi] ab incolis tepide suscepta sunt."

32. Gildas' source for this episode is the Latin translation by Rufinus of Eusebius' *Ecclesiastical History;* he avoids specifying the role of Roman authority in the persecution, and refers to the emperor Diocletian as a *tyrannus*, or illegal ruler.

33. See Jean Daniélou, *From Shadows to Reality*, pp. 261–75.

34. *De exc.*, 10 (pp. 24–26): "[Deus] gratuito munere . . . clarissimos lampades sanctorum martyrum nobis accendit . . .: sanctum Albanum Verolamiensem, etc."

35. *Ibid.*, 13. Gildas' implication that Maximus is a Briton is a distortion of his main source, Orosius; in the latter account, Maximus is a Spaniard.

36. Gildas refers to Britain in Chap. 12 as sick and poisoned, and speaks later (Chap. 21) of Christ as the true healer of all men ("vero omnium medico") whom the sinful Britons ignore.

37. See p. 54: "Inde germen iniquitatis, radix amaritudinis, virulenta plantatio nostris condigna meritis, in nostro cespite, ferocibus palmitibus pampinisque pullulat."

38. See p. 56: "Degeneraverat tunc vinea illa olim bona in amaritudinem, uti raro, secundum prophetam, videretur quasi post tergum vindemiatorum aut messorum racemus vel spica."

39. *De exc.*, 12, 16, 19, 21, 23.

40. At this point Gildas combines in one passage the main pejorative strains of imagery he has so far used: the Saxons are "dogs," and

grow like a "poisonous plant" in British soil (p. 54). The cumulative associations of each of the images impart great force to the passage in which they are brought together.

41. *De exc.*, 21, 22, 24 (prophecies fulfilled from Isaiah 1:5–6; 19:11, 13; 22:12–13; Psalms 74:7, 79:1).

42. See p. 60: "Ex eo tempore nunc cives, nunc hostes, vincebant, ut in ista gente experiretur dominus solito more praesentem Israelem, utrum diligat eum an non."

43. *De exc.*, 22.

44. *Ibid.*, 21. Gildas here describes the sins of the Britons in terms of the rhetorical *topos* of the "world turned upside down." On this *topos* see Curtius, pp. 94–98.

45. Gildas' knowledge of Eusebius (in the translation by Rufinus) is beyond dispute. He even mentions the work (*De exc.*, Chap. 9, p. 24, "ecclesiastica historia narrat"; see Williams' note to the passage).

46. *De exc.*, 25: "[Ambrosius] qui solus forte Romanae gentis tantae tempestatis collisione . . . superfuerat."

47. *Ibid.;* "Cuius nunc temporibus nostris suboles magnopere avita bonitate degeneravit."

48. See the opening words of the hortatory section of *De exc.* (Chap. 27): "Reges habet Britannia, sed tyrannos."

49. See Williams' note 1, p. 64.

50. *De exc.*, 25, p. 64; Gildas speaks of those whose prayers are supporting *nostra infirmitas*, which I read as referring collectively to Britain, not (as does Williams) simply to Gildas himself.

51. *De exc.*, 1 (pp. 2–4). The examples include: the denial to Moses of the sight of the promised land because of a moment of doubt (Num. 20:12); the punishment of the Israelites, in spite of God's promises to them, because of their transgressions; the sudden death of the two sons of Aaron for bringing strange fire to the altar of the Lord (Lev. 10:1–2); the disastrous consequences of Israel's breaking her oath to the Gibeonites (II Sam. 21:1); and the prophetic activities of Jeremiah and the other prophets, who were forced by the sins of Israel to utter their warnings.

52. See p. 7: "If the Lord did not spare a people, peculiar out of all the nations, the royal seed and holy nation . . . what will he do to such blackness as we have in this age?"

53. See p. 5: "These passages and many others I regarded as, in a way, a mirror of our life, in the Scriptures of the Old Testament, and then I turned to the Scriptures of the New; there I read things

that previously had perhaps been dark to me, in clearer light, because the shadow passed away, and the truth shone more steadily."

54. Paul uses it to refer to the way in which this life prefigures our life with God (I Cor. 13:12).

55. P. 7. He makes specific reference to Matthew, Acts, Romans, and Revelation. Note the appearance here of the (biblical) images of the sheep and the tree, which figure so largely in the rhetorical structure of the historical section of *De exc.*

56. Most of the New Testament texts cited by Gildas in this chapter have primarily an eschatological significance.

57. P. 7. The syntax is extremely tortured in this passage, but this seems the best sense.

58. Num. 22.

59. P. 8: "In zelo igitur domus Domini sacrae legis."

60. The story of Balaam's ass also serves as an expression of Gildas' modesty (he hesitates to speak as a man, "of a rational origin second to the angels"), and as a biblical *exemplum* of truth-telling to be imitated. In choosing the incident as a climactic one in his own life, Gildas undoubtedly did not analyze its various levels separately, as we must do today to understand its significance for him.

61. Constantine (Chaps. 28–29), Aurelius Caninus (30), Vortipor (31), Cuneglas (32), Maclocunus (33–36).

62. See *De exc.*, 29 (p. 71): "For if thou despisest these admonitions, know that thou shalt even soon be whirled around and burnt in hell's indescribable dark floods of fire." *Ibid.*, 30 (p. 73): "But if [you refuse to repent] eternal pains await thee, who shalt be always tormented, without being consumed, in the dread jaws of hell." Etc.

63. For an example of the interchangeability of levels in traditional exegesis, see *De exc.*, 36 (p. 84), where Gildas interprets a prophetic text (Lam. 18:8) addressed to the sinful Israel (*gens*) as applicable to the individual Christian (*peccator*).

64. *De exc.*, 32 (p. 75; italics mine).

65. See above, note 8.

66. Williams, n. 1, pp. 64–65, quotes a passage from a homily of Wulfstan, the 11th-century Anglo-Saxon bishop, in which Gildas is recognized as a prophet with a message for all time. See also two letters from Alcuin, the Anglo-Saxon companion of Charlemagne, which imply similar recognition (quoted in Williams, II, 415).

67. Bede refers to him as "historicus [Brittonum] Gildus" (*HE*, i. 22).

Chapter III. Bede's Historia ecclesiastica gentis
Anglorum: *Britannia Renovata*

1. All references to the *Historia ecclesiastica* (*HE*) and Latin quotations are to book and chapter numbers in Plummer's edition; all English translations are based on the Jane revision of the Stevens translation.

2. See, for example, R. W. Chambers, "Bede," *Man's Unconquerable Mind,* p. 26; C. W. Jones, ed., *Bedae opera de temporibus,* Introduction, p. 125; and E. W. Watson, "The Age of Bede," in A. H. Thompson, ed., *Bede, His Life, Times, and Writings,* pp. 39–59.

3. Daniélou and Marrou mention, as a comment on the connection, "the curious distinction" made in sixth-century Irish monasticism "between red martyrdom—the bloody martyrdom of persecution—and white or green martyrdoms, which were attained by a life of renunciation and mortification." (Jean Daniélou and Henri Marrou, *The First Six Hundred Years,* Vol. I of *The Christian Centuries: A New History of the Catholic Church,* p. 270.)

4. See especially Athanasius' *Life of St. Anthony* (*ca.* 360 A.D.?), and Jerome's *Life of Paul the Hermit* (*ca.* 380 A.D.?), both available in Roy J. Deferrari, ed., *Early Christian Biographies,* pp. 133–216, 225–38. Interestingly enough, the latter "biography" begins with accounts, unrelated to Paul's life, of two martyrdoms.

5. The chronological table provided by P. de Labriolle, *The Church in the Christian Empire,* pp. 447–54, and that of Décarreaux, pp. 372–77, summarize the order of events in the early history of monasticism, but disagree on the date of the foundation of Pachomius' first monastery, the former proposing 323, the latter 307.

6. See De Labriolle, *The Church,* pp. 482–91; Jean Décarreaux, *Les moines et la civilisation,* pp. 110–50.

7. See J. Leclercq, *The Love of Learning and the Desire for God,* pp. 19–32, and Décarreaux, pp. 204–23; M. L. W. Laistner, in *Thought and Letters in Europe, 500–900,* pp. 91–95, discusses the Rule of St. Benedict and gives further references in his notes.

8. See the forceful statements of this idea, based on Pope Gregory's *Life of St. Benedict,* by C. W. Jones, *Saints' Lives and Chronicles,* pp. 1–4, "Benedict leaves the world," and by Leclercq, pp. 19–20, 27–28.

9. "Indeed the one end of monastic life is the search for God. . . . In order to obtain eternal life, of which St. Benedict speaks so often as the only end which has any importance, one must become detached from all immediate interests, devoting oneself in silence and in withdrawal from the world to prayer and asceticism. . . . According to St. Benedict, monastic life is entirely disinterested; its reason for existing is to further the salvation of the monk, his search for God, and not for any practical or social end which, incidentally, is never even mentioned. The *conversatio* of the monk is presumed to be a *conversio* similar to St. Benedict's which entails total renunciation with the intention of pleasing God alone." (Leclercq, pp. 27–28.)

10. See Norman Cantor, *Medieval History*, pp. 119–31. According to Dom Ursmer Berlière, *L'ordre monastique des origines au XII*[e] *siècle*, p. 45, the Benedictine monastery "was a little State, which could serve as a model for the new Christian society which was arising from the fusion of the conquered and conquering races—a little State which had for its basis, religion; for its support, the honour given to work; for its crown a new intellectual and artistic culture." (Translated in R. W. Chambers, *Thomas More*, pp. 137–38.)

11. W. C. Bark, *Origins of the Medieval World*, pp. 110–16, stresses the "pioneering" work of the monks in spreading the new medieval social ideal along the frontiers of post-Roman Europe.

12. Leclercq, pp. 19–151, discusses the attention to learning inherent in the monastic discipline as it developed from the *Rule* of St. Benedict; on the preservation, study, and propagation of the classics, see especially pp. 116–51.

13. D. Knowles, *The Monastic Order in England*, pp. 3–25, emphasizes this point.

14. On the work of Cassiodorus (*ca.* 490–*ca.* 580), who stressed the preservation and study of literature in his approach to the monastic life, see Laistner, *Thought and Letters*, pp. 95–103, Décarreaux, pp. 223–35. Leclercq, pp. 76–115, 153–88, discusses the continuation and adaptation of patristic exegesis in monastic studies, and the consequent attitude of monastic writers toward history, hagiography, etc.

15. The brief account given here depends on the following works, which should be consulted for further details about the conversion of the Anglo-Saxons and the growth of the English church: Décarreaux, pp. 244–57; Peter Hunter Blair, *An Introduction to Anglo-Saxon England*, pp. 116–61; F. Stenton, *Anglo-Saxon England*, pp.

96–129; M. Deanesley, *The Pre-Conquest Church in England*, pp. 61–82.

16. Bede describes the circumstances under which the Scottish missionaries, headed by Aidan, were summoned to England by King Oswald of Northumbria in 635. See *HE*, iii. 3, and A. H. Thompson, "Northumbrian Monasticism," *Bede*, pp. 60–77.

17. Laistner, *Thought and Letters*, p. 103.

18. Cantor, pp. 201–12, speaks of the "colonial phenomenon" of the English church, on the edge of the civilized world, being so vigorous a supporter of Roman primacy.

19. See E. S. Duckett, *Anglo-Saxon Saints and Scholars*, pp. 217–24, 230–38, on Biscop.

20. See Duckett, *Saints and Scholars*, "Boniface of Devon," pp. 339–445, for the story of one such hero.

21. My references here are to the translation of O. M. Dalton. On Bede's knowledge of Gregory, see A. S. Cook, "Bede and Gregory of Tours," *PQ*, VI (1927), 315–16.

22. Laistner, *Thought and Letters*, p. 129, mentions the passage in Gregory's history in which the author dismisses a cleric, saying "the wretch was ignorant that all the bishops but five who held the see of Tours were connected with my family."

23. On the extent of Gregory's episcopal involvement in the life of his region, see R.-A. Meunier, *Grégoire de Tours et l'histoire morale du centre-ouest de la France*.

24. By W. Levison, "Bede the Historian," in Thompson, ed., *Bede*, p. 133. Cf. J. M. Wallace-Hadrill, "The Work of Gregory of Tours in the Light of Modern Research," *TRHS* (5th ser.), I (1951), 31: "Gregory became a historian because the Catholic communities in Gaul seemed to him to stand in imminent danger; the times were bad enough to call forth an explanation: his own church, the church of Tours, required it." Thus presented, Gregory's motives resemble those of Salvian and Gildas before him.

25. See the opening lines of Book ii., where Gregory uses examples drawn from historical narrative in the Bible to furnish support for the method he will follow in recounting the specifically Frankish history of the following books. Other authorities appealed to in this passage as precedents for his narrative method include Eusebius and Orosius.

26. Again he uses Orosius to buttress his analysis; see Dalton's tr. of Gregory's *Historia Francorum*, II, 168.

27. *Ibid.* (to the kings of the Franks): "Beware of discord, beware of civil wars that crush both yourselves and your people. . . . If thou, O king, hast delight in civil war, practise that war which, according to the apostle, is waged in the heart of every man, that the Spirit may strive against the flesh, that vices may yield before virtues, and thou thyself, as one set free, mayst serve thy head, which is Christ, even thou who once in thy chains didst serve the root of all evil."

28. On Gregory as hagiographer-historian, see J. M. Wallace-Hadrill, "Gregory of Tours," pp. 26–31.

29. *Historia Francorum*, ii. 18–32.

30. See L. Halphen, "Grégoire de Tours, historien de Clovis," *Mélanges d'histoire du moyen age*, pp. 235–44.

31. J. M. Wallace-Hadrill ("Gregory of Tours," p. 39) points out that Gregory shifted the conversion of Clovis from its actual date to one a decade earlier, "and by doing so made it appear that Clovis had undertaken all his great campaigns as a Catholic."

32. In the preface to Book i., Gregory says he will "write about the wars of the kings with hostile peoples, of the martyrs with the heathen, and of the churches with the heretics" (quoted by J. M. Wallace-Hadrill, "Gregory of Tours," p. 32). On Christian opposing Arian, see ii. 2; on bishop opposing king, v. 36; father opposing son and wife husband, iv. 13, iii. 5, v. 28, vi. 7; city opposing city, vii. 2—and on strife between factions of a convent, ix. 39 f.

33. See Erich Auerbach, "Sicharius and Chramnesindus," *Mimesis*, p. 79.

34. In the preface of Book ii., Gregory almost apologizes for his awareness of the dualities of history, and therefore of his work: "I think it will not be held unreasonable that I recount the happy lives of blessed men amid the disasters of the unfortunate, since this follows not from the carelessness of the writer but the course of events as they befell."

35. Auerbach, "Sicharius," pp. 77, 78, 79.

36. Cantor, p. 51, points out that in "a breakthrough of realism, . . . Gregory sometimes reveals Clovis as the thug he was."

37. See, for example, W. Levison, in Thompson, ed., *Bede*, pp. 132–45, *passim*, and F. J. Foakes-Jackson, *A History of Church History*, pp. 107, 119–22.

38. See especially Gregory's *Historia* v. 34, on his difficulties with the civil power.

39. Edmond Faral, *La légende arthurienne*, I, 40–55.

40. C. W. Jones, *Saints' Lives and Chronicles in Early England*, p. 85.

41. For more detailed information about sources see Levison, in Thompson, ed., *Bede*, pp. 132–42, and Laistner, "The Library of the Venerable Bede," *ibid.*, pp. 237–66. In Plummer's text many of Bede's direct borrowings are italicized and identified, but Jones (*Saints' Lives*, pp. 39–40) issues a *caveat* on the incompleteness of Plummer's attempt.

42. W. Levison, ed., *MGH* (*scriptores rerum Merovingicarum*), VII, 225–83.

43. See, e.g., Laistner, *Thought and Letters*, p. 165.

44. C. W. Jones edited *De temporum ratione* in *Bedae opera de temporibus*, pp. 175–291, but unfortunately omitted the chronicle and the eschatological chapters. See the edition of Bede's works by J. A. Giles, VI, 270–342.

45. The other, *De tempore* (*ca.* 703), is also edited by C. W. Jones in *Bedae opera de temporibus*, pp. 295–303.

46. Plummer, pp. xli–xlii, mentions all the places in Bede's works where the idea of the *aetates mundi* is mentioned. See also J. E. Cross, "Aspects of Microcosm and Macrocosm in Old English Literature," in *Studies in Old English Literature in honor of Arthur G. Brodeur*, pp. 1–22, on the common device in Old English literature of comparing the old (sixth) age of the world with that of man. Such a comparison appears in the *De temporum ratione* chronicle, and is translated by C. W. Jones in *Saints' Lives*, p. 23.

47. *Saints' Lives*, pp. 17–18.

48. Levison, in Thompson, ed., *Bede*, pp. 121–23, rightly sees the influence of Augustine here. Typically, Bede ends his eschatological consideration of Easter with these words: "Verum de mysterio temporis paschae si quis plenius scire vult, legat beati Aurelii Augustini ad Januarium epistolam de ratione paschali."

49. Bede's exegesis needs further scholarly attention. The commentaries of C. Jenkins, "Bede as Exegete and Theologian," in Thompson, ed., *Bede*, pp. 152–200, and Plummer, pp. xlvii–lxii, are handicapped by their authors' uneasiness with the methods of patristic exegesis, all of which they lump together under the term "allegory." E. S. Duckett, *Saints and Scholars*, is more sympathetic but not rigorous. Bede's exegesis is to my knowledge discussed competently only by H. de Lubac, *Exégèse médiévale*, but the plan of the

work makes it impossible to treat Bede's exegesis separately or consecutively. See the index to Vol. I.

50. See *HE*, v. 24: "From the time I received the orders of the priesthood until the fifty-ninth year of my age, I have endeavored, for the use of me and of mine, to compile out of the works of the venerable fathers, and to interpret and explain according to their meaning, these works on the holy scriptures: [there follows a list of exegetical works]." Plummer, p. l, n. 2 and 3, gives an exhaustive list of Bede's exegetical borrowings from the fathers.

51. Plummer, pp. lvi–lviii.

52. Jones explains, "Because the early Middle Ages conceived of historical and astronomical time as a unit, chronicle and theory naturally united under a single cover. . . . The union inevitably developed from the Christian calendars under the stimulation of the catholic doctrine that physical, moral, and spiritual worlds were one and inseparable;" i.e., under the stimulation of the Christian theology of history, based on multilevel scriptural exegesis (*Opera de temporibus*, p. 114). Cf. Levison, in Thompson, ed., *Bede*, p. 123: Bede is "a theologian even when writing history."

53. A. M. 3903, 4007, 4021, 4031, 4131, 4145, 4238, 4259, 4337, 4348, 4376 (two entries bear this date, both containing British matter), 4402, 4426.

54. A. M. 3903.

55. A. M. 4426; the source is Gildas, *De exc.*, 26.

56. A. M. 4337, 4348.

57. A. M. 4402.

58. *Historia adversum paganos*, vii. 34.

59. "Confirmant antistites fidem verbo veritatis simul et miraculorum signis" (A. M. 4402).

60. ". . . Qui deinceps ad Ravennam perveniens, et summa reverentia a Valentiniano et Placidia susceptus, migravit ad Christum . . ." (*ibid.*).

61. C. W. Jones, *Saints' Lives*, pp. 22–23: ". . . Bede wanted constantly to emphasize the artificiality of the whole time structure. With this point of view every act becomes simply a phenomenon and as nothing compared with God's eternal present. Bede and the chroniclers whom he represents no doubt felt eminently justified in selecting according to personal caprice and the needs of exegesis." In other words, history is presented in the chronicle to emphasize the divine providence which orders it.

62. See *ibid.*, pp. 21–22, for an analysis of the miraculous element (or rather the lack of it) in the whole post-incarnation section of the chronicle.

63. *HE*, preface: "For if history relates good things of good men, the attentive hearer is excited to imitate that which is good, or if it mentions evil things of wicked persons, nevertheless the religious and pious hearer or reader, shunning that which is hateful and perverse, is the more earnestly excited to perform those things which he knows to be good, and worthy of God." Bede's formulation of history's exemplary value is very similar to that of Livy, though this does not necessarily mean the two writers expected their histories to support the same moral outlook. On the tradition of exemplary historiography, both Christian and pagan, see below, Chapter V, pp. 124–26.

64. Cf. his dependence upon the methods and often the words of the fathers in interpreting the scriptures, discussed above in note 50 and corresponding text.

65. Cf. Orosius, *Historiarum*, vi. 7–10; vii. 6, 15, 17, 25; Eutropius, *Breviarium*, vii. 13, 14, 19; etc.

66. On the source of Bede's *Passio Albani*, see Levison in Thompson, ed., *Bede*, p. 135 and n. 4. Levison assumes that Bede and Gildas utilized the same text as a source, which makes their divergent treatment of Alban an important key to their attitudes.

67. *HE*, i. 22: "[Brittones] qui inter alia inenarrabilium scelerum facta, quae historicus eorum Gildus flebili sermone describit, et hoc addebant, ut numquam genti Saxonum sive Anglorum, secum Brittaniam incolenti, verbum fidei praedicando committerent. Sed non tamen divina pietas plebem suam, quam praescivit, deseruit, quin multo digniores genti memoratae praecones veritatis, per quos crederet, destinavit."

68. See above, Chapter II, pp. 52–53.

69. See the end of *HE*, i. 18, for example: "Quibus ita gestis, innumera hominum eodem die ad Dominum turba conversa est."

70. *HE*, i. 17.

71. *HE*, i. 20. This is the famous "Hallelujah victory" which is won by the strategem of placing men in the hills whose shouts of "alleluia" reverberate all around the Saxon and Pictish armies, convincing them they are outnumbered. The aggressors flee, leaving their arms behind, and many drown in trying to cross a river. The narrative continues: "Triumphant pontifices hostibus fusis sine

sanguine; triumphant victoria fide obtenta, non viribus." Cf. the brief
chronicle passage on this victory, cited on p. 74, above.

72. *HE*, l. 21: "Porro Germanus post haec ad Ravennam pro pace
Armoricanae gentis supplicaturus advenit, ibique a Valentiniano et
Placidia matre ipsius summa reverentia susceptus, migravit ad Christum. Cuius corpus honorifico agmine, comitantibus virtutum operi-
bus, suam defertur ad urbem. Nec multo post Valentinianus ab Aetii
patricii, quem occiderat, satellitibus interimitur, anno imperii Mar-
ciani VI°, cum quo simul Hesperium concidit regnum." This passage is inspired by the *De temporum ratione* chronicle, where, however, it has no structural significance for Bede's account of Britain.

73. *HE*, ii. 1.

74. *Ibid.:* "Thus much may be said of his immoral genius . . . ;
other popes applied themselves to building or adorning of churches
with gold and silver, but Gregory was entirely intent upon gaining
souls."

75. *HE*, i. 26: "At ubi datam sibi mansionem intraverant [Augus-
tine and his companions], coeperunt apostolicam primitivae ecclesiae
vitam imitari . . ."

76. "[n]ova Anglorum ecclesia" (from Gregory's letter to Augustine, *HE*, i. 29).

77. *HE*, i. 27.

78. *HE*, ii. 2. After writing the following passage, I read Prof. N.
K. Chadwick's treatment of the same incident in *Celt and Saxon*, and
was pleased to find that her analysis follows the same lines as mine.

79. *HE*, ii. 2: "[Augustinus] coepitque eis fraterna admonitione
suadere, ut pace catholica secum habita communem evangelizandi
gentibus pro Domino laborem susciperent."

80. *Ibid.:* ". . . deprecans, ut visum caeco, quem amiserat, resti-
tueret, et per inluminationem unius hominis corporalem, in pluri-
morum corde fidelium spiritalis gratiam lucis accenderet."

81. *Ibid.:* "Quibus vir Domini Augustinus fertur minitans prae-
dixisse, quia, si pacem cum fratribus accipere nollent, bellum ab
hostibus forent accepturi; et, si nationi Anglorum noluissent viam
vitae praedicare, per horum manus ultionem essent mortis passuri."

82. *Ibid.:* "Sicque conpletum est praesagium sancti pontificis Augustini, ut etiam temporalis interitus ultione sentirent perfidi, quod
oblata sibi perpetuae salutis consilia spreverant."

83. At the synod at Whitby Wilfrid, champion of the Roman
cause, refers to the Picts, Scots, and Britons as those who "in these

two remote islands of the ocean, and only in part even of them, oppose all the rest of the universe" (*HE*, iii. 25).

84. As Bede puts it, with deliberate casualness, "factumque est, ut venientibus illis sederet Augustinus in sella" (*HE*, ii. 2).

85. The anchorite is himself a figure of the isolated British church; Prof. Chadwick, *Celt*, p. 170, speaking of the incident, refers to "the pre-eminence accorded to the anchorite above all the *episcopi* and *viri doctissimi* as adviser to the Bangor monks in a matter of highest ecclesiastical importance, while at the same time his counsel is represented as the source of the ultimate disaster to the Britons." She suggests, though, that Bede was here merely reproducing the attitude of his source, which is perhaps a questionable conclusion considering Bede's attitude toward the British church throughout *HE*.

86. Plummer, p. lviii, mentions passages in Bede's exegetical works which reject a mere literal interpretation of the words of the scriptures as "Iudaico more"; the spirit of the Old Testament, revealed by multilevel exegesis, is what matters.

87. *HE*, iii. 25.

88. This was, in fact, a continual moot point throughout the early church. See the excellent discussion of this complicated matter in C. W. Jones, *Baedae opera de temporibus*, pp. 6–122. Jones points out (pp. 103–4) that the synod was also summoned to consider practical difficulties of a chronological nature: since the Roman and Celtic churches used different cycles to compute their liturgical calendars, a large scale divergence was imminent which would have introduced chaos into the English church's observances.

89. See *HE*, ii. 2 and iii. 26. Compare the less dramatic treatment in Eddius' *Life of Wilfred*, ed. by B. Colgrave, pp. 20–23, for an indication of how Bede's historical vision transformed this scene.

90. *HE*, iii. 25: "Primusque rex Osuiu praemissa praefatione, quod oporteret eos, qui uni Deo servirent, unam vivendi regulam tenere, nec discrepare in celebratione sacramentorum caelestium, qui unum omnes in caelis regnum expectarent."

91. *Ibid.*: "Neque haec evangelica et apostolica traditio legem solvit, sed potius adimplet, in qua observandum pascha a XIIII[a] luna primi mensis ad vesperam usque ad XXI[am] lunam eiusdem mensis ad vesperam praeceptum est; in quam observationam imitandam omnes beati Johannis successores in Asia post obitum eius, et omnis per orbem ecclesia conversa est."

92. Matthew 7:22–23.

93. Matthew 16:18–19.

94. Oswy says, *HE*, iii. 25, "And I also say unto you, that [Peter] is the door-keeper, whom I will not contradict, but will, as far as I know and am able, in all things obey his decrees, lest, when I come to the gates of the kingdom of heaven, there should be none to open them, he being my adversary who is proved to have the keys."

95. The "Hallelujah victory" of Germanus (*HE*, i. 20) is a possible exception, with its reminiscence of Joshua and the walls of Jericho. Bede, as we have seen, borrowed this episode for other reasons.

96. *HE*, i. 32. "For even so Constantine, our most pious emperor, recovering the Roman commonwealth from the perverse worship of idols, subjected the same with himself to our Almighty God and Lord Jesus Christ, and was himself with the people under his subjection, entirely converted to Him. Whence it followed, that his praises transcended the fame of former princes; and he as much excelled his predecessors in renown as he did in good works. Now, therefore, let your glory hasten to infuse into the kings and people that are subject to you, the knowledge of one God, Father, Son, and Holy Ghost; that you may both surpass the ancient kings of your nation in praise and merit, and become by so much the more secure against your own sins before the dreadful judgment of Almighty God, as you shall wipe away the sins of others in your subjects."

97. *HE*, i. 34.

98. *Ibid.*, iii. 1 ff.

99. *HE*, iii. 1: "impia manu, sed justa ultione."

100. *Ibid.*

101. *Ibid.*, iii. 2.

102. *Ibid.*, iii. 3.

103. *HE*, iii. 6: "King Oswald, with the nation of the English which he governed being instructed by the teaching of this most reverend prelate [Aidan, the Irish bishop], not only learned to hope for a heavenly kingdom unknown to his progenitors, but also obtained of the same one Almighty God, who made heaven and earth, larger earthly kingdoms than any of his ancestors."

104. *HE*, iv. 26 [28]: "When [Cuthbert] had served God in solitude many years, the mound which encompassed his habitation being so high, that he could from thence see nothing but heaven, to which

he so ardently aspired, it happened that when a great synod had been assembled in the presence of King Egfrid, near the river Alne, at a place called Twyford, which signifies 'the two fords,' in which Archbishop Theodore, of blessed memory, presided, Cuthbert was, by the unanimous consent of all, chosen bishop of the church of Lindisfarne. They could not, however, persuade him to leave his monastery, though many messengers and letters were sent to him; at last the aforesaid king himself, with the most holy Bishop Trumwine, and other religious and great men, passed over into the island; many also of the brothers of the same isle of Lindisfarne assembled together for the same purpose: they all knelt, conjured him by our Lord, and with tears and entreaties, till they drew him, also in tears, from his retreat, and forced him to the synod. Being arrived there, after much opposition, he was overcome by the unanimous resolution of all present, and submitted to take upon himself the episcopal dignity. . . ."

105. *HE*, iv. 25 [27].

106. The *Epistola ad Ecgberctum* appears in C. Plummer, ed., *Venerabilis Baedae opera historica*, I, 405–23.

107. See, for example, *Epistola*, ii, v, ix, xi ff.

108. *HE*, iv. 1 ff.

109. *Ibid.*, iv. 2: "Nor were there ever happier times since the English came into Britain; for their kings, being brave men and good Christians, they were a terror to all barbarous nations, and the minds of all men were bent upon the joys of the heavenly kingdom of which they had just heard; and all who desired to be instructed in sacred reading had masters at hand to teach them." Note the re-iterated parallel between the secure earthly kingdom, headed by Christian kings, and the "joys of the heavenly kingdom" which the inhabitants of the Christian society keenly anticipate; Bede obviously intends the first as an earthly prefiguration of the second, with the "good Christian" serving as the exegetical link between the two.

110. *Ibid.*, "Wilfrid . . . was the first of the bishops of the English nation that taught the churches of the English the Catholic mode of life."

111. *Ibid.* "Maxime autem modulandi in ecclesia more Romanorum, quem a discipulis beati papae Gregorii didicerat, peritum."

112. *HE*, iv. 16 [18].

113. *HE*, v. 20: "Nam et ipse episcopus Acca cantator erat peritis-

simus, quomodo etiam in litteris sanctis doctissimus et in catholicae fidei confessione castissimus, in ecclesiasticae quoque institutionis regulis solertissimus existerat; . . . cum [Wilfrido] etiam Roman veniens multa illic, quae in patria nequiverat, ecclesiae sanctae institutis utilia didicit."

114. C. L. Wrenn, "The Poetry of Caedmon," *Proc. Brit. Acad.,* XXXII (1946), 277–95.

115. *HE*, iv. 22 [24]: In his biblical songs, Caedmon "endeavored to turn away all men from the love of vice, and to excite in them the love of, and application to, good actions;" his task is the same as the historian's.

116. *HE*, v. 9: "At that time the venerable priest and servant of Christ, Ecgberct, whose very name should be held in esteem, and who . . . lived the life of a pilgrim in Ireland to obtain a final home [*patria*] in heaven, proposed to himself to do good to many, by taking upon him the apostolical work, and preaching the word of God to some of those nations that had not yet heard it. . . ." On Ecgberct see also iii. 4, 27; iv. 3, 24 [26].

117. See *HE*, iii. 4, where Bede describes how Ecgberct brings the Picts to the correct observance of the time of Easter, i.e., brings them into the universal church.

118. *Ibid.:* "Returning then to the beloved place of his peregrination [i.e., the cell in which he had previously resided], he gave himself up to our Lord in his wonted repose, and since he could not be profitable to strangers by teaching them the faith, he took care to be the more useful to his own people by the example of his virtue."

119. *HE,* v. 10–11.

Chapter IV. Historia Brittonum: *Heroes and Villains versus Saints and Sinners*

1. All references to the *Historia Brittonum* (*HB*) in this chapter, unless otherwise stated, are to chapter numbers in MS Harleian 3859, as printed in F. Lot, *Nennius et l'Historia Brittonum* (based on the edition of T. Mommsen in *MGH*). I have also consulted the Chartres MS in Lot, and Edmond Faral's printing of the Harleian and Chartres texts in *La légende arthurienne,* Vol. III. Translations are based on A. W. Wade-Evans, *Nennius' History of the Britons.*

2. Lot, pp. 1–143, takes note of all relevant scholarship to his day. On the most important recent studies, those of N. K. and H. M. Chadwick, see below, *passim*.

3. I adopt the categorization and symbols of T. Mommsen, pp. 112–42, which are summarized by Lot, pp. 1–5.

4. See Lot, p. 1.

5. Bishop of Bangor, who converted the British church to the observation of the Roman date of Easter in 768, and died in 809. See Wade-Evans pp. 7–8, and N. K. Chadwick, "Early Culture and Learning in North Wales," in N. K. Chadwick, *Studies in the Early British Church*, pp. 43–44, 91–93.

6. See Lot, p. 2. The text of MS Z stops in mid-sentence in Chap. 37.

7. The corrupt heading of the MS is printed by Lot, p. 227. On its interpretation, see *ibid.*, pp. 22–23.

8. See N. K. Chadwick, "Early Culture," pp. 112–15; Wade-Evans, pp. 11–12.

9. See Wade-Evans, pp. 9–10, 14–16; N. K. Chadwick, "Early Culture," pp. 37–46, and H. M. Chadwick, "Vortigern," p. 25, in N. K. Chadwick, *Studies in Early British History*. Lot's complicated consideration of dating and authorship, pp. 35–123, stresses the importance of a compilation (he thinks by Nennius) in 826, but does not deny the possibility of some bringing together of sources soon after 796. He also discusses later additions, pp. 124–28.

10. See N. K. Chadwick, "Early Culture," pp. 45–46; Wade-Evans, p. 7.

11. Zimmer, *Nennius Vindicatus*, and F. Liebermann, "Nennius the Author of the *Historia Brittonum*," in *Essays in Medieval History Presented to T. F. Tout*, give Nennius credit for the lion's share of the compilation; Lot, pp. 38–53, feels that Nennius was a late editor who added relatively little.

12. Mommsen's MSS CD² contain the reference to Nennius; see Lot, p. 3.

13. See Rachel Bromwich's comprehensive article, "The Character of Early Welsh Tradition," in N. K. Chadwick, *Studies in Early British History*, pp. 83–136, on the methods of transmission, etc.

14. Edmond Faral, *La légende arthurienne*, II, 56–220.

15. See especially her "Introduction" in *Studies in the Early British Church*, pp. 1–28. She indicates, pp. 45–46, that Nennius was credited

by his contemporaries with creating a Celtic alphabet, and mentions a similar story involving Celtic scholars and alphabets ("Early Culture," pp. 94 ff.) which underscores the keen propagandistic interest in glorifying British culture in eighth- and ninth-century Britain.

16. See "Early Culture," pp. 29–36: "Antiquarian Speculation. Origin Legends." On the culmination of this movement in the kingship of Rhodri Mawr, who unified many of the smaller Welsh kingdoms and fought vigorously against the Saxons, see *ibid.*, pp. 79–93.

17. *Ibid.*, pp. 93–118.

18. *Ibid.*, p. 36: "It would seem that about the beginning of the ninth century a new intellectual impetus was at work throughout the Celtic lands, resulting in the 'origin' stories discussed above. The effect of this new intellectual activity was the record of the native traditions and their expansion, by means of inference and speculation, with the aim of creating a great national past."

19. N. K. Chadwick, "Introduction" in *Early British Church*, pp. 16–17; "Early Culture," pp. 84 ff.

20. All references are to the translation of W. D. Foulke.

21. He was born *ca.* 720, and, after a life at court, became a monk at about age fifty, continuing, however, to involve himself in worldly activities, including a trip to Charlemagne's court. He died after 792. See M. L. W. Laistner, *Thought and Letters in Western Europe, A.D. 500–900*, pp. 268–71, on his various writings.

22. H. M. Chadwick, *The Heroic Age in Literature*, remains the standard work on the shared heritage of heroic tradition among the barbarian nations. According to Chadwick (pp. 9–10), Paul's history is the most valuable testimony to Langobardic involvement in the heroic legacy; he also notes that Paul's mention (*Hist. Lang.*, i. 27) of heroic songs sung in many nations about Alboin, a Langobardic king who died *ca.* 572, provides the latest known date for the existence of the international heroic tradition.

23. See *Hist. Lang.*, ii. 5 (the invitation sent to the Langobards by Narses, their reaction to it, and the heavenly portents of their invasion of Italy); i. 7 (the Langobard leaders "determine that it is better to maintain liberty by arms than to stain it by the payment of tribute"; cf. i. 10, 12, 13); i. 17 (the speech of king Lamissio to the Langobards), etc.

24. See, for instance, *Hist. Lang.*, iii. 1–2 (the story of St. Hospitius), which introduces briefly the themes of national punishment for national sin and of the historical importance of the saintly Chris-

tian who understands and implements the providential course of history; cf. *Hist. Franc.*, vi. 6.

25. *Hist. Lang.*, v. 10–11.

26. The action of the campaign covers the years 662–668.

27. See the opening words of *Hist. Lang.*: "The region of the north, in proportion as it is removed from the heat of the sun and is chilled with snow and frost, is so much the more healthful to the bodies of men and fitted for the propagation of nations, just as, on the other hand, every southern region, the nearer it is to the heat of the sun, the more it abounds in diseases and is less fitted for the bringing up of the human race." The barbarians, of course, are of northern origin.

28. It is ironic that, in Paul's view, the barbarians are defeated by the empire because of their sins; the position of Salvian and of Gildas has been completely reversed over the course of the centuries.

29. For two recent (and divergent) interpretations see Norman Cantor, *Medieval History*, pp. 214–24, and J. M. Wallace-Hadrill, *The Barbarian West*, pp. 113–16.

30. This idea developed in the dealings between the papacy and the Frankish mayors of the palace, who ousted the legitimate but feeble-minded Merovingian dynasty and pledged support to the pope, who, in return, had St. Boniface consecrate and crown Pepin the first Carolingian monarch in 753. See W. Mohr, *Die karolingische Reichsidee*, pp. 18 ff. Peter Munz (*The Origins of the Carolingian Empire*, p. 4) feels that Charles himself held a form of this theory.

31. See Munz, pp. 5–10; Mohr, pp. 58–61. J. M. Wallace-Hadrill, *West*, p. 113, assumes that Charles had fallen under the influence of Alcuin's imperial ideas by the time of his coronation.

32. See *De civ.*, v. 25; Mohr, pp. 42–44; J. M. Wallace-Hadrill, *West*, pp. 103–4. Einhard remarks in his *Vita Karoli Magni*, Chap. 24, that Charles was an avid student of *De civ.*

33. See Munz. His ingenious attempt suffers from a lack of equally convincing evidence for the existence of all the factions.

34. Mohr, pp. 39–47, emphasizes the anti-Byzantine policy of Charles in the last two decades of the eighth century; see also Munz, pp. 11–13.

35. In *Medieval History*, p. 213, Cantor states: "The solution to the enigmatic character of Carolingian history lies in perceiving that eighth- and ninth-century Europe belongs to the general form of an underdeveloped, preindustrial society which is only beginning to

benefit from intelligent leaders." He also speaks of "the deep traditions of disorder, localism, and violence in the underdeveloped society."

36. Cf. *De gestis Karoli,* the "imperial hagiography" written by a
monk of St. Gall in the second half of the ninth century. Its anti-
Byzantine feelings are precisely the same as Paul's.

37. J. M. Wallace-Hadrill, *West,* p. 108, concludes his discussion
of the studies of the day by saying, "Altogether, if attention is
focussed on Biblical studies as the central theme of the Carolingian
revival, its other facets fall into their proper places, and one begins
to see what is meant by calling it modest and practical, and how innumerable its roots were. This was no New Athens finer than the
Old: it was intellectual reform and textual criticism as the indispensable preliminary to the reform of the clergy and to the per-
formance of the *opus Dei.*"

38. H. M. Chadwick, "Vortigern," pp. 21–46.

39. *Germania,* ii, quoted by Edmond Faral in *La légende arthurienne,* I, 82–83.

40. I omit the genealogies of British and Saxon royal houses which
appear in the latter part of MS H, as these are more clearly factual.
See Lot, pp. 91–96; Wade-Evans, pp. 25–26, 32.

41. In what follows I have avoided the question of the order of
composition of these origin stories. Zimmer, Faral, Lot, and other
scholars all discuss this question, but their conclusions are very diverse.

42. The process of inventing national origin stories, to which I
refer here, is to be distinguished from the utilization by barbarian
historians of the heroic traditions of national antiquity. The former
is a conscious, learned act of literary creation growing out of what
N. K. Chadwick calls "antiquarian speculation," while the latter is a
shaping of an existing body of oral sources left as the legacy of what
H. M. Chadwick calls the "heroic age."

43. Lot, p. 228.

44. On the widespread creation of stories linking European nations to the Trojans, see Faral, I, 171 ff.

45. According to MS M, he is "consul imperii romani"!

46. MS M reads "et postea tenuit Britanniam insulam quam habita-
bant Britones filii Romanorum, olim Silvio Posthumo orti." The
other MSS are corrupt and unclear at this point (see Lot, p. 228, and
Faral, III, 8). At the end of the section in all MSS is the sentence,

"set a Bruto Britones et de stirpe Bruti surrexerunt." G. Thurneysen (in his review of H. Zimmer's *Nennius vindicatus* appearing in Z. f. d. Ph., XXVIII [1896], 87–89), first pointed out that this sentence may be a later insertion.

47. Faral, I, 172–74, attributes the inspiration for this episode to the Trojan origin of the Franks found in the second continuation of the Frankish chronicle of "Fredegarius" (seventh century). He also states his belief that the author was a cleric, and was expressing the ambitions of the papacy—ambitions which culminated in the coronation of Charles.

48. *HB*, 10. It begins, "In annalibus autem Romanorum scriptum est . . ."

49. Variant readings in some MSS make Silvius the son of Ascanius, son of Aeneas. See Faral, I, 193 ff. and Lot, p. 153, note 4.

50. "Exosus omnibus hominibus."

51. "[Brutus] expulsus est ab Italia . . . et venit ad insulas maris Tyrreni et expulsus est a Graecis causa occisionis Turni, quem Aeneas occiderat. Et pervenit ad Gallos usque et ibi condidit civitatem Turonorum, quae vocatur Turnis. Et poste ad istam pervenit insulam quae a nomine suo accepit nomen, id est Brittanniam, et implevit eam cum suo genere et habitavit ibi. Ab illo autem die habitata est Brittania usque in hodiernum diem."

52. The story of Brutus can actually be regarded as an interesting variant of the "loss and recovery" narrative pattern of romance. Brutus "recovers" his stature and home, but only by leaving his original environment forever and creating a new one as a pioneer hero.

53. *HB*, 17. Lot, pp. 10, 38 ff., claims that this list belongs in Chapter 10.

54. "Fraenkische Voelkertafel," ed. K. Muellenhof, *Abhandlungen der k. Akademie der Wissenschaften*, p. 532. See Faral, I, 82–84.

55. "Hessitio autem habuit filios quattuor, hi sunt: Francus, Romanus, Britto, Alamannus. . . . Ab Hisitione autem ortae sunt quattuor gentes: Franci, Latini, Alamanni et Britti."

56. The genealogy goes back to Adam, "filii Dei vivi."

57. *HB*, 18. See Faral, I, 183–84, on this combination of sources.

58. See Lot, p. 162, note 1.

59. I do not mean to imply that it was necessarily compiled last, but merely that its position in MS H is suggestive.

60. *HB*, 12.

61. *HB*, 13–15, headed "Concerning the experiences of the Scots at the time they occupied Hibernia."

62. "Et de familia illius ciulae quae relicta est propter fractionem tota Hibernia impleta est usque in hodiernem diem."

63. *HB*, 15: "The Scots from the west and the Picts from the north fought incessantly together and with one endeavor against the Britons, because the Britons were wont to be without arms."

64. There may be a comparison intended between the struggling Scots and Brutus, who, like Abraham, has a new nation grow up from his seed in Britain (the New Israel?).

65. Cf. the origin story of Brutus the consul in MS Z, and MS H, Chap. 7: "Brittannia insula . . . a quodam Bruto consule romano dicta."

66. On this section see Wade-Evans, pp. 19–20, and footnotes, pp. 45–53. My comments depend on his analysis, which illustrates how Nennius (?) combined bits of information from Gildas with a list of seven Roman emperors reputed to have come to Britain.

67. *HB*, 15, 19; cf. Gildas, *De exc.*, 5.

68. *HB*, 19; cf. *De exc.* 4–6.

69. *HB*, 27; cf. *De exc.* 13–14. Note, however, that *HB* attributes the colonization of Brittany by "Brittones armorici" to the soldiers of Maximianus, a detail not in Gildas, and one which Geoffrey of Monmouth was later to utilize.

70. *HB*, 30; cf. *De exc.*, 15–17.

71. Wade-Evans, p. 16, characterizes *HB* as "a commentary on the 'Story of the Loss of Britain' [i.e., Gildas' historical chapters]," referring no doubt to sections like this one. But such an appellation certainly oversimplifies the relationship between the two texts.

72. The exception is Tiberius (*De exc.* 8), who grants freedom to the new religion of Christ.

73. *HB*, 21: "In tempore [Claudii] quievit dare censum Romanis a Brittannia, sed Brittannicis imperatoribus redditum est."

74. *HB*, 23: "et non multo post intra Brittanniam Severus reversus apud Eboracum cum suis ducibus occiditur." On this invented career of Severus see Lot, p. 58; Wade-Evans, p. 20.

75. *HB*, 26: "Maximus imperator regnavit in Brittania," and cf. "Claudius imperator venit et in Brittannia imperavit . . ."; "Severus, qui transfretavit ad Brittanos"; "Caritius imperator et tyrannus, qui et ipse in Brittanniam venit tyrannide." (*Ibid.*, 21, 23, 24)

76. *HB*, 27: "Propter hoc Brittannia occupata est ab extraneis

gentibus et cives expulsi sunt, usque dum Deus auxilium dederit illis."
The invocation of God's aid here seems little more than a pious turn
of phrase, indicating uncertainty of the duration of occupation.

77. *HB*, 31: "Factum est autem post supra dictum bellum quod fuit
inter Brittones et Romanos. . . ."

78. *HB*, 30: "While the Britons were being harassed by barbarian
nations, that is the Scots and the Picts, they used to solicit the aid of
the Romans. And while ambassadors were being sent with much sor-
row and were entering with dust on their heads and carrying rich
presents with them to the Consuls of the Romans to expiate the admitted crime of the murdering of the leaders, the Consuls used to
receive the gifts from them with favour, whilst they were promising
with an oath to take the yoke of Roman rule, however hard it might
be."

79. *Ibid.:* "Et Romani venerunt cum maximo exercitu ad auxilium
eorum et . . . spoliata Brittannia auro argentoque cum aere et omni
pretiosa veste et melle cum magno triumpho revertebantur.'

80. On the sources of the episode, see Lot, p. 178, note 3; on the
learned and clerical elements, see Faral, I, 118–21; and L. A. Paton,
"The Story of Vortigern's Tower," *Radcliffe College Monographs*,
XIII, 13–23.

81. Here called "Angli," an appellation otherwise foreign to *HB*.

82. *HB*, 41; his mother, when questioned, says, "I know not how
he was conceived in my womb, but one thing I know, that I have
never known a man." One would expect this parallelism with the
birth of Christ to be developed in some specifically Christian manner; in the text as we have it, this is not the case. But see note 85,
below.

83. *HB*, 42: "Et puer respondit: 'en revelatum est mihi hoc mys-
terium et ego vobis propalabo: regni tui figura tentorium est; duo
vermes duo dracones sunt; vermis rufus draco tuus est et stagnum
figura huius mundi est. At ille albus draco illius gentis quae occupavit
gentes et regiones plurimas in Brittannia et paene a mari usque ad
mare tenebunt.' "

84. *Ibid.:* "Et rex ad adolescentem dixit: 'quo nomine vocaris? '.
Ille respondit: 'Ambrosius vocor. . . . Unus est pater meus de con-
sulibus Romanicae gentis.' " Wade-Evans (p. 65, note 5) remarks
that according to *HB*, 26, "Caesars were called consuls after the time
of Maximus."

85. *Ibid.:* The text is contradictory; Ambrosius tells Guorthigirn

that the latter will not be able to build the fortress, but a few lines later we read, "Et [Guorthigirn] arcem dedit illi cum omnibus regnis occidentalis plagae Brittanniae. . . ." There may be the marks of a conflation of sources at this point.

86. See "Early Culture," pp. 83 ff., on the culmination of this nationalism and its expectations in Rhodri Mawr (d. 878).

87. Compare the figure of Brutus in the second origin story discussed above. Insofar as Brutus is isolated—and expelled—from his Italian homeland, he assumes an individuality quite distinct from the framework of Christian or national destiny. But as an eponymous hero who both founds and gives his name to a new nation, Brutus is a typical figure embodying and originating an imagined set of national virtues. He partakes of both individual excellence and national ideals, and emerges as an ambivalent figure of a kind which has always troubled categorizing critics (the enigmatic Aeneas being the prime example of the type, though not himself eponymous). The close relationship between individual excellence and traditions of national glory has always figured in western considerations of the formation of nations; it repeatedly takes the form of a parent-child relationship, either literally, as in the Brutus narrative, or metaphorically (the founding *fathers;* the *father* of his country, etc.).

88. Significantly, neither Gildas nor Bede speaks of political deposition in his consideration of the past. In their Christian systems only God can depose a king, directly or indirectly, to punish him and the nation for accumulated sins.

89. It is actually two subvariants of one Christian story; see Wade-Evans, p. 70, n. 2.

90. *HB*, 48: "Others give a different account. After all the men of his nation had risen against him on account of his crime, both the powerful and the weak, both slave and free, both monks and laity, both small and great, and whilst he himself is wandering vagrant from place to place, at last his heart broke and he died without praise."

91. *HB*, 31: "Guorthigirnus regnavit in Brittannia et dum ipse regnabat, urgebatur a metu Pictorum Scottorumque et a Romanico impetu necnon et a timore Ambrosii." Faral, I, 94, rightly remarks that the fear of Ambrosius refers back to Gildas' Ambrosius, hero of the Britons' resistance to the Saxons, and not to *HB*, 42. That the secularized Ambrosius of the latter chapter is also Roman, despite the national anti-Roman feelings revealed in the earlier secular chap-

ters, cannot be explained, except by the hypothetical conflation of sources suggested in notes 82 and 85.

92. "And in his accustomed manner St. Germanus followed him, and fasted there with all his clergy, remaining three days and as many nights on his account. And in the fourth night about the hour of midnight the whole citadel fell by fire sent suddenly from heaven, the heavenly fire burning it. And Guorthigirn, together with all who were with him and together with his wives, perished."

93. On the sources and meaning of these chapters, see further Faral, I, 92–130, and H. M. Chadwick, "Vortigern," pp. 21–46, including a "Note on the name Vortigern" by N. K. Chadwick.

94. See *HB*, 32: "Aliquanta miracula quae per illum fecit Deus scribenda decrevi." The heading of MS Z speaks of a *liber sancti Germani* from which excerpts have been taken for *HB*.

95. Countless examples of this type of hagiographic narrative were produced in early medieval Britain, with protagonists including (St.) Gildas, and with heroes such as Arthur assuming the role of sinful king! See C. G. Loomis, "King Arthur and the Saints," *Speculum*, VIII (1933), 478 ff.; J. S. P. Tatlock, *The Legendary History of Britain*, pp. 188–90.

96. "Guorthigirn received them kindly and turned over to them the island called Thanet in their language, and Ruoihm in the British language."

97. A genealogy inserted at this point traces the Saxons' leaders, Hengist and Horsa, back to a *filius Dei*, a device reminiscent of the genealogies of the Britons in *HB*, 17–18. But the difference is clear: "Non ipse est Deus Deorum . . . sed unus est ab idolis eorum quod ipsi colebant."

98. ". . . Saxones a Guorthigirno suscepti sunt, anno CCCXLVII post passionem Christi."

99. ". . . Et multi per eum salvi facti sunt et plurimi perierunt." Germanus is a type of Christ, at whose final coming many will indeed be saved and many damned. See, for example, Matt. 25:31–46. As a forerunner of the eschatological Christ, he is also a new John the Baptist, who came to preach the word in Judaea (Matt. 3:1) as Germanus does in Britain. The baptizing activities of Germanus in this episode are perhaps best viewed in this exegetical light.

100. Faral, I, 103, points out the parallels between this story and the story of Lot's rescue from Sodom in Genesis 9.

101. *HB*, 35: "Et sic evenit, et impletum est quod dictum est per

prophetam dicentem: 'suscitans de pulvere egenum, et de stercore erigens pauperem, ut sedeat cum principibus et solium gloriae teneat.' " The reference is to Psalms 102:7, 8.

102. Cf. Exodus 12:46, and John 19:36, where the prescription for the paschal lamb is shown to be a prefiguration of the crucified Christ.

103. *HB,* 39.

104. *Ibid.,* 37.

105. *HB,* 37 begins, "Hencgistus autem, cum esset vir doctus atque astutus et callidus, cum explorasset super regem inertem et super gentem illius, quae sine armis utebatur . . ." Note the close identification of ruler and subjects, probably suggested by the Gildas tradition.

106. "Postquam autem venissent ciulae, fecit Hencgistus convivium Guorthigirno et militibus suis et interpreti suo. . . . Et puellam iussit ministrare illis vinum et siceram et inebriati sunt et saturati sunt nimis."

107. "And Hengist, having taken counsel with his elders who came with him from the island of Oghgul as to what they should ask of the king in return for the girl, there was one opinion among all of them, that they should ask for the region called Canturguoralen in their language, but Chent in ours. And Vortigern gave it to them, although Guoyrancgono was the ruler of Kent, and he knew nothing of the fact that his realm had been given to the pagans, and that he himself was secretly surrendered into their power. And thus the girl was given to Vortigern in marriage and he slept with her and loved her greatly."

108. *HB,* 45, begins, "At barbari reversi sunt magno opere, cum Guorthigirnus amicus illis erat propter uxorem suam."

109. The play on words in the signal—"Eu Saxones eniminit saxas" (Saxons, draw your knives)—is identified as a learned pun rather than a folk tradition by N. K. Chadwick, "Early Culture," pp. 44–45.

110. *HB,* 46: Hengist tells his followers in arranging for the massacre, "Et regem illorum nolite occidere, sed eum, pro causa filiae meae quam dedi illi in coniugium, tenete, quia melius est nobis ut ex manibus nostris redimatur."

111. *Ibid.:* "Et [Guorthigirnus] solus captus et catenatus est et regiones plurimas pro redemptione animae suae illis tribuit. . . ."

112. MSS MN are more explicit, adding after "by the will of God": "and whoever reads this should realize that not by their

strength did they overcome Britain, but because of the great sins of
the Britons, as God permitted."

113. *HB,* 44: "Et ante mortem suam ad familiam suam dixit
[Guorthemir] ut sepulchrum illius in portu ponerent a quo exierant
[Saxones], super ripam maris: 'in quo vobis commendo: quamvis in
alia parte portum Brittanniae teneant et habitaverint, tamen in ista
terra in aeternum non manebunt.' "

114. See above, Chapter IV, notes 84–87 and corresponding
text.

115. For a recent summary of criticism and a reinterpretation, see
K. H. Jackson, "The Arthur of History," *ALMA,* pp. 1–11.

116. "And thus St. Patrick . . . gave sight to the blind, cleansed
lepers, made the deaf hear, drove demons from the bodies of those
possessed by them, raised the dead, nine in number, redeemed many
captives of both sexes at his own charge, wrote three hundred and
sixty-five alphabetical textbooks [*abegetoria*] or more; he also
founded three hundred and sixty-five churches, and ordained the
same number of bishops, or even more, in whom was the Spirit of
God. He ordained three thousand priests, and converted to the faith
of Christ twelve thousand persons in the one region of Conachta,
and baptized them, and baptized also in one day seven kings, who
were the sons of Amolgith."

117. Note the intimate connection between national victory and
personal or national eschatology.

118. "St. Patrick and Moses are alike in four ways: first, an angel
addressed them in a burning bush; in the second place, each fasted on
a mountain forty days and forty nights; thirdly, they were alike in
age, 120 years; finally, no one knows the sepulchre of either, for
each was buried secretly."

119. *HB,* 56: "Then Arthur fought against the Saxons in those
days with the kings of the Britons, but he was the leader in battle
[*sed ipse dux erat bellorum*]." Concerning Arthur's holiness we are
told that at his eighth battle with the invaders "Arthur carried an
image of holy Mary ever virgin on his shoulders [*super humeros
suos*] and the pagans were turned back in flight in that day and
there was a great slaughter of them through the power of our Lord
Jesus Christ and through the power of holy Mary, his virgin
mother." Lot, p. 195, note 8, gives a later addition copied into MS L
which tells of Arthur's trip to the Holy Land to obtain some pieces

of the true Cross, through which he wins victory over the pagan Saxons.

120. For example, in the final battle at *mons badonis*, "there fell in one day nine hundred and sixty men in one onset of Arthur, and no one laid them low save Arthur alone."

121. A similar impulse to place British history within the scheme of the history of salvation explains the *aetates mundi* chapters included at the beginning of *HB*.

Chapter V. Geoffrey of Monmouth's Historia regum Britanniae: *Great Men on a Great Wheel*

1. All references to *Historia regum Britanniae (HRB)* are to the edition of Acton Griscom. Translations are my own, though I have consulted the rendering of Sebastian Evans. The complete surprise of Geoffrey's contemporary, the historian Henry of Huntingdon, on discovering a MS of *HRB* (reported in a letter of 1139 as quoted in E. K. Chambers, *Arthur of Britain*, pp. 251–52) may fairly be called representative of the effect Geoffrey's work must have had on the learned, courtly-clerical audience among whom it was first circulated, despite T. D. Kendrick's reference (*British Antiquity*, p. 11) to "a background of antiquarian expectancy" in Geoffrey's day, and to his "waiting public." As I shall point out later, the interests of the Anglo-Norman historians whose works prompted *HRB* were historical, psychological, and philosophical rather than "antiquarian."

2. A number of works on Geoffrey's influence have been written including H. Brandenburg, *Galfrid von Monmouth und die frühmittelenglischen Chronisten* and L. Keeler, *Geoffrey of Monmouth and the Late Latin Chroniclers*. See also the relevant sections of R. H. Fletcher, *Arthurian Material in the Chronicles*, pp. 116 ff., and of the works mentioned in note 5, below.

3. See J. S. P. Tatlock, *The Legendary History of Britain*, p. 439; Edmond Faral, *La légende arthurienne*, II, 1–38; J. E. Lloyd, "Geoffrey of Monmouth," *EHR*, LVII (1942), 460–68; and J. J. Parry and R. A. Caldwell, "Geoffrey of Monmouth," *ALMA*, pp. 72–75, for summaries and varying interpretations of the available information about Geoffrey's antecedents and activities. Geoffrey's signatures on charters establish his residence in Oxford at least from 1129 to 1151.

4. *Vita Merlini* was edited by J. J. Parry (*Illinois Studies*, X, 243–

380), who established beyond doubt the previously disputed attribution of the work to Geoffrey.

5. The vicissitudes of Geoffrey's reputation have proven a popular topic with students of history and of British *Kulturgeschichte*. See, for example, R. F. Brinkley, *Arthurian Legend in the Seventeenth Century*, pp. 60–88, and E. Jones, *Geoffrey of Monmouth, 1640–1800*. Kendrick, pp. 78–104, describes "the battle over the British History" (and therefore over Geoffrey's credibility) in the sixteenth and seventeenth centuries; he also outlines, on pp. 11–13, the earliest doubt concerning, and opposition to, the presentation of the British past in *HRB*. The two famous twelfth-century denunciations of Geoffrey as a fraudulent historian (by William of Newburgh, in the *proemium* of *Historia rerum Anglicarum*, and Giraldus Cambrensis, *Itinerarium Kambriae*, i. 5) are printed by Chambers, *Arthur*, pp. 268, 284.

6. Almost, but not quite. There are still those who, like R. S. Loomis, prefer the language of pejoration when speaking of *HRB*. See *The Development of Arthurian Romance*, p. 35: ". . . Geoffrey was quite unscrupulous, for the *History of the Kings of Britain*, which he claimed to have translated from an ancient book imported from Brittany, was one of the world's most brazen and successful frauds."

7. *HRB*, i. 1. In xii. 20 Geoffrey adds that Walter brought the book "ex britannia"; scholarly opinion is divided over a correct translation of *britannia* as Wales or Brittany. See Griscom, Introduction, p. 22, n. 1; W. F. Schirmer, *Die frühen Darstellungen des Arthurstoffes*, p. 35, "Exkurs I"; Tatlock, *Legendary History*, pp. 422–23; A. W. Wade-Evans, tr., *Nennius's "History of the Britons,"* p. 17; and G. H. Gerould, "King Arthur and Politics," *Speculum*, II (1927), 37.

8. See Griscom's introduction to his edition, and R. S. Loomis' writings on the subject in *Speculum*, including "Geoffrey of Monmouth and Arthurian Origins," III (1928), 16–33, and a review of Schirmer's book, XXXIV (1959), 677–82.

9. The leading opponents of the "Celtic tradition" theory have been Faral, Chambers, and Tatlock. W. L. Jones, in "Latin Chroniclers from the Eleventh to the Thirteenth Centuries," *CHEL*, I, 169–71, exonerated Geoffrey as a harmless romancer whose "*History* can be adequately explained only as the response of a British writer, keenly observant of the literary tendencies of the day, to the grow-

ing demand for romance." H. Pilch, "Galfrid's *Historia*. Studie zu ihrer Stellung in der Literaturgeschichte," *Romanische Monats-schrift*, N.F. VII (1957), pp. 254–73, thinks of Geoffrey as an historical novelist, while Kendrick, p. 10, proposes that "he may after all have been doing no more than write a book of antiquarian interest for fellow antiquaries. . . ." Gerould and Tatlock incline toward divergent interpretations of *HRB* as propaganda, while Schirmer insists that the work was intended as a topical political warning.

10. *HRB* was most probably written somewhere between the years 1135 and 1138. Griscom, comparing the content of the various dedications which Geoffrey wrote to public figures of his day, opts for a date nearer the beginning of this period, while Schirmer's theories of the work's meaning are best supported by the latest possible date. Tatlock, pp. 433–37, cautiously suggests 1130 and 1138 as outer limits.

11. Geoffrey's systematic secularization of British history in a work of literary polish and pretensions is to be distinguished from the political and nationalistic developments which, as we have seen in the preceding chapter, led to the appearance of the secular episodes of the *Historia Brittonum*. The appeal to the *vetustissimus liber*, of which he is but the translator, is very possibly an indication that Geoffrey was aware of the radical nature of his departure from the fall of Britain tradition and sought to soften the impact of his approach by giving it a pedigree of its own.

12. See H. Richter, *Englische Geschichtschreiber des 12. Jahrhunderts*, pp. 170–71.

13. I do not mean to impute frivolity to Geoffrey in calling his work a parody; rather, I refer to the process whereby he took certain models, distorted them significantly, heightened and emphasized their nontraditional features, and produced thereby a fictional copy in which all lines are more sharply etched than those of the "originals"—and in which, consequently, the genius of the genre is isolated and magnified.

14. I exclude from this section any account of early medieval universal chronicles or rehandlings of Roman history. There is some discussion of these works and of Geoffrey's relationship to them in two unpublished University of California dissertations: F. P. Colligan, "The Historiography of Geoffrey of Monmouth," pp. 82–88, and L. M. Myers, "Universal Histories in the Early Middle Ages."

15. See above, Chapter I, notes 35–38 and corresponding text.

16. The practice continued on into the Tudor period and beyond, a famous case being the introduction to Sir Walter Raleigh's history of the world. In fact, it can be argued that Collingwood's statement on the uses of history (quoted above, Chapter I, note 1) is itself exemplary, and that it proposes to regard history as a storehouse of metaphysical rather than moral *exempla*.

17. One is constantly made aware of this difficulty in attempting to make students realize that today's "scientific" and "critical" history, or social and intellectual history, far from being "objective," reflect the humanistic, sociological, psychological, and psychoanalytical insights and preoccupatons of contemporary society.

18. This is also true of those sections in which the historian's aims were not specifically Christian. The unhorsing of the "little Greek" by a Langobardic warrior in Paul's *Historia Langobardorum* is patently exemplary (see above, Chapter IV, note 27 and corresponding text).

19. The prefaces of the histories of William of Malmesbury, Henry of Huntingdon, and Ordericus Vitalis contain conventional references to the exemplary uses of history, and Orderic again takes up the theme in the first chapter of his sixth book: "It is every man's duty to be daily learning how he ought to live, by having the examples of ancient worthies ever present before his eyes, and profiting thereby."

20. The efflorescence may be studied in Richter, and in H. Lamprecht, *Untersuchungen über einige englische Chronisten des 12. und beginnenden 13. Jahrhunderts,* and set within the context of twelfth-century historiography generally in C. H. Haskins, *The Renaissance of the Twelfth Century*, pp. 224–78, and F. Heer, *The Medieval World*, pp. 227–38.

21. On the dating of the work's successive stages, see R. W. Southern, *St. Anselm and his Biographer*, pp. 298–300. Eadmer's work covers a shorter period of time than the other histories here under consideration, and poses certain special problems to the investigator as well; I have therefore reluctantly decided to exclude it from the present discussion. See Richter, pp. 20–53.

22. The dating of the various parts and reworkings of Orderic's work is an extremely complicated process. See the masterful summary in H. Wolter, *Ordericus Vitalis*, pp. 65–71. References to Orderic follow the edition of A. Le Prevost; translations are based on that of Thomas Forester.

23. References are to the edition of T. Arnold (*R.S.*), and the translation is once again Forester's.

24. References are to the text of *Gesta Regum Anglorum* edited by W. Stubbs (R.S.); translations are based on J. A. Giles' revision of the Sharpe rendering. The *Historia Novella* has been edited with a translation by K. R. Potter.

25. See Haskins, pp. 93–126, 193–223.

26. Orderic is especially exemplary of this intoxication; a perfect example is the speech of Robert of Normandy to his father, the Conqueror (*Hist. Eccl.*, v. 10), in which he says he will undertake the life of a voluntary exile and become a mercenary soldier, thereby imitating Polyneices the Theban. Cf. Henry's preface, in which he proves the great exemplary value of history by adducing the Homeric heroes as great examples of virtue and vice. The historians' knowledge of Greek literature was all secondhand, of course.

27. Orderic compares the Norman barons to the Roman senate (*Ibid.*, iii. 11); he and Henry, borrowing from early medieval chronicles, recapitulate the complete series of Roman emperors in the west, which Henry prefaces with a word of praise for the emperors (*Hist. Eccl.*, i. 23; *Hist. Ang.*, i. 15 ff.).

28. There are many examples of the traditional patriotic exhortation, notably Caesar's to his troops when they invade Britain (*Hist. Ang.*, i. 13); also traditional is the speech of Tostig, who in his complaint to the king of Norway (*Hist. Eccl.*, iii. 11), excoriates his brother Harold, king of England, for his tyranny; on the other hand, the confrontation of Robert and William, mentioned in note 26, and William's deathbed speech (*Hist. Eccl.*, vii. 15; see below, pp. 132 ff.) are innovations and striking indications of Orderic's art.

29. William speaks in his preface of his desire to "season the crude materials" of his history "with Roman salt" ("exarata barbarice Romano sale condire").

30. Norman Cantor, *Medieval History*, p. 255, feels that "the . . . most decisive stage in the emergence of Normandy was involved in the relationship between the Norman dukes and the church in their territory." To D. C. Douglas, "the ecclesiastical development of Normandy during the earlier half of the eleventh century was almost as remarkable as the growth at the same time of its secular strength . . ." (*William the Conqueror*, p. 105).

31. See Douglas, pp. 83–155, esp. "The Duke in his Duchy," p. 155, for a penetrating assessment of William's preconquest achievements, which Douglas considers were "among the most remarkable political

phenomena of eleventh-century Europe, . . . [and] the basis of . . . [William's] establishment of the Anglo-Norman kingdom."

32. Heinrich Pähler, *Strukturuntersuchungen zur Historia Regum Britanniae des Geoffrey of Monmouth*, p. 58, shows how the histories of William and Henry are constructed around the central, elaborate sections dealing with the Anglo-Norman monarchs.

33. See, for example, *Hist. Eccl.*, iii. 8, v. 2; Orderic stresses the great virtues of William which make him beloved of God. Henry, on the other hand (*Hist. Ang.*, vi. 27, 38) sees the Normans primarily as the instrument chosen by God "because he perceived that they were more fierce than any other people." They carry out God's revenge on the sinful English, whom God gives up "to destruction by the fierce and crafty race of the Normans." William of Malmesbury (*Gesta*, iii. 238, 244) speaks of "the prudence of William, seconded by the providence of God," and thinks that God especially protected the Conqueror in the battle of Hastings.

34. William especially paints a gloomy picture of the decadence of the English, one which has too frequently been taken literally, even until the present century. See *Gesta*, iii. 245. Henry (*Hist. Ang.*, vi. 38) sees the English defeat to be the result of "the righteous will of God." Orderic is more impartially providential, and says of Hastings (*Hist. Eccl.*, iii. 14), "Thus did Almighty God . . . punish in various ways the innumerable sinners in both armies."

35. *Hist. Ang.*, vi. 1; in vii. 1, he says further that God, having punished the Saxons, "now began to afflict the Normans themselves, the instruments of his will, with various calamities."

36. See *Hist. Eccl.*, iv. 3, 4, 8; vi. 2; Orderic says that "Under [William's rule] the native inhabitants were crushed, imprisoned, disinherited, banished and scattered beyond the limits of their own country"; he tells frequently how "the English deeply lamented the loss of their freedom" and, "sighing for their ancient liberties," were "provoked to rebellion by every sort of oppression on the part of the Normans" who "had crushed the English and were overwhelming them with intolerable oppression." Cf. *Gesta*, ii. 207; and *Hist. Ang.*, vi. 38, where Henry characterizes the Normans as a people who fight until they have "so crushed their enemies that they can reduce them no lower," at which point they turn against each other.

37. Orderic says of the barons that they are "always restless [and] longing for some disturbance" (v. 10); describes one as "a brave soldier, lavish in his liberalities, [taking] great delight in riotous

sports, in jesters, horses, and dogs, with other vanities of that sort" (vi. 2); and, when an Anglo-Norman party sets out for Italy, remarks, "The Normans are ever given to change and desirous of visiting foreign lands, and they therefore readily joined themselves to the aspiring prelate whose ambition was not satisfied by the dominion of England and Normandy" (vii. 8). Like William (see *Gesta*, ii. 227), Henry stresses the great greed of the Norman lords (vii. 19) as well as their rebelliousness (vii. 2), and tells us that when the Conqueror was exhorting his forces to victory before the battle of Hastings, "all the squadrons, inflamed with rage, rushed on the enemy with indescribable impetuosity, and left the duke speaking to himself!" (vi. 30). On the cruelty of the Normans, see the preceding note.

38. Henry of Huntingdon inclines more toward the former view (vii. 1–2), Orderic the latter. See for example *Hist. Eccl.*, v. 10: "Thus Normandy had more to suffer from her own people than from strangers, and was ruined by intestine disorders."

39. *Eccl. Hist.*, v. 1; Orderic returns to this point again in vi. 1.

40. Preface: "I shall search out and give to the world the modern history of Christendom, venturing to call my unpretending work 'An Ecclesiastical History.' "

41. See another important passage, *Hist. Eccl.*, viii. 15, where Orderic notes, "I see many passages in the sacred writings which are so adapted to the circumstances of the present times, that they seem parallel. But I leave to studious persons the task of inquiry into these allegorical quotations [allegoricas allegationes] and the interpretations applicable to the state of mankind, and will endeavor to continue the history of Norman affairs a little further in all simplicity." Here the writer overtly disassociates himself from the methods, if not the beliefs, of national-ecclesiastical historiography, preferring a record of the present human condition not overtly organized around the history of salvation.

42. See the section headed "Vera lex historiae" in C. W. Jones, *Saints' Lives and Chronicles in Early England*, pp. 81–85, for a brief analysis of the historical method of the early medieval historian.

43. *Gesta*, ii. 167 ff.

44. *Ibid.*, iii. 237, 268. Cf. *Hist. Eccl.*, viii. 17 (a vision of purgatory).

45. *Gesta*, ii. 207.

46. *Ibid.*, iv. 343 ff.; *Hist. Ang.*, vii. 5 ff.

47. As Richter (p. 65), puts it, "[William] berichtet von den grossen Menschen, die Geschichte machten, denn sie erlebten die Möglichkeiten des Daseins tiefer und voller als die Masse der Unbekannten; aber er erzählt auch von denen, denen sich irgendwie einmal das Tor zu der anderen Welt auftat."

48. An amusing and perhaps significant example of the historians' awareness of the problem of reconciling national and personal desires is Orderic's mention (*Hist. Eccl.*, iv. 4) of the perplexity of Norman barons in England whose wives insisted that they return to Normandy or risk conjugal infidelity, while William urged them to remain in England and become his lieutenants in ruling and controlling the newly conquered nation.

49. See William's preface to the third book of *Gesta* where, speaking of the Conqueror, he says, "where I am certified of his good deeds, I shall openly proclaim them; his bad conduct I shall touch upon lightly and sparingly [leviter et quasi transeunter], just enough that it may be known."

50. See especially William of Malmesbury on William Rufus, *Gesta*, iv. 312–14, 333.

51. See *Gesta*, iv. 333 (of William Rufus): "He formed mighty plans, which he would have brought to effect, could he have spun out the tissue of fate or broken through, and disengaged himself from, the violence of fortune." See Henry's similar reflections on the death of Ralph, the powerful and unscrupulous bishop of Salisbury, *Hist. Ang.*, viii. 11, in which the *rota volubilis* of fortune is specifically mentioned, and Orderic's comment on the Norman Conquest, iii. 14: "Inconstant fortune frequently causes adverse and unexpected changes in human affairs; some persons being lifted from the dust to the height of great power, while others, suddenly falling from their high estate, groan in extreme distress."

52. See vii. 15.

53. Orderic, *Hist. Eccl.*, vii. 15. Note the almost psalmic quality of William's confession that "I became . . . an object of jealousy to all my neighbours, but by His aid in whom I have always put my trust, none of them were able to prevail against me."

54. Henry of Huntingdon strives briefly for the same effect in describing the death of Henry I, *Hist. Ang.*, viii. 2; the account stresses the stench exuded by the corpse, and Henry counsels his readers, "Observe, I say, what horrible decay, to what a loathsome

state, his body was reduced . . . and learn to despise what so perishes and comes to nothing."

55. See Pähler, pp. 58–60.

56. See Tatlock, pp. 392–95; Colligan, pp. 22–24, and, most thoroughly, Pähler, pp. 87–126.

57. See above, note 35 and corresponding text.

58. W. F. Schirmer first noted this important passage and correctly interpreted it. See Schirmer, pp. 25–27, and *Exkurs IV*, "Geoffrey und Gildas," pp. 38–39. Where Gildas' words condemned his nation for its sins, Geoffrey interrupts the narrative to upbraid the Britons for the political strife which is leading them to national catastrophe. He could have found many models for this interruption and its point of view in the Anglo-Norman historians; see above, note 38.

59. Pähler, pp. 95 ff., demonstrates the structural importance for *HRB* of the "Wechsel von Aufstieg und Niedergang" in the narrative, but never completely subscribes to the idea that the entire work is organized around the rise and fall of the Britons.

60. E.g., *HRB*, vi. 2, when the Romans leave Britain for the last time. The basis for this scene is Gildas (cf. *De exc.*, 18), but Geoffrey inserts a long speech by Guethelin, bishop of London, who urges the inhabitants to fight for their freedom. The insertion effectively modifies the pathos which the scene has in *De exc.*, and takes away from the Romans the prominence given them in the older narrative.

61. See *HRB*, xi. 12, 13 (the destruction of the British monks by the Saxons under Ethelfrid after the Britons refuse to cooperate with St. Augustine; cf. Bede, *HE*, ii. 2 ff.); etc.

62. Cf. *HRB*, xii. 14 ff. and *HE*, iv. 15; v. 7. With typical self-assurance, Geoffrey remarks of Cadwaladrus, "quem beda clieduallam iuvenem vocavit" without mentioning, of course, his metamorphosis in nationality.

63. HB, 10–11, 19–30, 40–42.

64. Schirmer, p. 29, sees in Geoffrey's placement and use of the prophecies the influence of Anchises' prophecies in the sixth book of the *Aeneid* which connect the story of Aeneas directly to the greatness of the Augustan present. On Geoffrey's reasons for wanting to establish a line between the story of the Britons and the present, see below, p. 171.

65. The arrival and *gesta* of St. Germanus in Britain are men-

tioned in *HRB*, vi. 13, but not recounted. In the narrative of Vortigern's destruction (*HRB*, viii. 2), Geoffrey adapts the violent, "religious" tradition of *HB*, 47, but removes St. Germanus from the story and replaces the fire that descends from heaven by fires set by the Britons who have besieged the sinful monarch in his castle.

66. William of Malmesbury prefaces his history with an epistle to Robert, Earl of Gloucester (also a dedicatee of *HRB*) which begins by extolling "the virtue of celebrated men" ("virtus clarorum virorum") and their "great actions."

67. In *HRB*, ix. 13 Geoffrey apostrophizes the Britons under Arthur's rule in an analogous fashion. See Arthur's speech to his army before the battle with the Romans at Siesia (x. 7), Brutus' threats to Anacletus (i. 8), and the cruelty of Arthur's Britons in ravaging Normandy (ix. 11) for further examples of "Norman" pride, vigor, and cruelty as adapted by Geoffrey.

68. It may be precisely the arbitrariness and inexplicability of Fortune to which Geoffrey alludes when he interrupts the narrative of *HRB* immediately following the announcement of Modred's treason, which forces Arthur to turn back from Rome and go to his death in Britain; addressing his words to his patron (xi. 1) Geoffrey says that he will not comment on this turn of events ("De hoc Galfridis munomotensis tacebit") but will confine himself to rendering his source as briefly as possible.

69. Geoffrey includes a fourth nation, Brittany, in the cycle; see below, p. 167.

70. In recounting the final destruction of the kingdom of the Britons, Geoffrey borrows from Gildas an account of plagues which ravage the nation (cf. *De exc.*, 22). Once again his treatment of his source is revealing: in Gildas, the plagues are sent by God as warnings to the sinful Britons before the final punishment, the Saxon invaders; in *HRB* the plagues, coming after the Saxon arrival and not sent by God, represent the final fury of amoral nature, stamping out the doomed nation of the Britons who have reached the end of their cycle.

71. *HRB*, xii. 17.

72. Among them is the return to Britain of relics of the saints carried off during the Saxon invasions. Before this can happen, however, a fated time must come ("postquam fatale tempus supervenisset . . .").

73. See above, Chapter I, pp. 17–20.

74. It is as old as Herodotus' portrayal of the struggle between Persian might and Greek freedom in the seventh and eighth books of his history. See M. Ritter, "Studien über die Entwicklung der Geschichtswissenschaft. I: Die antike Geschichtsschreibung," *Hist. Zeit.*, LIV (1885), pp. 1–41.

75. See Schirmer, pp. 26–28, and Pähler, pp. 92–107, *passim*.

76. *HRB*, i. 3.

77. *Ibid.*, iv. 8–10.

78. *Ibid.*, iii. 1–7.

79. E.g., Porrex (*ibid.*, ii. 16); Maximianus (v. 9–16); etc.

80. On the topical import of the name, see Tatlock, "Contemporaneous Matters in Geoffrey of Monmouth's *Historia Regum Britanniae*," *Speculum*, VI (1931), 206–23: Anacletus II was the name taken by an antipope who "reigned" from 1130–1138.

81. *HRB*, i. 8–9.

82. There is a striking parallel between this development in *HRB* and the *Chanson de Roland*, where a relationship between godfather and godson (Ganelon and Roland) leads to the former's treason and consequent national disaster. In the *chanson*, Charlemagne represents the nation and its historical destiny and, like Britain in *HRB*, undergoes rise and fall dependent upon the behavior of his vassals. Charles is on the threshold of great national triumph in his Spanish campaign when Ganelon's treason brings about the loss of Roland and the twelve peers and raises for Charles the specter of future national hardships and defeats (see *Roland*, lines 2887 ff., Charles' lament for Roland and for his own power).

83. Of course, the range of relationships is very limited; again we may cite as a parallel the nonfeudal relationships of the *chanson de geste*. It remained for the romance to discover a new world of interpersonal relationships by its exaltation of love to a new level of psychological and narrative importance. To Geoffrey, as we shall see, love is still primarily the madness it was to the ancients.

84. Of course, these characters often help to bring about that national condition which they represent; still, as Pähler says (p. 97), "Das Reich steht als Realität hinter den Königen; die britische Geschichte Geoffreys ist unter dem Gesichtspunkt des Reiches, nicht der einzelnen Könige geschreiben. . . ." And (p. 29) to Schirmer, "Held der Historia ist das regnum, nicht die reges." Arthur, then, is not Geoffrey's hero but Britain's, and Britain is Geoffrey's. The extra level in the narrative allows for considerable

irony, as is especially evident in the "trip to Rome" episodes, which will shortly be discussed.

85. A few exceptions will be noted. The angelic voice, already mentioned, which dissuades Cadwaladrus from returning to Britain, is a convenience rather than a *testamentum fidei* on Geoffrey's part, and is designed, as I have indicated, to remind us once again of the cycles of history.

86. The contrary view is held by Schirmer, pp. 23–30. But it fails to take into account factors, such as the cyclical view of history, which militate against the prescriptive value of Geoffrey's presentation and analysis. It should be noted as well that the great reversal for the Britons—the fall of Arthur through the treachery of Modred —is not provided by Geoffrey with a motive. Only in later Arthurian story was Modred supplied with a character befitting the betrayer of Arthur.

87. *HRB*, iii. 1–10.

88. Not only does Briton fight Briton in the course of the fraternal strife, but Brennius invites Norwegians into Britain to aid his cause, and is about to invade with a Burgundian force when he is reconciled with his brother. Cf. the story of Tostig and Harold in Oderic's *Hist. Eccl.*, iii. 11, a possible source for Geoffrey's story.

89. In *HRB*, iii. 1, he is convinced by wicked advisers that he is equal in valor and nobility to his brother, and that his dignity has been injured by his acceptance of the smaller portion of the kingdom. Cf. the "factious young men" who convince Robert, son of William the Conqueror, to demand from his father the rule of the duchy of Normandy, *Hist. Eccl.*, v. 10.

90. *HRB*, iii. 10: "Habita ergo victoria remansit brennius in italia populum inaudita tyrande afficiens."

91. Brennius' career is an odyssey in search of *dignitas;* he visits Norway, Scotland, Gaul, and Burgundy in his campaign against Belinus.

92. Belinus is successor to Dunwallo Molmutius, the great lawgiver, and we are told (*HRB*, iii. 5) that he is a zealous interpreter and protector of his predecessor's achievement.

93. The contrast between the two brothers—and national attitudes—is well summarized by Geoffrey in iii. 6: "While Belinus was ruling his kingdom in peace and tranquility, his brother Brennius, exiled to the shore of Gaul, was racked by internal anxieties. For he

took very badly his banishment from his native land, and his inability to return to enjoy his lost dignity."

94. *HRB*, v. 6–8.

95. *Ibid.*, v. 6: Constantine, "when he was impowered with the honors of the throne, began in a few years to possess great prowess, to demonstrate the fierceness of a lion, and to maintain justice among the people. He restrained the rapacity of robbers, suppressed the cruelty of tyrants, and sought everywhere to reestablish peace."

96. *Ibid.*, v. 7: The refugees ask Constantine, "For what prince is there who may be compared to the King of Britain, either in the strength of his hardy soldiers or in the quantity of his gold and silver?"

97. (*Ibid.*, v. 8). It is led by Trahern, a Briton and the uncle of Constantine's mother, Helena.

98. *Ibid.* "[Octavius] returned to Britain, and having dispersed the Romans recovered the throne of the kingdom. After which he demonstrated such prowess and such plentiful supplies of gold and silver that in a short time he feared no one at all. And so he possessed happily the kingdom of Britain from that time until the days of Gratian and Valentinian."

99. *HRB*, v. 9–16; he is modeled on Gildas' Maximus (*De exc.*, 13) and the Maximianus of *HB*, 27.

100. *HRB*, v. 9. His motivation is similar to that of Brennius: he has been denied the share of rulership in Rome that he feels owing to him. "There was a great disturbance at that time between Maximianus and the two emperors, Gratian and his brother Valentinian; Maximianus had been repulsed in seeking to obtain a third part of the empire."

101. Like Caesar before him and Vortigern after him. See *HRB*, iv. 5, vi. 6 ff., and below, pp. 151 ff., 164–66.

102. See, *HRB*, v. 9, the advice given Maximianus by the Briton Mauricius, who comes to Rome to persuade him to take the crown: "Come with me to the island of Britain and there you will possess the crown of the kingdom. . . . If therefore you will come with me, you will at once achieve this undertaking: with the copious gold and silver of Britain, and the great multitude of warlike soldiers living there, you will be able to return to Rome, subjugate it, and cast out the emperors. Your relative Constantine and many of our kings have done just this, and attained the imperial throne." The

reference to former Britons who have taken Rome is an ironic touch on Geoffrey's part, since, like former Roman adventures, this one will bring trouble to the island.

103. *Ibid.*: "Alii vero censebant conacum meridiacum nepotem suum [i.e., of King Octavius] in solium regni initiandum . . . indignatus est conanus nepos regis [at the choice of Maximianus] qui omni nisu in regnum anelabat, totamque curiam propter talia turbavit."

104. Note the parallel to the Gallic expedition of Belinus and Brennius after their reconciliation.

105. *Ibid.*, v. 12: "For the land is fertile with grain and the rivers full of fish, the forests fair and the meadows beautiful; there is nowhere, in my judgment, a more pleasing land." The description recalls a similar praise of the beauty of Britain by Geoffrey himself in i. 2, and is possibly yet another cyclic reference.

106. Geoffrey alludes briefly to his death in v. 16. Pähler comments on the limited, symbolic role of Maximianus, pp. 103–4.

107. On the relationship between Britain and Brittany, see below, note 198 and corresponding text.

108. *HRB*, ix. 15–x. 13. Actually, Arthur never reaches Rome, since he receives news of Modred's treason while en route there from Siesia, where he has defeated the Romans. See *HRB*, x. 13.

109. *HRB*, xi. 1–2.

110. The retrograde motion of the nation is not continuous; there are episodes of British recovery and efflorescence. As Pähler has indicated, pp. 110–26, there are several subsidiary ascents and declines within the span of British history. Until Arthur the general trend of national fortunes is upward; after him, it is downward. Of course, as the nation rises higher, the effects of temporary setbacks become correspondingly more severe; Maximianus and Vortigern hurt Britain more than does Brennius.

111. Just as Mauricius reminds Maximianus (and Geoffrey's audience) of the previous British trips to Rome, Arthur reminds his barons (and Geoffrey's audience) of the Britons who had taken the imperial throne before him, leaving no doubt that Arthur's career is to be considered in the context of all the trips to Rome. Once again, there is in Arthur's reminder, as there was in Mauricius', great irony.

112. Cf. *HRB*, i. 16 and x. 3.

113. *HRB*, i. 17–18: Immediately following the successful dispatch

of the giant, Brutus establishes his capital city and gives its citizens laws.

114. Pähler, pp. 105–6. Geoffrey says of Arthur's prowess at this point, "Secure in his great power he was unwilling to lead an army against such monsters, when he might encourage his men by showing that he was capable of destroying the creatures alone."

115. *HRB*, x. 3: ". . . concurrebant ei [Arthur] ascribentes laudes qui patriam a tanta ingluvie liberaverat."

116. See *ibid.*, ix. 16, where the Romans complain of Arthur's having usurped their European domains.

117. See Tatlock, *Legendary History*, pp. 388–89, for possible sources and analogues in various folk literatures.

118. On the youthful spirits of the Britons in their war with the Romans immediately after this episode, see below, p. 169.

119. *HRB*, ii. 2–5.

120. Pähler, p. 92, makes this point.

121. *HRB*, vi. 12; cf. *HB*, 37.

122. See *HRB*, vi. 8–9.

123. *Ibid.*, vi. 12. "Hengist, who was a prudent man, perceiving the inconstancy of the king's mind, took counsel with his brother Horsa and the other elders who were with him as to what demands they should make of the king [in exchange for the daughter of Hengist]. And all agreed that they should give the girl to the king in return for a gift of the province of Kent. Soon the girl was given to Vortigern and the province to Hengist, without the knowledge of Count Gorangon, who ruled Kent. That same night the king married the pagan girl, who pleased him exceedingly."

124. *Ibid.*, vi. 12–15.

125. See *HB*, 47.

126. *HRB*, vi. 15–16; cf. *HB*, 45. Geoffrey places the scene of the massacre at Kaercaradoc.

127. The Saxons are only able to return to Britain because Vortigern surreptitiously invites them. See *HRB*, vi. 15: "After the death of Vortimer, Vortigern was reinstated on the throne; he, moved by the petitions of his wife, sent messengers to Hengist in Germany and bade him to return to Britain."

128. Geoffrey follows Gildas in portraying the Britons as cowards after Maximianus has stripped the nation of its soldiery (see *HRB*, vi. 1–4); once Vortigern has murdered the monk Constans and declared himself king (vi. 8), the Britons, united in their opposition

to the new monarch, become progressively braver. At Kaercaradoc, when the Saxons draw their hidden knives and fall on the unarmed Britons, the latter snatch sticks and stones ("eripiebant enim britones ex tellure lapides et fustes") and fight back lethally. Eldol, Earl of Gloucester, seizing a stake, wreaks havoc on the attackers, breaking limbs and sending souls to hell. ("Quemcunque attingebat cum illo confringens ei membrum quod percuciebat dirigebat confestim ad tartara.") Finally Eldol escapes and the Saxons win the victory, but at great cost to them, and with considerable glory for the surprised and outnumbered Britons.

129. See *HRB*, vi. 17–19; borrowing from *HB*, 40–42, Geoffrey has Vortigern attempt to build a stronghold, the foundations of which repeatedly sink into the earth. The king consults his *magos*, who tell him the foundation stones must be sprinkled with the blood of a fatherless boy. Merlin is discovered and brought to Vortigern, and to save his life reveals his great powers, by which he utters his prophecies to the king.

130. *HRB*, viii. 10–12. Before Merlin performs his feat of magic in moving the huge stones, the Britons display their valor by destroying an Irish army which attempts to prevent them from reaching the Giants' Dance.

131. See Schirmer, p. 13: "Nun besteht eine Diskrepanz zwischen dem Handlungshöhepunkt (Arthur) und dem strukturellen Zentrum (den Weissagungen Merlins). Zwischen diesen beiden Polen sind verbindende Fäden gesponnen, und durch die Mitwirkung Merlins bei der Zeugung Arthurs erhält dieser von vornherein besondere Bedeutung."

132. *HRB*, viii. 19.

133. *Ibid.* "[Eius] pulcritudo omnes mulieres britannie superabat."

134. *Ibid.* ". . . novibus artibus et tempore tuo inauditis."

135. *Ibid.* "Concepit quoque eadem nocte celeberrimum virum illum arturum qui postmodum ut celebris foret mira probitate promeruit." On the parallels between the birth of Arthur and that of Alexander, as told in the main medieval sources of the Alexander legend, see Tatlock, pp. 312–20; E. Greulich, *Die Arthursage in der Historia Regum Britanniae*, pp. 47–88.

136. *HRB*, viii. 22–23. Uther's indomitable energy may be Geoffrey's response to the Anglo-Norman historians' fascination with the same quality in the Conqueror and his heirs.

137. *Ibid.*, 24. The "fons nitidissime aque quam [Uther] solitus

erat bibere" by which Uther is poisoned may be intended to recall Ygerna, by whom the king was also wont to satisfy a natural desire.

138. See Merlin's denunciation of Vortigern and prediction of his death in *HRB*, viii. 1.

139. See *ibid.*, 10: "The king [Ambrosius] gladly received Merlin, and commanded him to reveal the future, being anxious to hear of marvellous happenings. Merlin replied to him, 'Mysteries of this kind are not to be revealed except when a great emergency dictates.' " (The Latin, "nisi cum summa necessitas incubuerit," implies an almost involuntary obedience by Merlin to the prophetic power liberated in him by the crisis.)

140. See *ibid.*, 15, where Merlin, summoned to explain the significance of a strange star seen over Britain, reveals the death of Ambrosius, at the same time forecasting the coming of Arthur. Corroboration of this interpretation of the prophetic office may be drawn from the early prophecy about Britain uttered to Brutus by the goddess Diana (*ibid.*, i. 11), who leaves no doubt that Fate has chosen for the Britons a glorious history.

141. Merlin speaks of his "novae artes" (see above, note 134) and when he moves the stones of the Giants' Dance, Geoffrey remarks that Merlin has "proved that wit [*ingenium*] outdoes strength."

142. He passes unnoticed from the story after the birth of Arthur. It is noteworthy that Merlin, like Arthur, has a more-than-natural origin. He was conceived as a result of an affair between an invisible *incubus* and his mother, who had never known the love of men (see *HRB*, vi. 18). Geoffrey may have been inspired in his portrait of the prophet-wonderworker who acts as *genius regni* by the role of St. Dunstan in William of Malmesbury's *Gesta*, ii, *passim*. Dunstan is active in several reigns, foretelling the fate of kings, saving them from sins which have national consequences, etc. Dunstan is himself obviously modeled on the prophets of the Old Testament, who guided and judged Israel and her rulers. Merlin, however, is a secularized prophet.

143. See *HRB*, x. 2, where Modred is suddenly introduced as the nephew to whom Arthur entrusts his realm and his queen Ganhumara when the Britons embark with their king to fight the Romans on the continent

144. See *ibid.*, 13: "When summer had come and Arthur, wishing to travel on to Rome, began to cross the mountains, it was announced to him that his nephew Modred, to whom he had entrusted Britain,

had treacherously and tyrannically crowned himself king and had joined himself in an illicit union with Ganhumara, thereby violating her previous marriage vows."

145. See below, notes 167–69 and corresponding text, for a consideration of some instances of treason in *HRB*.

146. In *HRB*, xi. 1 Modred sends for Chelric, leader of the Saxons, to return quickly from Germany with his army, and promises to requite the Saxons for their aid by gifts of land, including Kent, which Hengist and Horsa ruled in the time of Vortigern ("tempore vortegirni horsus et hengistus possederant"). Note the recall of Vortigern's earlier betrayal of Britain in this passage. For other instances of the disastrous effects of inviting foreign troops into Britain, see *HRB*, iii. 3, iv. 9, v. 2–3, vi. 10 ff.

147. See *HRB*, xi. 1.

148. *Ibid.*, 3 ff.

149. Cf. *HRB*, ii. 17 (the establishment of the law) and xi. 4, where Constantine kills one of the sons "before the altar of the church of St. Amphibalus, to which he had fled," and the other in London before the altar of a convent of monks.

150. On this passage and its significance see above, note 58.

151. Cf. Brutus' role as lawgiver in *HRB*, i. 18. The lawgiver as a figure representing the rise of the young nation is noted by Schirmer, pp. 29–30.

152. See, for example, Orderic's apostrophe to the Norman baron, William Fitz-Osborn (*Hist. Eccl.*, iv. 14), on the latter's death: "The righteous Judge, who seeth all things, rewards every man according to his deserts. . . . Many had fallen by his sword, and by the sword he himself was suddenly cut off."

153. *HRB*, i. 3–18.

154. On the sources of the adventures of Brutus, especially the *Aeneid*, see Pähler, pp. 68–70; H. Tausendfreund, *Vergil und Gottfried von Monmouth;* Faral, II, 69–92; Heeger, *Ueber Die Trojanersage der Britten*, pp. 63–72; etc.

155. See *HRB*, i. 3: Brutus finds in Greece "the progeny of Helenus, son of Priam, who were held in servitude by the power of Pandrasus, king of the Greeks. For Pirrus, son of Achilles carried away from Troy with him after its destruction Helenus and many others, whom he ordered kept in captivity so that he might exact vengeance upon them for the death of his father."

156. Note, for example, the correspondence between the growth

of the Trojans in their captivity ("They had multiplied so much in that country [Greece] that they numbered seven thousand, not including women and small children") and the growth of Israel in Egypt (Exodus 1); in both cases it is a factor in bringing about the crisis which results in freedom for the captive nation.

157. See *HRB*, i. 3: Brutus, after his arrival in Greece, shows such prowess, skill in warfare, wisdom, and generosity that young and old alike love him. "When his fame had spread among all nations, the Trojans began to flock to him, praying that he should lead them to freedom from Greek slavery" ("orantes ut ipso duce a servitute grecorum liberarentur"). On Geoffrey's models for the tyranny versus freedom *topos* in Anglo-Norman historiography, see above. Geoffrey refers constantly to freedom during the British struggle against Roman domination and the Saxons, e.g., in *HRB*, iv. 1, vi. 2–3, etc. On the opposition between national disorder and freedom as the key to HRB, see Schirmer, pp. 25–30. One can acknowledge the force of Schirmer's argument without agreeing with him that the theme of freedom versus disorder makes *HRB* an allegory of Geoffrey's own day and nation.

158. See *HRB*, iv. 1, the letter of Cassibelanus to Caesar, and below, pp. 164–66.

159. *HRB*, i. 4: The great nation of the Trojans "preferred to live a free life like animals [ferino ritu], nourished by the flesh of beasts and by wild plants, rather than remain in the yoke of slavery, pampered with complete luxury."

160. *Ibid.*, 5: Pandrasus is amazed and angered that a nation enslaved by him should dare to send such a request for freedom to him. ("Pandrasus . . . ammiratus est ipsos quos in servitutem tenuerat tanta audacia abundasse ut ei talia mandata dirigerent.")

161. See *De exc.*, ii. 20, 25; in each case the Britons flee to the woods in the face of their enemies and, with God's aid, return to their cities after the defeat of the foreign oppressors. Bede's holy hermits appear to be Christians who forsake society, but this is only an appearance. The hermit in his cell is still part of the *ecclesia*, and remains in an intimate relation with all other Christians. With the *ecclesia*-society no longer a factor in *HRB*, real opposition between city and forest life becomes possible.

162. *Gamelyn*, ed. by W. W. Skeat. Indirectly, this romance is one of the sources of *As You Like It*.

163. *HRB*, i. 3: ". . . erat quidam nobilissimus iuvenis in grecia

nomine assaracus qui partibus eorum favebat. Ex troiana namque matre natus erat fiduciamque in illis habebat maximam ut auxilio eorum inquietudini grecorum resistere quivisset. Arguebat enim eum frater suus propter tria castella quae sibi moriens pater donarat et ea auferre conabatur quia ex concubina natus fuerat. Erat autem frater patre et matre grecus asciveratque regem ceterosque grecos parti sue favere."

164. Perhaps it would be more nearly accurate to say that Brutus himself, forced to leave his homeland because of the hatred of society despite his innocence, is the first example.

165. See *HRB*, ii. 15 (Marganus and Cunedagius); ii. 16 (Ferrex and Porrex); iii. 1 (Brennius and Belinus); v. 9 (Conan); etc.

166. See the story of Geta and Bassianus (*Ibid.*, v. 2), in which Geta, the brother of pure Roman descent, is placed in charge of Britain by the Romans; but the Britons give their allegiance to Bassianus, who is of British blood on his mother's side. The brothers fight, and Geta is killed, whereupon Bassianus ascends the throne.

167. *HRB*, i. 7.

168. *Ibid.*, iv. 8–9.

169. Cf. the games of *Aeneid*, v, *Iliad*, xxiii, etc.

170. See *HRB*, iv. 3, where Androgeus, commanding a troop of Londoners, attacks the bodyguard of Caesar.

171. *HRB*, i. 12.

172. *Ibid.*: "They asked him with whose permission he had entered the king's forest to kill beasts; for it was an ancient law that no one could hunt without the approval of the ruler."

173. See *ibid.*, 15, where Goffarius tells his soldiers that they will capture the Trojans like sheep and hold them captive within the Aquitanian kingdom.

174. On the forest law see Poole, *From Domesday Book to Magna Carta*, pp. 29–35. He quotes Richard Fitz Neal, twelfth-century treasurer of the realm, as saying that the kings of England enjoyed the forest as a relief from the court and a place where they could enjoy "natural freedom" (p. 29); yet this is precisely what was denied Corineus, and what William of Malmesbury complained was denied the nobility of England by William Rufus; see *Gesta*, iv. 319, on the tyranny of the forest laws.

175. On the novelty of primogeniture as a policy of the Normans in England, see Tatlock, p. 291.

176. See, for example, the amusing story in Thucydides' *Peloponnesian Wars*, i. 134, in which the oligarchs of Sparta let a criminal die of exposure by lifting the roof off a temple in which the culprit has taken refuge, rather than violate the sanctity of the shrine.

177. See Tatlock, *Legendary History*, pp. 281–82.

178. William of Malmesbury is especially outspoken on the subject of royal greed, which leads to insupportable taxes. See, for example, *Gesta*, iv. 318.

179. In this light, it is difficult to agree with Tatlock's judgment (p. 278) that Geoffrey "usually favors kings over people and wholly ignores the extortions which were such a grievance against the Norman kings." It would be more nearly correct to say that Geoffrey generalizes the grievances of the day into a subtle philosophical attitude toward the limitations of laws.

180. *HRB*, i. 11.

181. *HRB*, ii. 1.

182. Ibid., v. 16.

183. Some love their families and country and do not wish to leave them (cf. Innogen—Geoffrey cannot resist recalling by his very language incidents placed earlier in the cycle of British history); others prefer virginity to marriage; etc.

184. On the hagiographical sources of this incident, see Tatlock, pp. 236–41.

185. See above, p. 127, on the positive response to Rome of the Anglo-Norman historians.

186. See, for example, *Gesta*, ii. 201, iv. 351–53, where William contrasts the glories of ancient Rome with the meanness of her present inhabitants, and *ibid.*, iv. 357, where William alludes, as he often does, to the freedom of the Franks, which sets them sharply in contrast to the absolutist eastern empire. See above, Chapter Four, on anti-Roman (Byzantine) sentiment stretching back to the eighth century.

187. It is, of course, possible that Geoffrey was thinking of the Holy Roman Emperor Charlemagne, and striking a blow at French claims to superiority over the Anglo-Norman kings. Gerould suggests this possibility in "King Arthur and Politics" (see above, note 8), pp. 33–52. See also W. T. H. Jackson, *The Literature of the Middle Ages*, p. 83, for possible literary stimuli to an anti-Charlemagne response by Geoffrey.

188. *HRB*, iv. 1–10.

189. E.g., Orosius, Bede, etc. Cf. Bede, *HE*, i. 2, which is largely drawn from Orosius' *Historia*, vi. 7, 9, 10.

190. *HRB*, iii. 20: "As soon as he was crowned, Cassibelanus began to shine so brightly both in prowess and in liberality that his fame spread to faroff lands. Whence it happened that the control of the entire realm passed to him rather than to his nephews."

191. All three kings are brave and generous, and all three become widely known throughout Europe. Cf. *ibid.*, i. 3, ix. 11.

192. This part of the episode is discussed above, p. 160.

193. *HRB*, iv. i.: Caesar says he will suggest to the Britons "ut cetere etiam gentes subiectionem senatui faciant ne nos ipsorum cognatorum nostrorum sanguinem fundentes antiquam nobilitatem patris nostri priami offendamus."

194. Geoffrey may here be referring ironically to the masterful set-speech which Caesar delivers at this point in Henry of Huntingdon's recapitulation of British history, and which is mentioned in note 28, above.

195. See *HRB*, iv. 5: "Apertis thesauris quosque nobiliores adire ut singulis munificatis in concordiam reduceret. Plebi libertatem pollicetur, ex hereditatis amissas possessiones servis autem libertatem."

196. See *ibid.*, vi. 17.

197. See above, pp. 146–47, on Constantine's trip to Rome, epitomizing the main themes of this portion of *HRB*.

198. Tatlock, *Legendary History*, pp. 396–400, has given a complete summary of the role of Brittany and the Bretons in British history as presented in *HRB*. Arthur himself is of Breton stock on his father's side; see *HRB*, vi. 5.

199. See especially Lloyd, pp. 460–68.

200. In *HRB*, vi. 4, Aldroenus, King of Brittany, tells Guethelinus, Archbishop of London, "I possess the kingdom which is under my rule with honor and without owing tribute to anyone. I have chosen to govern it above all other nations because I govern it in freedom."

201. *HRB*, ix. 15–x. 12.

202. Geoffrey says in ix. 13 that Britain at that time also excelled all other realms in luxury and in courtly behavior; knights performed great deeds in honor of ladies, and ladies honored with their love the boldest warriors. "[The ladies] grew chaste and more perfect, and the knights grew nobler out of love for them."

203. Geoffrey took the idea for this ceremony from the crown-wearing ceremonies of the Anglo-Norman kings. See Poole, pp. 4–5, and Tatlock, *Legendary History*, pp. 270–74. The latter also mentions court ritual at Constantinople as a possible source for some of the features of Geoffrey's description.

204. See, e.g., Charles' council in the *Chanson de Roland*, ll. 166 ff.

205. On the crusading "flavor" of the names used by Geoffrey to give Arthur's battle the atmosphere of a holy war against the pagans, see Tatlock, "Contemporaneous Matters."

206. In *HRB*, ix. 1, Geoffrey praises Arthur's valor and generosity, and remarks that Arthur was handicapped early in his reign by a lack of funds, owing to his over-liberal largesse to his followers! William of Malmesbury, *Gesta*, iv. 313, blames William Rufus for a similar extravagance.

207. See *HRB*, ix. 11. The result of these fears is a continental mobilization which, of course, proves futile.

208. *Ibid.* The Britons invade Norway and "having won the victory, they set fire to the cities and scattered the rural population; nor did they desist from their cruelty until all of Norway and Denmark had been brought under Arthur's sway."

209. *Ibid.* After Arthur has subdued Gaul later in the same expedition, he goes to Paris, where he holds a council of clerks and laymen and "established the realm in peace and justice." The juxtaposition of cruelty in war and justice in peace which distinguishes Arthur's Britain distinguished the Anglo-Norman monarchy as well. Henry of Huntingdon's final estimation of the achievement of William the Conqueror mingles blame for his cruelty, and for his oppression of the English through his officials, with the recognition (*Hist. Ang.*, vi. 39) that "he so firmly preserved the peace that a girl laden with gold could pass in safety from one end of England to the other." Even more apposite is Orderic's account (*Hist. eccl.*, iv. 1), of William's behavior after he has defeated the English and been crowned their king. The new monarch ruled with justice and moderation, "erected some laws founded on admirable principles," and brought peace and security to all. "Thus the first acts of his reign were all excellent, and eminent for the great benefits flowing from good government conferred upon his subjects."

210. See *HRB*, ix. 15: ". . . twelve men of ripe age and worshipful mein entered with measured steps [moderatis passibus],

carrying in their right hands an olive branch, the sign of a peaceful embassy." The description recalls an embassy sent to the Britons by Maximianus when he arrives in Britain (*HRB*, v. 10), also of old men bearing olive branches; like its predecessor, the embassy to Arthur promises danger to Britain from a trip to Rome, and hence this verbal recall of the earlier event.

211. The letter protests the astonishment of Lucius, the Roman emperor (rei publice procurator), at Arthur's tyranny, and at the injuries done Rome by Arthus ("Admiror inquam et iniuriam quam rome intulisti"). Cf. the opening of Cassibelanus' letter to Caesar in *HRB*, iv., 2: "Miranda est cesar romani populi cupiditas. . . ." The roles of the two nations have been reversed.

212. *HRB*, x. 4.

213. *Ibid.* Boso says, "Since we began this fight without Arthur's knowledge, let us take care not to finish on the losing end [in peiorem partem] of what we started. . . . Regain your boldness [audatiam] and follow me into the ranks of the Romans."

214. *Ibid.*, 8.

215. See his speech to his council in *ibid.*, ix. 16; he says that Julius Caesar and his successors were invited to Britain by "the discord of our ancestors" ("discidio veterum nostrorum").

216. "For five years have passed during which, given over to such [peacetime] pleasures, we have absented ourselves from the exercises of war."

217. See *ibid.*, x. 7. Arthur also distinguishes between the strength and freedom of the western nations over which he rules and the cowardice of eastern nations, among which he obviously includes Rome and her foes. On this distinction between new west and old, corrupt east, see above, Chapter IV; cf. William of Malmesbury, *Gesta*, iv. 360, where William observes that, because of the western love of freedom, empires continually change hands and succeed one another, while the Persian empire (and by implication the Byzantine empire) remains stable because its inhabitants do not object to bondage. This passage may have helped to determine the system of *HRB*, in which the continual wish for personal and national freedom (or dignity) results in the cycle of history.

218. *HRB*, x. 12. The Britons, refusing to pay the tribute unjustly demanded by Rome, defend the freedom which the Romans wished to end ("libertatem quam illi eisdem demere affectabant"), and revenge their ancestors (veteres eorum) whom the ancestors

of the Romans (avos istorum) used to persecute with hateful dep-
redations (invisis inquietationibus).

219. *HRB*, vi. 10. There is no parallel for this speech in *Historia
Brittonum*, but Geoffrey took the matter of it from William of
Malmesbury, *Gesta*, i. 5: "For almost all the country lying to the
north of the British ocean, though divided into many provinces,
is justly denominated Germany, from its germinating so many
men. And as the pruner cuts off the more luxuriant branches of
the tree to impart a livelier vigour to the remainder, so the inhabitants of this country assist their common parent by the expulsion
of a part of their members, lest she should perish by giving sus-
tenance to too numerous an offspring; but in order to obviate
discontent, they cast lots who shall be compelled to migrate. Hence
the men of this country have made a virtue of necessity, and, when
driven from their native soil, they have gained foreign settlements
by force of arms." William inserted the comment as a rhetorical
flourish (note the simile drawn from husbandry), and made no
attempt to fit it into a system as Geoffrey does.

220. "Consuetudo ab antiquo statuta."

221. Geoffrey speaks of the Saxons as "agros colentes, civitates
et opida reedificantes. . . ." Cf. *HRB*, i. 16, where the Britons,
newly arrived in Albion, "agros incipiunt colere, domos edificare
ita ut brevi tempore terram ab evo inhabitatam censeres."

222. See Geoffrey's two mentions of the Normans, in *HRB*, i. 2
and iii. 20 (where he remarks that the name of the city founded
by Brutus as Trinovantum, and changed by Lud to Kaerlud, became London in later years, and finally Londres "by the foreigners
who later subdued the nation for themselves." The reference to
the changing name of the same city as it is occupied by different
nations is an excellent self-analysis of Geoffrey's view of history.

223. *HRB*, vii. 4. I follow Pähler, p. 134, in accepting the prophecies of Merlin as an integral part of *HRB* rather than as a careless
insertion by Geoffrey to capitalize on the popularity of the Welsh
bard and prophet in Geoffrey's day.

224. *HRB*, vii. 4. It is possible to find a reference to cyclical
rebirth even in this passage, if one reads with Griscom's Bern MS
"pulvis veterum renovabitur," instead of "pulvis ventorum renovabitur" as in the Cambridge MS.

Chapter VI. Conclusion: Metamorphosis of the Vision

1. For the last years of the "anarchy" in England (the twenty years from the death of Henry I in 1135 to the accession of Henry II in 1154), Poole must rely almost entirely on the anonymous _Gesta Stephani_, and he says that "there are no adequate contemporary sources for the early years of the reign of Henry II." See his bibliographical section, "Narrative Sources," pp. 494–95.

2. The term "romance" as used here refers to any work written in the vernacular. Wace's verse form, however, is the same as that used by Chrétien in his romances and Marie de France in her _lais_. Henry also commissioned Wace to write a _Roman de Rou_, a vernacular retelling of the deeds of the Norman dukes beginning with Rollo; the commission was later transferred to a clerk named Benoit, probably the Benoit de St. Maur who wrote one of the first _romans d'antiquité_. A vernacular version of _HRB_ by Geoffrey Gaimar had been composed before Wace's translation, but the popularity of the later work apparently drove it quickly into oblivion, and no manuscripts are extant today. On Gaimar's lost translation, see M. Dominica Legge, _Anglo-Norman Literature and its Background_, (Oxford, 1963), pp. 28–30.

3. On Wace's courtly, popularizing changes in the "atmosphere" of Geoffrey's history see W. F. Schirmer, _Die frühen Darstellungen des Arthurstoffes_, pp. 44–53.

4. There is no good study of the historiography of the later Middle Ages and its treatment of the Christian assumptions of early medieval historians. While there was obviously much continuity, there were undoubtedly also considerable changes and developments, in keeping with the evolution of medieval biblical studies and specifically the progressive modification of the patristic exegetical tradition after the twelfth century. The latter phenomenon, which is briefly summarized by Charles Donahue in _Critical Approaches to Medieval Literature_, pp. 75–78, and studied in greater detail by Smalley, pp. 112 ff., raises _a priori_ doubts about the integral survival into the later medieval centuries of an historical imagination formed and conditioned by a theology of history resting on scriptural exegesis.

5. We can again cite a parallel with the _chanson de geste_. The

equilibrium in the *Roland,* an early *chanson,* between the historical or "Charles" level and the personal or "Roland-Ganelon" level of the narrative is so precarious that many scholars have found it difficult to imagine the work as the product of one author. In the later *chansons de geste* the "Charles" level tends to suffer further diminution, and the emperor becomes a *roi fainéant* analogous to the Arthur of the romances, or even a comic figure, while the epic deeds of the baronial heroes come more and more to be the main concern of the narrative.

6. Erich Auerbach's essay "The Knight Sets Forth," *Mimesis,* pp. 107–124, stresses the limited segment of social experience drawn on in the French courtly romance.

7. I speak here of general and generic principles, not of the history of Old French literature; at a later date, the romance assumptions were synthesized in a variety of ways with the traditions of Arthurian history founded upon *HRB,* especially in the *morte Arthur* tradition given definitive form by Malory.

8. There is a vestigial sense of Arthur the historical and political hero in the first lines of Marie's *Lanval,* although the idea is never developed; in her *Guigemar,* on the other hand, Arthur's court has become simply the proving ground of the chivalric hero.

9. Honor being by its very nature a social value, some social setting is necessary to establish it. See the remarks on the "shame culture" of honor-centered literature in G. F. Jones, *The Ethos of the Song of Roland,* pp. 97–98.

10. The *Vita Merlini* approaches the same problem from a very different point of view, that of the individual rather than of the nation. The fact that the individual in question is Merlin, the figure whom Geoffrey endowed in *HRB* with such important quasi-allegorical powers, indicates the depth of Geoffrey's interest in the problem.

Bibliography

Texts

Athanasius, St. *Life of St. Anthony*. Translated by M. E. Keenan. See *Early Christian Biographies*.

Augustine, St. *De civitate Dei*. Edited by B. Dombart, 2 vols. Leipzig, B. G. Teubner, 1918.

Augustine, St. *The City of God*. Translated by D. Honan, D. Zema, and G. Walsh. Vols. VI, VII, and VIII in *Fathers of the Church: The Works of St. Augustine*, edited by R. J. Deferrari. New York, Fathers of the Church, 1950, 1952, 1954.

—— *Collected Letters*. Translated by W. Parsons. Vols. IX–XIII in *Fathers of the Church: The Works of St. Augustine*, edited by R. J. Defarrari. New York, Fathers of the Church, 1951–1956.

Bede. *De temporum ratione*. Edited by J. A. Giles in Vol. VI, pp. 270–342, *The Complete Works . . . in the original Latin*. London, Whittaker, 1843–1844.

—— *De temporum ratione*. See Jones, Charles W., ed., *Baedae opera de temporibus*.

—— *Epistola ad Ecgberctum*. See Plummer (I, 405–423).

—— *Historia ecclesiastica gentis Anglorum*. See Plummer (I, 1–360).

—— *Opera de temporibus*. See Charles W. Jones, *Baedae opera de temporibus*.

Biblia Sacra, Vulgatae editionis editio emendatissima . . . cura et studio Monachorum Abbatiae Pontificae Sancti Hieronymi in Urbe Ordinis Sancti Benedicti. Rome, Marietti, 1959.

Holy Bible. Translated from the Latin by Ronald Knox. London, Burns, Oates and Washbourne, 1955.

La Chanson de Roland. Edited by F. Whitehead. (Blackwell's

French Texts, edited by Alfred Ewert) Oxford, Basil Blackwell, 1942, reprinted 1957.

Constantius Lugdunensis. *Vita Germani Episcopi Autissiodorensis.* Edited by W. Levison in *Passiones vitaeque sanctorum aevi Merovingici.* Published as Vol. VII of *Monumenta Germaniae historica: Scriptores rerum Merovingicarum.* Hannover and Leipzig, Hahn, 1920. Pp. 225–283.

Eadmer. *Historia novorum in Anglia.* Edited by Martin Rule. (*Chronicles and Memorials of Great Britain and Ireland during the Middle Ages,* No. 81) London, Longman, 1844.

Early Christian Biographies. Edited by R. J. Defarrari. New York, Fathers of the Church, 1952

Eddius Stephanus. *The Life of Bishop Wilfred.* Edited with a translation by Bertram Colgrave. Cambridge, Cambridge University Press, 1927

Einhard. *The Life of Charlemagne.* Translated by S. E. Turner. Ann Arbor, University of Michigan Press, 1960.

Eusebius Pamphili. *Ecclesiastical History.* Translated by R. J. Deferrari. Vols. XIX and XXIX in *Fathers of the Church,* edited by R. J. Deferrari. New York, Fathers of the Church, 1953, 1955.

—— *Histoire ecclésiastique.* Edited and translated by G. Bardy. Vols. XXXI, XLI, LV, and LXXIII in *Sources chrétiennes.* Paris, Les Editions de Cerf, 1952–1960.

—— *Die Kirchengeschichte.* Vol. II, pts. 1–3, in *Eusebius Werke,* edited by Eduard Schwartz and Theodor Mommsen. Leipzig, J. C. Hinrich, 1903, 1908, 1909.

—— *Life of Constantine.* Translated by E. C. Richardson. Pp. 481–559. (A Select Library of Nicene and Post-Nicene Fathers of the Christian Church, Second Series, Vol. I, edited by P. Schaff and H. Wace) New York, Christian Literature; Oxford and London, Parker, 1890.

Eutropius. *Breviarium historiae romaniae.* Edited by W. H. S. Jones. Blackie's Latin Texts, edited by W. H. D. Rouse. London, Blackie, 1905.

Faral, Edmond. *La légende arthurienne.* (Bibliothèque de l'école des hautes études, Vols. CCLV–CCLVII) Paris, Honore Champion, 1929.

Fraenkische Voelkertafel. Edited by K. Muellenhof in *Abhandlungen der königliche Akademie der Wissenschaften für 1862:*

Historisch-philologische Classe. P. 532. Berlin, Akademie der Wissenschaften, 1863.

Gamelyn. Edited by W. W. Skeat. London, Oxford, Clarendon Press, 1884, reprinted 1893.

Geoffrey of Monmouth. *Historia regum Britanniae.* Edited with an introduction by Acton Griscom, and a translation of the Welsh manuscript no. LXI of Jesus College, Oxford, by Robert Ellis Jones. New York, Longman's Green, 1929.

—— *Historia regum Britanniae.* See Faral (III, 63–303).

—— *Historia regum Britanniae, a Variant Version.* Edited by J. Hammer. (Medieval Academy of America, Publication 57) Cambridge, Mass., Medieval Academy, 1951.

—— *History of the Kings of Britain.* Translated by Sebastian Evans, rev. by Charles W. Dunn. (Everyman's Library) New York, Dutton, 1958.

—— *Vita Merlini.* Edited with a translation by John Jay Perry. Pp. 243–380 (Illinois University Studies in Language and Literature, Vol. X, no. 3) Urbana, University of Illinois Press, 1925.

—— *Vita Merlini.* See Faral (III, 306–52).

Gesta Stephani. Edited with a translation by K. R. Potter. (Medieval Texts) London and New York, Nelson, 1955.

Gildas. *De excidio et conquestu Britanniae.* See Mommsen; Williams.

Gregory of Tours. *Historia Francorum.* Translated with an Introduction by O. M. Dalton. 2 vols. London, Oxford, Clarendon Press, 1927.

—— *Opera omnia.* Edited by T. Ruinart in Vol. LXXI of *Patrologia Latina.* Edited by J. P. Migne. Paris, 1879.

Henry of Huntingdon. *Historia Anglorum.* Edited by Thomas Arnold. (Chronicles and Memorials of Great Britain and Ireland during the Middle Ages, No. 74) London, Longman, etc., 1879.

Henry of Huntingdon. *Chronicle [Historia Anglorum].* Translated by Thomas Forester. London, Bohn, 1853.

Herodotus (Histories). Translated by G. Rawlinson. New York, Random House, 1942.

Historia Brittonum. Edited by Ferdinand Lot in *Nennius et L'Historia Brittonum.* (Bibliothèque de l'école des hautes études, Vol. CCLXIII) Paris, Honoré Champion, 1934.

—— See Mommsen.

—— See Wade-Evans.

Jerome, St. *Life of Paul the Hermit.* Translated by M. L. Ewald.

See *Early Christian Biographies.*

Jones, Charles W., ed., *Baedae opera de temporibus* (containing *De temporum ratione*). (Medieval Academy of America, Publication 61) Cambridge, Mass., Medieval Academy, 1943.

Jordanes. *Gothic History.* Translated by C. C. Mierow. 2d ed. Princeton, Princeton University Press, 1915.

Livy. *History of Rome* (*ab urbe condita libri*). Translated by B. Foster, *et al.* (Loeb Classical Library) London, Heinemann; New York, Putnam; 1919–1959.

Marie de France. *Lais.* Edited by Alfred Ewert. (Blackwell's French Texts) Oxford, Basil Blackwell, 1947, reprinted 1952.

Mommsen, T., ed. Gildas, *De excidio et conquestu Britanniae:* pp. 1–85. *Historia Brittonum:* pp. 143–222. *Chronica minora saec. iv, v, vi, vii,* Vol. III. Published as Vol. XIII of *Monumenta Germaniae historica: auctores antiquissimi.* Berlin, Weidmann, 1898.

Monk of St. Gall, a. *De Gestis Karoli.* Translated by A. J. Grant in *Early Lives of Charlemagne.* (Medieval Library, No. 14.) London, Chatto and Windus, 1926.

Nennius. *History of the Britons, together with The Annals of the Britons.* See Wade-Evans.

Ordericus Vitalis. *Historia ecclesiastica.* Edited by A. Le Provost for the Société de l'histoire de France. 5 vols. Paris, 1838–1855.

Ordericus Vitalis. *Ecclesiastical History of England and Normandy.* Translated by Thomas Forester. 4 Vols. London, Bohn, 1854.

Orosius, Paulus. *Historiarum adversum paganos libri VII.* Edited by Carl Zangenmeister. Leipzig, B. G. Teubner, 1889.

—— *History Against the Pagans.* Translated by I. W. Raymond. (Records of Civilization, No. 26) New York, Columbia University Press, 1936.

Paulus Diaconus. *Historia Langobardorum.* Edited by G. Waitz. Pp. 12–187. *Monumenta Germaniae historica,* Scriptores rerum langobardicarum et italicarum saec. vi–ix. Hannover, Hahn, 1878.

—— *History of the Langobards.* Translated by W. D. Foulke. Philadelphia, University of Pennsylvania Press, 1907.

Plummer, Charles, ed. *Venerabilis Baedae opera historica.* 2 vols. London, Oxford, Clarendon Press, 1896, reprinted 1901.

Salvian. *De gubernatione Dei.* Edited by F. Pauly in *Salviani Presbyteri Marsiliensis opera omnia,* Vol. VIII of *Corpus scriptorum ecclesiasticorum latinorum.* Vienna, C. Gerold, 1883.

—— *De gubernatione Dei.* Translated by Eva M. Sanford. (Records of Civilization, No. 12) New York, Columbia University Press, 1930.

Tacitus. *Germany and its Tribes.* In *The Complete Works of Tacitus.* Translated by A. J. Church and W. J. Brodribb. New York, Random House, 1942.

Thucydides. *Peloponnesian Wars.* With an English translation by C. Forster Smith. 4 vols. (Loeb Classical Library) London, Heinemann; New York, Putnam; 1928–1935.

Thucydides. *History of the Peloponnesian War.* Translated by Rex Warner. Baltimore, Penguin Books, 1954.

Vergil. *Aeneid.* With an English translation by H. Rushton Fairclough, in *Works.* 2 vols. Revised ed. (Loeb Classical Library) London, Heinemann; Cambridge, Mass., Harvard University Press; 1946, 1950.

Wace. *Le roman de Brut.* Edited by I. Arnold. 2 vols. Paris, Société des anciens textes français, 1938–1940.

Wade-Evans, A. W., tr. *Nennius, History of the Britons, together with The Annals of the Britons* . . . London, Society for the Promotion of Christian Knowledge, 1938.

William of Malmesbury. *Gesta Regum Anglorum.* Edited by William Stubbs. 2 vols. (Chronicles and Memorials of Great Britain and Ireland during the Middle Ages, No. 90) London, Eyre and Spottiswoode, 1887, 1889.

William of Malmesbury. *Chronicle of the Kings of England.* Translated by John Sharpe, revised by J. A. Giles, London, George Bell, 1904.

—— *Historia Novella.* Edited with a translation by K. R. Potter. (Medieval Texts) London and New York, Nelson, 1955.

Williams, Hugh, ed. Gildas, *De excidio et conquesto Britanniae,* I, 2–252. *The Works of Gildas,* 2 vols. (Cymmrodorian Record Series, No. 3, Parts I and II). London, David Nutt, 1899–1901.

Studies

Auerbach, Erich. *Dante.* Translated by R. Manheim. Chicago, University of Chicago Press, 1961.

Auerbach, Erich. "Figura," in *Scenes from the Drama of European*

Literature: Six Essays. Translated by R. Manheim. New York, Meridian Books, 1959.

—— *Mimesis.* Translated by Willard Trask. New York, Doubleday, 1957.

Bailey, Cyril, ed. *The Legacy of Rome:* Essays by C. Foligno, *et al.* London, Oxford, Clarendon Press, 1923.

Bark, William Carroll. *Origins of the Medieval World.* New York, Doubleday, 1960.

Barker, E. "The Conception of Empire," C. Bailey, ed., *The Legacy of Rome.* London, Oxford, Clarendon Press, 1923.

Baron, Salo W. *To the Beginning of the Christian Era.* Vol. I of *A Social and Religious History of the Jews (Ancient Times).* 2d ed. revised. New York, Columbia University Press, 1952.

Barrett, C. K. *The New Testament Background.* New York, Harper and Row, 1961.

Blair, Peter Hunter. *An Introduction to Anglo-Saxon England.* Cambridge, Cambridge University Press, 1956, reprinted 1959.

Blair, Peter Hunter. *Roman Britain and Early England.* Edinburgh, T. Nelson, 1963.

Bourke, Myles M. *Passion, Death and Resurrection of Christ.* New York, Paulist Press, 1963.

Brandenburg, Hertha. *Galfrid von Monmouth und die frühmittelenglischen Chronisten.* Berlin, Mayer, 1918.

Brinkley, Roberta F. *Arthurian Legend in the Seventeenth Century.* Baltimore: Johns Hopkins Press; London, Oxford University Press, H. Milford; 1932.

Bruce-Mitford, R. L. S., ed. *Recent Archaeological Excavations in Britain.* London, Routledge and Kegan Paul, 1956.

Bury, J. B. *Ancient Greek Historians.* New York, Dover, 1958 (original edition, 1908)

Cantor, Norman F. *Medieval History: The Life and Death of a Civilization.* London and New York, Macmillan, 1963.

Chadwick, H. M. *The Heroic Age in Literature.* Cambridge, Cambridge University Press, 1912.

Chadwick, Nora K., ed. *Studies in the Early British Church.* Cambridge, Cambridge University Press, 1958.

—— *Studies in Early British History.* Cambridge, Cambridge University Press, 1954, reprinted 1959.

Chadwick, Nora K., *et al. Celt and Saxon.* Cambridge, Cambridge University Press, 1963.

Chambers, E. K. *Arthur of Britain*. London, Sidgwick and Jackson, 1927.

Chambers, Raymond Wilson. *Man's Unconquerable Mind: Studies of English Writers from Bede to A. E. Housman and W. P. Ker* London, Cape, 1939.

—— *Thomas More*. London, Cape, 1935, reprinted 1948.

Cochrane, C. N. *Christianity and Classical Culture*. London and New York, Oxford University Press, 1940, reprinted 1957.

Colligan, F. P. "The Historiography of Geoffrey of Monmouth." Unpublished Ph.D. dissertation, Department of English, University of California, 1941.

R. G. Collingwood. *The Idea of History*. New York, Oxford University Press, 1956.

Collingwood, R. G., and J. N. L. Myres. *Roman Britain and the English Settlements*. 2d ed. (Oxford History of England, edited by G. N. Clark) London, Oxford, Clarendon Press, 1936, 1937.

Cook, Albert S. "Bede and Gregory of Tours," *Philological Quarterly*, VI (1927), 315–16.

F. M. Cornford. *Thucydides Mythhistoricus*. London, Edward Arnold, 1907.

Cross, J. E. "Aspects of Microcosm and Macrocosm in Old English Literature," in S. B. Greenfield, ed., *Studies in Old English Literature in Honor of Arthur G. Brodeur*. Eugene, University of Oregon Press, 1963.

Curtius, Ernst R. *European Literature and the Latin Middle Ages*. Translated by Willard Trask. (Bollingen Series, No. 36) (First published as *Europäische Literatur und lateinisches Mittelalter* in 1948: Bern, A. Francke AG Verlag) New York, Pantheon Books, 1953.

Daniélou, Jean. *From Shadows to Reality: Studies in the Biblical Typology of the Fathers*. Translated by W. Hibberd. London, Burns, Oates and Washbourne, 1960.

—— *Origen*. Translated by W. Mitchell. New York, Sheed and Ward, 1955.

—— *The Salvation of the Nations*. Translated by A. Bouchard. London, Sheed and Ward, 1949.

Daniélou, Jean, and Henri Marrou. *The First Six Hundred Years*. Translated by Vincent Cronin. Volume I of *The Christian Centuries: A New History of the Catholic Church*. New York, McGraw-Hill, 1964.

Davis, Charles Till. *Dante and the Idea of Rome*. London, Oxford, Clarendon Press, 1957.

Dawson, Christopher. "St. Augustine and His Age," in M. C. D'Arcy, *et al.*, *A Monument to St. Augustine: Essays on Some Aspects of His Thought Written in Commemoration of His 15th Centenary*. London, Sheed and Ward, 1945.

Deanesley, Margaret. *The Pre-Conquest Church in England*. New York, Oxford University Press, 1961.

Décarreaux, Jean. *Les moines et la civilisation en occident*. (Collection signe des temps, Vol. XIII) Paris, B. Arthaud, 1962.

Delehaye, Hippolyte. *The Legends of the Saints*. Translated by D. Attwater. 4th ed. (First published as *Les legendes hagiographiques* in Brussels, 1905) New York, Fordham University Press, 1962.

Donahue, C. "Patristic Exegesis in the Criticism of Medieval Literature: A Summation," in D. Bethurem, ed., *Critical Approaches to Medieval Literature*. (Selected Papers from the English Institute, 1958–1959) New York, Columbia University Press, 1960.

Douglas, D. C. *William the Conqueror*. Berkeley and Los Angeles, University of California Press, 1964.

Driver, Tom F. *The Sense of History in Greek and Shakespearian Drama*. New York, Columbia University Press, 1960.

Duckett, E. S. *Anglo-Saxon Saints and Scholars*. New York, Macmillan, 1947.

—— *Gateway to the Middle Ages*. New York, Macmillan, 1938.

—— *Latin Writers of the Fifth Century*. New York, Holt, 1930.

Enslin, M. S. *The Literature of the Christian Movement*. Part three of *Christian Beginnings*. New York, Harper and Row, 1956.

Faral, Edmund. *La légende arthurienne*. (Bibliotheque de l'école des hautes études, Vols. CCLV–CCLVII) Paris, Honoré Champion, 1929.

Feuerherd, Paul Otto. *Geoffrey of Monmouth und das Alte Testament*. Halle, E. Karras, 1915.

Finley, John H. *Thucydides*. Ann Arbor, University of Michigan Press, 1942, 1963.

Fletcher, Robert Huntington. *Arthurian Material in the Chronicles, Especially Those of Great Britain and France*. ([Harvard] Notes and Studies in Philology, No. 10) Boston, Harvard University Press, 1906; reprinted New York, Burt Franklin, 1958.

Foakes-Jackson, F. J. *A History of Church History*. Cambridge, W. Heffer, 1939.

Gamble, W. M. T. "Orosius," in P. Guilday, ed., *Church Historians.* (American Catholic Historical Association Papers, No. 1) New York, P. J. Kennedy and Sons, 1926.

Gerould, G. H. "King Arthur and Politics," *Speculum,* II (1927), 33–52.

Gilson, Etienne. *The Christian Philosophy of St. Augustine.* Translated by L. E. M. Lynch. New York, Random House, 1960.

Greulich, E. *Die Arthursage in der "Historia Regum Britanniae" des Galfred von Monmouth.* Halle, Hohmann, 1916.

Halphen, L. "Grégoire de Tours, historien de Clovis," *Mélanges d'histoire du moyen age, offerts à M. Ferdinand Lot par ses amis et ses élèves.* Paris, E. Champion, 1925.

Hardy, E. "The City of God," in R. W. Battenhouse, ed., *A Companion to the Study of St. Augustine.* New York, Oxford University Press, 1955.

Haskins, Charles Homer. *The Renaissance of the Twelfth Century.* Cambridge, Mass., Harvard University Press, 1927; reprinted New York, Meridian Books, 1957.

Heeger, G. *Ueber die Trojanersage der Britten.* "München, Oldenbourg, 1886.

Heer, Friedrich. *The Medieval World: Europe 1100–1350.* Translated by Janet Sondheimer. New York, World, 1962; reprinted New York, Mentor, 1963.

Hodgkin, R. H. *A History of the Anglo-Saxons.* 2 vols. 3d ed. London, Oxford, Geoffrey Cumberlege, 1952.

Jackson, Kenneth Hurlstone. "The Arthur of History," in R. S. Loomis, ed., *Arthurian Literature in the Middle Ages: A Collaborative History.* London. Oxford, Clarendon Press, 1959.

Jackson, W. T. H. *The Literature of the Middle Ages.* New York, Columbia University Press, 1960, reprinted 1961.

Jones, Charles W. *Saints' Lives and Chronicles in Early England.* Ithaca, Cornell University Press, 1947.

Jones, Ernest van B. *Geoffrey of Monmouth, 1640–1800.* (University of California Publications in English, Vol. V, No. 3, Studies in the Geoffrey of Monmouth Tradition, III) Berkeley and Los Angeles, University of California Press, 1944.

Jones, G. F. *The Ethos of the Song of Roland.* Baltimore, Johns Hopkins University Press, 1963.

Jones, W. L. "Latin Chroniclers from the Eleventh to the Thirteenth Centuries," Vol. I, *From the Beginnings to the Cycles of*

Romance, in *The Cambridge History of English Literature.* Edited by A. W. Ward and A. R. Waller. Cambridge, Cambridge University Press, 1907, reprinted 1920.

Keeler, Laura. *Geoffrey of Monmouth and the Late Latin Chroniclers, 1300–1500.* (University of California Publications in English, Vol. XVII, No. 1, Studies in the Geoffrey of Monmouth Tradition, IV) Berkeley and Los Angeles, University of California Press, 1946.

Kendrick, T. D. *British Antiquity.* London, Methuen, 1950.

Knowles, David. *The Monastic Order in England.* Cambridge, Cambridge University Press, 1940, reprinted 1949.

de Labriolle, P., *et al. The Church in the Christian Roman Empire.* Vols. III and IV of *L'histoire de l'Eglise.* Edited by A. Fliche and V. Martin. Translated by E. Messenger. New York, Macmillan, 1953.

—— *The History and Literature of Christianity from Tertullian to Boethius.* Translated by Herbert Wilson. New York, Knopf, 1924.

Laistner, M. L. W. *The Greater Roman Historians.* Berkeley and Los Angeles, University of California Press, 1947, 1963.

Laistner, M. L. W. *The Intellectual Heritage of the Early Middle Ages: Selected Essays.* Edited by Chester Starr. Ithaca, Cornell University Press, 1957.

—— *Thought and Letters in Western Europe,* A.D. 500–900. 2d ed. revised. Ithaca, Cornell University Press, 1957.

Lamprecht, Hans. *Untersuchungen über einige englische Chronisten des 12. und des beginnenden 13. Jahrhunderts.* Torgau, Torgauer Druck- und Verlaghaus, 1937.

Lebreton, J. and Zeiller, J. *The History of the Primitive Church.* Vols. I and II of *L'histoire de l'Eglise.* Edited by A. Fliche and V. Martin. Translated by E. Messenger. New York, Macmillan, 1949.

Leclercq, Jean. *The Love of Learning and the Desire for God: A Study of Monastic Culture.* Translated by C. Misrahi. New York, Mentor, 1962.

Leff, Gordon. *Medieval Thought from Saint Augustine to Ockham.* Harmondsworth, Middlesex, Penquin Books, 1958.

Legge, M. Dominica. *Anglo-Norman Literature and its Background.* London, Oxford, Clarendon Press, 1963.

Levison, W. *England and the Continent in the Eighth Century.* London, Oxford, Clarendon Press, 1946.

Lieberman, F. "Nennius the Author of the *Historia Brittonum*," in *Essays in Medieval History Presented to T. F. Tout.* Printed for subscribers, Manchester, 1925.

Lietzmann, H. *From Constantine to Julian.* Vol. III of *A History of the Early Church.* Translated by B. L. Woolf. New York, Scribner, 1950.

Litchfield, H. W. "National *Exempla Virtutis* in Roman Literature," *Harvard Studies in Classical Philology*, XXV (1914), 1–71.

Lloyd, J. E. "Geoffrey of Monmouth," *English Historical Review*, LVII (1942), 460–68.

Loomis, C. Grant. "King Arthur and the Saints." *Speculum*, VIII (1933), 478–82.

Loomis, Roger Sherman, ed. *Arthurian Literature in the Middle Ages: A Collaborative History.* London, Oxford, Clarendon Press, 1959.

Loomis, Roger Sherman. *The Development of Arthurian Romance.* (Hutchinson University Library: Modern Languages and Literature) London, Hutchinson, 1963.

—— "Geoffrey of Monmouth and Arthurian Origins," *Speculum*, III (1928), 16–33.

—— Review of *Die frühen Darstellungen des Arthurstoffes* by W. F. Schirmer, *Speculum*, XXXIV (1959), 677–82.

de Lubac, Henri. *Exégèse Médiévale: les quatre sens de l'Ecriture.* 2 vols. (Vol. II is subtitled "Seconde Partie: I") (Etudes publiées sous la direction de la faculté de théologie s. J. de Lyon-Fourvière, Vols. XLI and XLII) Paris, Aubier, 1959, 1960.

McKenzie, John L. *Myths and Realities.* Milwaukee, Bruce, 1963.

Manitius, Maximilianus. *Geschichte der lateinischen Literatur des Mittelalters.* 3 vols. München, Beck, 1911–1931.

Meunier, René-Adrien. *Grégoire de Tours et l'histoire morale de centre-ouest de la France.* (Publications de l'Université de Poitiers. Série des sciences de l'homme," IX) Poitiers, chez l'auteur, 1944.

Milburn, R. L. P. *Early Christian Interpretations of History.* (Bampton Lectures, 1952) London, A. and C. Black, 1954.

Mohr, Walter. *Die Karolingische Reichsidee.* (Aevum Christianum: Salzburger Beiträge zur Religions- und Geistesgeschichte des Abendlandes, Vol. V) Münster, Aschendorff, 1962.

Mommsen, T. E. *Medieval and Renaissance Studies.* Edited by Eugene F. Rice. Ithaca, Cornell University Press, 1959.

Munz, Peter. *The Origins of the Carolingian Empire.* Leicester, Leicester University Press; University of Otago Press; 1960.

Myers, L. M. "Universal Histories in the Early Middle Ages." Unpublished Ph.D. Dissertation, Department of English, University of California, 1935.

Myres, J. N. L. "The English Settlements," in *Roman Britain and the English Settlements.* 2d ed. (Oxford History of England, edited by G. N. Clark) Oxford, Clarendon, 1936, 1937.

Pähler, Heinrich. *Strukturuntersuchungen zur Historia Regum Britanniae des Geoffrey of Monmouth.* Bonn, Rheinische Friedrich Wilhelms-Universität, 1958.

Parry, John Jay, and Robert A. Caldwell. "Geoffrey of Monmouth," in R. S. Loomis, ed., *Arthurian Literature in the Middle Ages: A Collaborative History.* London, Oxford, Clarendon Press, 1959.

Paton, L. A. "The Story of Vortigern's Tower," *Studies in English and Comparative Literature.* (Radcliffe College Monographs, no. 15) Boston, Ginn, 1910.

Pilch, H. "Galfrid's *Historia.* Studie zu ihrer Stellung in der Literaturgeschichte," *Romanische Monatsschrift,* N. F. VII (1957), 254–73.

Pöschl, Viktor. *The Art of Vergil.* Ann Arbor, University of Michigan Press, 1962.

Poole, Austin Lane. *From Domesday Book to Magna Carta, 1087–1216.* 2d ed. (The Oxford History of England, edited by G. N. Clark) London, Oxford, Clarendon Press, 1955.

Quasten, Johannes. *Patrology.* 3 vols. Utrecht/Antwerp, Spectrum Publisher; Westminster, Maryland, Newman Press, 1960–1962.

Richter, Heinz. *Englische Geschichtschreiber des 12. Jahrhunderts.* (Neue deutsche Forschungen, Vol. CLXXXVII: *Abteilung mittelalterliche Geschichte,* Vol. IV) Berlin, Junker und Dünnhaupt Verlag, 1938.

Ritter, M. "Studien über die Entwicklung der Geschichtswissenschaft. I: Die antike Geschichtschreibung," *Historische Zeitschrift,* LIV (1885), 1–41.

—— "Studien über die Entwicklung der Geschichtswissenschaft. II: Die christlich-mittelalterliche Geschichtschreibung," *Historische Zeitschrift,* CVII (1911), 237–63.

Schirmer, Walter F. *Die frühen Darstellungen des Arthurstoffes.*

(Arbeitsgemeinschaft für Forschung des Landes Nordhein-West-falen: Geisteswissenschaften, Vol. LXXIII) Köln and Opladen, Westdeutscher Verlag, 1958.

Shotwell, James T. *The Story of Ancient History.* 2d ed. New York, Columbia University Press, 1961.

Smalley, Beryl. *The Study of the Bible in the Middle Ages.* Notre Dame, University of Notre Dame Press, 1964.

Southern, R. W. *St. Anselm and His Biographer.* Cambridge, Cambridge University Press, 1963.

Stenton, F. M. *Anglo-Saxon England.* 2d ed. (The Oxford History of England, edited by G. N. Clark) London, Oxford, Clarendon Press, 1947, reprinted 1955.

Stevenson, J., ed. *A New Eusebius: Documents Illustrative of the History of the Church to* A.D. *337.* London, Society for the Promotion of Christian Knowledge, 1957, 1960.

Tatlock, J. S. P. "Contemporaneous Matters in Geoffrey of Monmouth's *Historia regum Britanniae,*" *Speculum,* VI (1931), 206–23.

—— *The Legendary History of Britain: Geoffrey of Monmouth's Historia Regum Britanniae and Its Early Vernacular Versions.* Berkeley and Los Angeles, University of California Press, 1950.

Tausendfreund, H. *Vergil und Gottfried von Monmouth.* Halle, Hohmann, 1913.

Thompson, A. H., ed. *Bede, His Life, Times, and Writings.* London, Oxford, Clarendon Press, 1935.

Thompson, J. W., and B. J. Holm. *A History of Historical Writing.* Vol. I: *From the Earliest Times to the End of the Seventeenth Century.* New York, Macmillan, 1942.

Thurneysen, G. Review of *Nennius vindicatus,* by H. Zimmer, *Zeitschrift für deutsche Philologie,* XXVIII (1896), 80–113.

Versfeld, Marthinus. *A Guide to the City of God.* New York, Sheed and Ward, 1958.

Wallace-Hadrill, D. S. *Eusebius of Caesarea.* London, A. R. Mowbrey, 1960.

Wallace-Hadrill, J. M. *The Barbarian West,* A.D. *400–1000: The Early Middle Ages.* London, Hutchinson, 1952; New York, Harper, 1962.

—— "The work of Gregory of Tours in the light of modern research," *Transactions of the Royal Historical Society* (5th series), I (1951), 25–45.

Whitman, Cedric. *Sophocles.* Cambridge, Mass., Harvard University Press, 1951.

Willaert, Benjamin. "Jesus as the 'Suffering Servant,'" *Theology Digest,* X (1962), 25–30.

Wolter, Hans. *Ordericus Vitalis.* Wiesbaden, Steiner, 1955.

Wrenn, C. L. "The Poetry of Caedmon," *Proceedings of the British Academy,* XXXII (1946), 277–95.

Zimmer, Heinrich. *Nennius vindicatus: über Entstehung, Geschichte und Quellen der Historia Brittonum.* Berlin, Weidmann, 1893.

Index